D0404437

WILL TO BE WELL

WILL TO BE WELL

The Real Alternative Medicine

Neville Hodgkinson

Samuel Weiser, Inc.
York Beach, Maine

To Dadi Janki
who shows through her own being
how beauty in thought, word and deed
transcends physical infirmity

First published in 1984 by
Rider and Company, London, England

First American paperback 1986 by
Samuel Weiser, Inc.
Box 612
York Beach, Maine 03910

ISBN 0-87728-659-0

Library of Congress Cataloging-in-Publication Data

Hodgkinson, Neville.
  Will to be well.

    1. Sick--Psychology. 2. Medicine and psychology.
3. Mind and body. I. Title.
R726.5.H63 1986   616'.001'9   85-26472
ISBN 0-87728-659-0

Printed in the United States of America

Contents

Preface

This book contains information that shocked the author; it may well shock the reader. Long-held beliefs about the self, and illness, and doctors, and medicine, are liable to be undermined by it, and to begin to change in a fundamental way. Disillusionment is involved, but this paves the way for a change of attitude – a change of mind – so profound as to be capable of bringing about an immediate improvement in health and health prospects.

The information is accurate in so far as it has been culled from a very wide variety of scientific studies and sources. The fact that science is its support does not give it any absolute authority, of course. Much of it concerns the intricate mechanisms through which mind, brain and body are linked; this is a relatively new field for scientific exploration and one in which discoveries are being made almost daily.

The framework of ideas within which these discoveries are placed is not new. It is in fact very ancient. But it had almost disappeared from view in western society, and although growing numbers of people are now inquiring into it, it remains distinctly unorthodox at present. It is the author's conviction that great distress results from this state of affairs. Truths about life and health that are essential to our happiness have been lost or grossly neglected. *Will To Be Well* has the aim of contributing to the stream of ideas springing from this distress – that offers the prospect of a much brighter future.

One of these ideas is that happiness itself is essential to health, and that a lack of it is probably the biggest cause of illness and premature death in our society. The author has become convinced that this is the case, surprising though it seems to those accustomed to thinking of disease as an unfortunate affliction unrelated to our states of mind. The notion has long found more favour among poets and priests than practising physicians, but current advances in medical science are forcing doctors to begin to take it seriously.

The unhappiness that can threaten health is a subtle force, and is not necessarily recognized consciously by the person it afflicts. It has more to do with a deep feeling of unease about his or her place in the world – a sense of displacement, rather than obvious displeasure – and also with an inability to behave as the world would seem to require. When this unease becomes too strong or goes on for too long, it gives rise to physiological disorder that sooner or later is liable to trigger overt disease.

We shall be examining the idea that this kind of unhappiness springs primarily from a lack of understanding about the relationship between the mind, or self, and the body. Although the things that are said and done to us by fate and other people are almost bound to affect our state of mind, through self-knowledge it is possible to take charge of our thoughts and emotions in such a way that they become health-promoting rather than illness-inducing. While negative emotions such as sorrow, anger, self-hatred or hopelessness are antagonistic to life and health, a positive outlook actually heals and protects. Even when there is irreversible damage to the body, a person can recover happiness by learning to live within the disability, and in that way stop the disease from progressing.

We shall also be seeing that because of an enormous over-reliance by both patients and doctors on technological methods of tackling disease, millions of people unnecessarily become the victims of chronic illness.

Part One of the book introduces these themes in a general way, and looks at some current efforts to escape from the blind alley of symptom-suppression through drugs. The heart of the book then follows. There are descriptions of nine of the most pervasive or worrying present-day disease conditions and analyses of the mind-body links prevalent in each one. These accord with the most up-to-date scientific information available. In every case, the analysis gives rise to the most profound challenges to orthodox treatment methods and approaches, which are frequently seen to be harmful and even life-threatening. In particular, it is argued that the search for purely physical causes and cures has led to many patients being deemed incurable and sentenced to lifelong treatment, when with a different way of viewing and tackling the illness their symptoms could disappear.

In order that the challenges made should not easily be dismissed, detailed physiological descriptions of the mechanisms involved in each kind of illness are included. The general reader who follows these descriptions progressively through the book should find that they gradually interlink to form a picture relevant to many forms of illness, not just those specifically examined. But patients with one of the particular diseases explored – or their friends or relatives – may prefer to turn straight to the section that most concerns them. In almost all cases, a summary of the main findings appears at the end of each analysis.

The nine conditions examined are, in their groupings: angina, heart attack, and hypertension (high blood pressure); arthritis, diabetes, kidney failure, migraine and multiple sclerosis; and finally, cancer.

The book ends by pointing the reader towards territory that is not physical at all, but spiritual – not in an other-worldly sense, but concerning the spirit in which we live. This, ultimately, is seen to be the main determinant of health.

Part One

A Change of Attitude

1 Disillusionment

An indication that a 'change of mind' about our selves and the lives we have been leading is needed, and indeed yearned for, is provided by the present huge consumption of mind-affecting drugs. There is nicotine from tobacco, for example, affecting the brain in such a way as to be both stimulating and deeply satisfying to the smoker. There is alcohol, a multi-billion-pound industry ministering to a widespread human need to find a relaxed state of consciousness quite different from that which normally prevails. There are the tranquillizing drugs, which until recently were being swallowed by a fifth of British women and a tenth of men at some time each year, according to one survey.

The mass consumption of these powerful chemicals demonstrates that millions of people regularly feel a need to alter their state of mind. But the question arises, when are they in their 'right' mind – drugged or sober? Clearly it cannot be the former, but what is there about the 'sober' condition prevailing in so many people that they should need to take these drugs? Very large numbers of people appear to sense some deficiency in their normal state of mind sufficiently distressing for them to want to modify it chemically, despite the known risks to health and the economic penalties in so doing. At the extreme, some people indulge in these chemical supports in an obviously excessive and self-destructive way, and yet they may still offer reasons for this behaviour which to them seem perfectly sound: life would 'just not be worth living', they may say, without their beer and fags. 'Eat, drink and be merry, for tomorrow we die' can become a self-fulfilling prophecy.

When people behave in ways that seem superficially to be self-destructive, often they are actually striving to 'be themselves', to be true to themselves, in a way that is otherwise eluding them. An inability to be true to ourselves is at the root of much human distress. Chronic suffering springs from falsehood, from mistaken ideas about who and what we are, and from wrongful habits stemming from the wrong ideas.

Distress is a condition not of the body or the brain, but of the mind or self or soul – the thinking and feeling essence of the human being. But we have been tending to deny the existence of this 'self' as an independent, decision-making entity with a nature and needs of its own. We have been denying our own humanity, and identifying ourselves merely with body and brain as rather clever but essentially reactive machines. Not recognizing our true selves, we have been blind to distress. We have not realized how much we have been suffering, nor how much suffering we have been causing to each other.

Wrong ideas about the nature of the self mean that conflict and tension arise without our realizing why, and then cannot be corrected. Failure to understand the importance of distress as a cause of illness – a failure perfectly embodied by modern medicine, which sees illness as arising from mechanical defects or invasion by germs – adds very greatly to the sum of unhappiness and illness that a society experiences.

It is true that the condition of the body does also affect the mind. So when mechanical failure can be corrected by technological medicine, such as through the replacement of a painful hip, or the removal of an arterial blockage, or the reinstallation of a severed limb, distress is likely to be relieved and a genuine benefit experienced. Similarly, when antibiotics are used to help the body remove an overwhelming infection, the body thereby becomes a far more congenial abode for the self. But it is equally true, as I hope to illuminate, that the condition of the mind or self profoundly affects the state of the body – and not just in an occasional crisis, but in every second of our existence. Each thought that springs to mind, each reaction made in response to external stimuli, as well as each action performed, has immediate consequences for the body. The mind creates its own physiological environment. And when this environment becomes polluted by chronic mental distress, physical disease is an almost inevitable result.

The body itself is like a garden, and the mind a gardener. Feelings of contentment and happiness promote balance and harmony in our inner ecology. The soil is made fertile for fruitful action. By contrast, feelings of distress and unhappiness drain the land of its energy and productive capacity.

Just as there are times of growing, picking, and replenishing in a garden, so a balance has to be found in the body between activity and rest. Human beings have an intricate system of nerve and hormone controls through which the mind can galvanize the body into effort, or relax it while the potentials for activity are restored. There are feedback circuits that help to sustain this balance without conscious thought in normal circumstances. But these can be by-passed by mechanisms that in recent years have been traced right to the heart of the brain, systems over which the mind has the overriding control.

When people feel at ease and at one with their environment, they enable their body systems to move into action and out again into rest in an easy and natural way. When they face novel, threatening, or otherwise demanding challenges requiring special attention, they bring the override mechanisms into operation in an effort to learn how to master the situation or to find some other strategy for handling it. Brain and body are aroused into an elevated level of activity. This prolonged arousal increases the chances of coping successfully – but only as long as it is appropriately directed. If the efforts are misplaced, or go on for so long that there are diminishing returns and coping ability falls, there can become established a vicious circle which provokes deep exhaustion, distress, and vulnerability to illness. Disease, by bringing symptoms of this inner sickness to the surface, can actually provide a way of breaking through the vicious circle. Other people, as well as the self, are alerted to the need for rest and comfort and a change of strategy.

Or, at least, they should be. But the personal and emotional factors in illness have been sorely neglected by doctors and patients alike in recent years. Because of difficulties in examining these factors scientifically – measuring them, pinning them down, controlling them – theories of illness pointing to the role of the mind and the emotions have been very much out of fashion. In fact, for many years they have been considered disreputable by orthodox medicine, despite their ancient and honourable history.

The result, as is rapidly being realized, and as I hope will be seen with incontrovertible clarity in the analyses of various diseases that form the main part of this book, has been an enormous overreliance by both patients and doctors on technological methods of tackling disease. We have asked modern medical technology to perform feats that are way beyond its capacity.

Disillusionment is growing fast. More and more people are seeing that the 'pill for every ill' syndrome is accompanied by an ill from every pill. Drug side-effects put hundreds of thousands of people into hospital and are contaminating the lives of millions. Family doctors find their surgeries overrun with people who are unquestionably suffering but for whom their training has not equipped them to offer real help. Huge technological hospitals gobble vast resources yet, relative to the sums involved, do not seem to make any real progress in the quest for the ability to enhance or extend life.

Britain's National Health Service, founded with the idea that by conquering illness it would eventually do away with the need for its own existence, has grown into a £15,000-million-a-year industry with more than a million employees. In a nation of only fifty million people, a million prescriptions – costing on average £6 apiece – are written out every day, producing a total drugs bill of over £2,000 million a year. Wealthier countries spend even more. In the United States the annual bill for health care is an astronomical £300,000 million, and it has been rising at about thirteen per cent a year. Public demand for health care, and the health-care industry's demand for public funds, both seem insatiable.

Doctors and other health professionals are not happy with this state of affairs. Their discontent has been reflected for some years in high rates of suicide and alcoholism. More recently, it has shown itself in the formation of bodies such as the British Holistic Medical Association, and the International Society for Humanism in Cardiology – the latter title carrying the clear implication that much existing cardiological practice is inhuman. In the field of cancer treatment, too, it is now increasingly recognized that orthodox medical approaches often add to the patient's suffering, and that more humane, person-centred methods need to be explored.

The Prince of Wales, 1982–83 President of the British Medical Association, has spoken of 'the sickness of the spirit proliferating with horrific swiftness all around us' and has urged doctors not to underestimate the importance of 'an awareness of what lies beneath the surface of the visible world and of those ancient, unconscious forces which still help to shape the psychological attitudes of modern man'. Prince Charles also suggested gently in a speech to the BMA that 'the whole imposing edifice of modern medicine, for all its breathtaking successes is, like the celebrated Tower of Pisa, slightly off balance'.

This book seeks to demonstrate that despite their growing recognition of the need for a change of outlook, today's doctors are probably worse equipped than at any previous time in the profession's history in really understanding why people fall ill – and why they become well again. It argues that scientific methods have been embraced in medicine with an extreme faith and fervour that actually betray the spirit of science itself, since this extremism has blocked consideration of the most important factors in health and illness. It also seeks to show that because a process of misunderstanding and misdiagnosis is operating right across a huge range of conditions, millions of patients are being trapped in disease unnecessarily. The process does not end with people being unnecessarily drugged, pernicious though that is when the drugs are taken for life, or when they are used to suppress symptoms of an illness which nevertheless continues to grow and eventually becomes chronically disabling. It extends to enormous numbers of unnecessary operations, from the removal of tonsils and appendices to coronary by-pass surgery and kidney transplants. Literally billions of pounds are being wasted, and lives put unnecessarily at risk. So are billions of dollars, and of every other currency in those countries where the arts of staying well and helping others to recover health have almost been extinguished by the expansion of technological medicine.

I learned about this extraordinary situation, with growing astonishment, while working as the medical and science correspondent of one of Britain's national newspapers. This job gave me access to all the leading medical and scientific journals, and it was mainly from these – from the many self-critical articles written by doctors themselves – that I pieced together a picture of the huge waste involved.

At first I felt rather angry and disillusioned – partly with myself for having previously shared the excessive faith in science and technology and the discounting of emotional factors in illness, and partly with doctors and drug companies for perpetuating what I now know to be dangerous myths about disease. Later I realized that it is both useless and wrong to direct blame towards any particular body. We are all in this together – including patients, many of whom, seemingly lacking any alternative strategy, not only fail to resist being declared sick or diseased, but often invite the doctor to confer some official disease label upon them and perhaps a powerful drug or an operation to go with it.

It came home to me that people can 'will' their illnesses upon themselves when I made a series of visits to the heart ward of one of London's big teaching hospitals. I spent some hours with a cardiologist there who tries to persuade patients to accept their own share of responsibility for their health – and for their illness. He does not always have an easy time of it. Some patients bitterly resist the suggestion that there has been anything wrong in their lives, and do not want to alter their routine at all to get well. Their attitude is: 'Can't you just give me something for it?'

Family doctors often meet the same attitude. It can seem much easier, in the short term, for patients to shift responsibility for their illnesses on to someone or something else, to blame some 'disease' for their illness, as if it does not belong to them but has invaded them from outside, and to place the burden for removing that disease on to their doctors. And the doctors, not only because of the narrowness of their training but also out of the strong sense of duty many of them share, have been trying to accept that burden, only to find, in time, to their chagrin and frustration, that this is rarely an effective way to improve the patient's lot.

So if ever this book sounds like an attack on doctors, or drug companies, or patients, or anyone at all, I apologize in advance. Its main aim is to provide a guide to the dynamics of habitual patterns of thought, feeling, action and physiological reaction that usually lie behind the most common illnesses. It seeks to show how, with a better knowledge of the choices available, patients may be able to steer themselves back into an acceptable and sustainable level of health, avoiding the hazards and expense of unnecessary medical treatment and the vicious trap of a drug-dependent and doctor-dependent life.

Everyone longs for that state of mind which promotes health rather than illness. Just by recognizing that our intrinsic self-healing potential vastly outweighs the therapeutic contribution of modern medicine, we will have taken a crucial step towards rediscovering and recapturing that state. Without rejecting the good that modern medicine can do, and without blaming anyone, including ourselves, for past mistakes, we need to turn our attention right away from doctors, hospitals and drugs and learn how to regain control of our own fate.

2   Confusion

When one begins to awaken to the fact that modern medicine has nothing like the power to repair or heal generally ascribed to it, a natural reaction is to seek to become stronger in oneself. But a common mistake is to think that this strength can be found mainly through increased physical fitness, to be brought about through exercise and a more prudent diet. This is putting the cart – the physical body – before the horse, which is the individual package of emotional tendencies or 'drives' with which each human being is equipped. If the horse is behaving wildly and stupidly, threatening to tear the cart apart, no amount of repair or reinforcement to the cart itself will be capable of providing a long-term solution. In fact, such reinforcement may simply mean that the horse and cart between them are enabled to rush around causing trouble for longer than might otherwise have been the case. Clearly, it would be far better if the horse were to be brought under control so that the process causing all the damage can be halted.

The emotions are the means by which thoughts and feelings are translated into action, or into the potential for action. In a sense they are actions. When a thought springs to mind that triggers an emotion, there is chemical and electrical movement within the brain and body. The chemicals that are set in motion in this way affect us just as profoundly as chemicals taken in the form of drugs – in fact more so in many cases, because the naturally occurring chemical processes are perfectly arranged to respond quickly and efficiently to orders received.

Sometimes the emotions find easy and natural expression whether through speech or bodily movement. In terms of the analogy, horse and cart move forwards together (even though the direction may ultimately not prove to be a healthy one) and strain is minimized for the time being at least. More liable to cause serious wear and tear is the situation where an emotion constantly surges up only to be denied expression, either because the body is too weak or disabled to respond, or because there is a simultaneous pull in a different direction by a conflicting emotional drive.

I know from experience that when inner conflict and frustration are building up in this way, physical exercise can provide relief. I took up jogging myself over a two-year period recently. Pounding around a local park, it was as though the 'horses' of the emotions were being let loose in a field to burn off their excess energy in harmless activity (although foot and ankle sprains were common). Made docile in this way, the emotions could cease to be troublesome – for a while. Exercise mobilizes and utilizes the 'effort' hormone noradrenalin, amongst others, and this seems to have a cleansing effect on body and mind. It is as though one is able to run one's cares away.

But the effect is fairly short-lived. After the effort-induced euphoria has died down, underlying worries remain. This is why exercise can be so addictive, as most joggers and runners know. It conceals rather than removes underlying causes of agitation. As the anaesthetizing effect wears off, the need for a new 'fix', perhaps bigger than the last one, becomes more and more urgent. Some people do run purely for pleasure, enjoying the sense of freedom, challenge, and self-control. But there is something driven about the behaviour of many joggers that makes one suspect they may eventually be doing themselves more harm than good. *En masse*, they make an even more poignant scene than the lone, worn-looking individual. There is definitely something rather sad and desperate about 'fun runs', though marathon runners do earn a measure of admiration for the heroic scale on which they are willing to take their self-inflicted punishment.

Similarly mixed feelings arise about the dance and exercise classes that have become such a craze in the 1980s, especially among women. Dance is potentially a most joyful human activity, yet here again the joy sometimes seems decidedly artificial: partly in that it is usually made clear that this is how you are supposed to feel, and partly in that there is only a short-term reward for the punishingly disciplined routines imposed.

Health Education – or Misinformation?

Health education in general has taken off in a big way in recent years, but it seems to me to have been tainted with the same kind of paradoxes and inadequacies as the joggers and dancers. To be more accurate, I should say that spending on health education has taken off, with multi-million-pound government-backed campaigns and a brisk market in do-it-yourself health and fitness books. Evidence that there may be something fundamentally ill-conceived about these efforts to date comes from their singular lack of success.

Children are indoctrinated in schools on the perils of cigarette smoking, but the habit is still ubiquitous – and particularly prevalent, and rising, among the young. Adults are constantly urged to change their eating habits and take more exercise. Going on a diet of one sort or another has become a national sport, indulged in regularly by forty per cent of women and fifteen per cent of men. But over-eating and obesity remain rife: according to a 1983 report from the Royal College of Physicians, more than a third of the British population is overweight, and the problem is worsening. Medical experts repeatedly exhort us to drink sensibly and warn of the perils of not doing so, but alcohol problems are at record levels, as are the number of addicts taking 'hard' drugs such as heroin.

Since the aims of health education are to promote self-care, shouldn't such efforts at least be a useful step in the right direction? Two main reasons come to mind as to why this is not so. One is that most of the campaigns to date have not offered true education, which helps one to make sense of experience, but manipulative propaganda. They are misleading rather than enlightening. The benefits that can be obtained from tobacco, for example, are rarely if ever acknowledged in such propaganda, yet nicotine affects the brain in such a way as to be both stimulating and deeply satisfying to the smoker. There is no way that nearly half a nation would take up an expensive habit (which is also obviously physically harmful, for how can taking smoke into the lungs be otherwise?) merely because it was there, or because it was cleverly advertised, or even because of its addictive qualities. People begin to smoke regularly when they discover that they like the effect it has on the way they think and feel. And many are unable to give up, even when the harm they are doing to themselves has become clearly apparent, because they do not want to be deprived of that effect and have not found any alternative way to obtain it. For as long as these positive effects are ignored in the advice that schools and doctors and other professionals offer on smoking, young people especially will know they are being hoodwinked and will be liable to reject as lies or discount as unimportant even the established facts about the hazards of smoking.

Another reason why propaganda urging individual responsibility in health matters can be counterproductive is that such messages and exhortations can actually undermine what they are purporting to promote. If you tell me what to do in relation to my health, I am encouraged to think myself absolved of real responsibility for taking care of it myself. If I follow your advice blindly, and try to give up smoking or cut down on my drinking or favourite foods, I shall be unlikely to find sufficient motivation for the change and so will soon revert to my old habits – only feeling more impotent than ever. Alternatively, and probably preferably, tired of being told what to do at every turn, I shall reject your advice completely and continue to eat, drink and smoke with a determinedly light heart.

Personal responsibility has been eroded on many fronts in the rather impersonal modern world, and some people appear to have abandoned the attempt to be self-directing. Perhaps this is why so many accept so meekly or even welcome the 'do-gooding' campaigns. They find some strange kind of security in being told repeatedly what harm they are inflicting on themselves. Like slaves who fear freedom, they half enjoy being confronted – each time they try and fail to give up smoking or cut down on the drink – with renewed evidence of their supposed inadequacy, confirming in their minds the belief that nothing can change.

In the long run, however, such failure of self-determination is liable to lead to mounting unhappiness. It can become an addiction itself, as with cigarettes, only in this case demanding ever-bigger doses of self-doubt, self-criticism or self-dislike. It is morally debilitating, and often accompanied by general physical neglect and deterioration. In the end, bitter, unloving and unloved, we may feel we might just as well die of lung cancer or alcohol poisoning or a road accident as carry on living in hell. Or we may try to make life more bearable by forcing others to give us attention because of a series of constant ills. When the health educators offer only glib and condescending exhortations to 'look after ourselves', their apparent interest in our welfare is a curse in disguise.

The Mirage of Preventive Medicine

Along with health education, the concept of 'preventive medicine' has become fashionable, especially since it began to become apparent that modern medical technology, for all its real achievements in patching up our injuries, was proving incapable of having any kind of impact on the main killer conditions. Doctors have become extremely perplexed to find that, despite the ever-increasing spending on drugs and hospitals, surveys show patients to be reporting high levels of illness, and to be dissatisfied with the treatment services on offer. Life expectancy for adults has increased only marginally in recent decades, and there is good evidence for attributing what increases there have been to continuing improvements in prosperity rather than to medical intervention in disease. The biggest advances have tended to be in those countries whose economies have performed best, while in countries such as Poland, where standards of living have fallen both quantitatively and qualitatively, death rates have increased. With many economic commentators predicting hard times ahead, we can expect to see increases appearing elsewhere in forthcoming years, and disillusionment with modern medicine will continue to grow.

So the emphasis has been shifting, in theory at least, to prevention. There has been a growing fashion within medicine itself to argue that if only people would in general be more responsible about the way they live, a lot of sickness and premature death could be avoided. But the idea generally only extends as far as responsibility for physical habits, rather than for the way we think and feel; and to avoid making the profession redundant, the argument is linked to the idea of catching disease early, so that remedial action – which usually means drugs – can be taken. People should allow doctors to 'screen' them regularly, it is said, and then either submit to the necessary drugs or surgery or follow the doctor's orders on eating, drinking, or smoking less. Thus, women are urged to attend cancer-screening clinics, and men to have their blood-pressure and blood-chemistry checked regularly. But since for the vast bulk of the conditions that might be detected there are no long-term cures, it is not at all surprising that such screening has not been proved to save lives.

On the other hand, there are definite costs attached to these 'preventive' efforts, apart from the financial ones. Anxieties about health are fuelled, to the detriment of our ability to face and tackle real problems. Guilt feelings are induced. Self-respect diminishes, as patients try in vain to cut down on their supposedly life-threatening indulgences. The happiness – albeit short-lived – to be obtained from these indulgences may be reduced, without any compensatory benefit. And since a foremost theme of this book is that unhappiness, born of wrong thinking, lies at the root of most illness, it can be argued that the misled and misleading efforts of doctors and health educators to persuade us to live differently are a definite threat to health rather than an aid to fitness.

This is not a facetious suggestion. The philosopher Dr Ivan Illich, author of *Limits to Medicine* (Marion Boyars, London, 1976), has been claiming for years that the world is suffering from so much medical interference as to make it a threat both to the physical and spiritual lives and comfort of human beings. He was among the first to point out that vast numbers of 'iatrogenic' or doctor-induced illnesses arise as side-effects from drugs and operations and mechanical tests. Even more significantly, he described how dependence on professional intervention in health matters was undermining the ability of ordinary people to cope with illness, and with life's problems generally. This intervention, he says, also weakens society's non-medical systems of providing support in times of trouble. In Dr Illich's eyes, we have become ill-informed, passive, fearful, disciplined consumers of medical products and services, desperately in need of 'a new courage to recover power for self-care'.

Alternative Medicine is no Panacea

A flight to 'alternative' or fringe medicine is no panacea for these problems. Its practitioners tend not to have the same degree of arrogance as the mainline professional, and therefore to have greater respect for the patient as an individual and less of a propensity to cause direct physical harm. But there is probably a greater danger of patients becoming trapped into a personal dependency by such therapists, who are often hungry for acceptance and acclaim and may not have that detached professionalism that is so often a real strength in western medicine. The trap of dependence can be time-consuming, expensive, and a hindrance to true recovery.

Furthermore, the effectiveness of alternative therapies often depends strongly on the personality of the individual therapist. This is true in orthodox medicine too, but at present the mainstream medical profession does have better-established institutional systems for regulating the patient's progression through different sources of potential help. The 'alternative' field is an enormous arena and it can be difficult for the patient seeking help to know where to begin.

Alternative practitioners tend to put more of an emphasis on the 'whole person' than orthodox doctors: that is, they are more likely to have some understanding of the importance of the patient's mind and emotions and circumstances in contributing to disease. But there is a trap in this too. Patients may find that on top of being ill, they are being blamed or encouraged to blame themselves for their illness – with no clear indication as to where they went wrong and how to avoid making the same mistakes again. Some even welcome this, as they also welcome their prescribed remedies, however way-out. Having found that a punishing course of drugs or operations or hospital tests has failed to solve their problems, and that a highly restrictive diet, say, has also provided only short-term relief, they may turn to punishing themselves mentally, thinking this will somehow absolve them of their sins and earn them a reprieve from their physical suffering or impending death.

The truth is that such self-reproach only adds to the burdens which the individual faces and may further weaken the body's ability to recover. Although I do hope to persuade readers that their state of mind, and the thoughts and actions that spring from and contribute to that state of mind, are most important in generating illness or maintaining health, this is not to place criticism or blame over past errors. Rather, the aim is to point the way towards self-realization, and through that, towards greater self-control in every sphere. *That* is the most powerful 'preventive medicine'.

Rather than being the passive consumers of medical products and services, whether alternative or orthodox, and rather than pounding around parks in order to divert troublesome emotional drives into otherwise purposeless physical activity, how much better to identify the roots of the malaise and distress which, as we shall see in our studies of individual diseases, underlie most physical disorders. Even if these roots go deep, identifying them would at least present the individual with the opportunity to prevent their further growth and perhaps to gain control over them. Gradually this would improve the chances of remaining free from illness. With this knowledge and realization we would also be in a far better position to know what best to do if our defences fail and disease strikes.

3   Taking Control

Over the past ten years, biochemists have learned how to measure blood levels of just about every known hormone. They have established that, not surprisingly, most of the hormones that increase when a person becomes aroused for effort are the ones that promote processes directed at mobilizing energy. More significantly for health, they have found that while these 'catabolic' or 'doing' hormones are breaking down fats and sugars for immediate use, the production of anabolic, 'building up' substances that promote energy storage and the synthesis of body materials tends to be suppressed. The anabolic hormones are concerned with growth, renewal, and repair. They are also implicated in the maintenance of body defences against infectious and malignant cells. So to remain healthy, periods of active 'doing' *must* be balanced by periods of relaxed 'being'.

The greater the ease with which an individual performs action, and the greater the satisfaction received as a result of these efforts, the quicker and deeper the ability to relax and recover afterwards. This is one reason why successful people are often able to take on so much. Success breeds success. But the reverse is also true: self-doubt and an inability to find the means of true self-expression bring about a distressed state that forbids true relaxation, encourages chronic emotional arousal, and thus fosters ill-health. Many people in modern society, feeling constantly troubled or dissatisfied, override the natural protective checks on physiological activity and engage in what may so often become an unceasing, health-threatening struggle.

Success and acceptance in the eyes of others helps us to regard ourselves as successful, encouraging us to permit ourselves to achieve metabolic balance and to stay well. But no matter how successful we may be in others' eyes, if we do not satisfy ourselves, a feedback circuit running between mind and body stays uncompleted and nerve and hormone activity stays chronically high, putting health at risk in a multitude of ways.

People spend their lives both 'doing' and 'being', moving into action and then – if all goes well – relaxedly enjoying the fruits of their efforts. But individuals differ in the emphasis they give to these different states. Some people feel that the whole purpose of their being is to act; while others feel that they only act in order that they should continue to 'be'. Although both states are essential for the continuance of life, there are extremes in which the one or the other pole on this spectrum of existence is lost sight of or greatly neglected. Western society, with its individualistic, fiercely competitive ways, is inclined strongly towards doing rather than being. Within it, many people successfully lead busy and active, if rather self-centred, lives, their appreciation of a wider world being limited to the needs of their family, perhaps, or business organization. But there are also considerable numbers of westerners who, because of an eventual intolerance of such high levels of activity, or an inability to find satisfaction for the soul in such a competitive, fast-moving world, suffer a crisis of 'being'. Eastern society, on the other hand, tends to enjoy stronger religious and philosophical traditions that emphasize a view of society as a single organism rather than a collection of warring parts, thereby giving more scope for the experience of the 'being' aspect of life. But along with this relatively passive, outlook it has tended to be more vulnerable to poverty and disease and to an inability to act against these ills.

Nervous and hormonal mechanisms associated with 'doing' have been clearly identified. Broadly, the strategy rests on calling up the catecholamines – adrenalin and noradrenalin – to produce to a lesser or greater degree the range of bodily responses known familiarly as the 'fight or flight' syndrome, though that description is inadequate since it only applies to the extremes. Sugars and fats are released into the bloodstream as fuels for effort and action, the heart beats faster, and blood-pressure rises. The system comes into effect semi-automatically, triggered through the autonomic nervous system, when someone sees a task or challenge which he knows or believes he can handle straightforwardly. The person who is ready and able to give an instant response to the situations that come in front will react predominantly in this way: thought and action are as one. Accompanying emotions may range from a simple alertness through to aggressiveness, fear or anger. Then, with the task completed, the individual can relax. Muscle tension is relieved, blood-pressure falls, energy stores are replenished through anabolic hormone activity and any damage done is repaired.

To a considerable extent the 'doing' system is capable in a sense of running itself, through the information-feedback loops of the nervous system, for as long as the challenges faced are familiar and capable of being handled through the exercise of previously learned skills. Sometimes a quick succession of challenges may put the system under excessive strain, and tiredness or minor illness forces temporary withdrawal to allow regeneration of coping resources. Here, a return to an increased level of physical fitness through rest and exercise, and perhaps the acquisition of relaxation skills and some modification of demanding living habits, may well be enough to let the individual carry on 'doing' more successfully than ever.

The physiological dynamics become more complex when deeper levels of our being are involved, and the 'automatic pilot' of the autonomic nervous system is no longer up to the task of giving expression to our thoughts and feelings. Triggered deep in the brain, the pattern of response in this case includes production by the pituitary gland at the base of the brain of a messenger chemical called ACTH (adrenocorticotropic hormone). This travels to the adrenal glands, where it stimulates the outer rim, or cortex, into stepping up the manufacture of a host of chemicals, notably the corticosteroid hormones cortisol and cortisone. These chemicals, travelling through the bloodstream, are capable of bringing about a generalized alert in body processes.

The 'pituitary adreno-cortical system', as it is technically known, is a powerful 'overdrive' arousal mechanism that can serve to give expression to both positive and negative feelings, and can be involved in both pleasant and unpleasant experiences. On the positive side, it may for example accompany the surge of effort that allows a concert pianist to concentrate his or her 'all' into giving a scintillating performance; or it may fuel the thrill of self-transcendence experienced by lovers as they exchange a passionate kiss; or the intense emotional outflow that can be a precursor to the state of bliss associated with religious ecstasy. These positive experiences all involve a kind of overflowing of the self towards others, a powerful outward movement, as the 'part' that is an individual human being takes a step or several steps towards becoming more closely integrated with the 'whole' that is human society. They are experiences that satisfy that deep aspect of the human psyche or soul that strives towards abandoning narrow and selfish behaviour and becoming lost in love.

When such desires are fulfilled, ego boundaries melt away to a greater or lesser degree. At one level, people feel more secure in the knowledge of their place in society. At another, they feel integrated not only into their immediate social surroundings but into a wider world as well. At its extreme the condition involves a transcendental consciousness where the individual feels at one with the rest of creation.

Corticosteroid production fuels the high-arousal process that may be needed to propel the individual towards such heights of integration and security. But in the achievement of the integrated state, the need for arousal ends. As the circuit is completed, there is the experience of joy – almost certainly transmitted by the endorphins, the naturally occurring, pleasure-giving, opiate-like substances whose role in the brain and body has only quite recently begun to be investigated. With that joy, an inner stillness and peace descend which permit total physiological relaxation and regeneration.

When the hyper-aroused condition is associated with negative feelings, however, it is much less likely to produce such a swift and satisfactory conclusion. In this case, the circumstances demanding a response are seen as threats to our being, events or challenges which we fear will weaken us, cutting us off from others and even putting at risk our *raison d'être*. If the threat is overcome, the unpleasantness passes and the reaction ends. But if it is not, the body stays on 'red alert', freezing restorative functions and mobilizing all available resources in the continuing search for a resolution of the threat. The resolution may eventually be achieved through extra-hard physical or mental activity, or through the learning of new skills, the development of new relationships, or the abandonment of ideas or aims previously held dear. The process is an adaptive one, seeking to remove barriers and friction and to ensure that the individual continues to have a well-defined place within society.

But when the process fails, and a person continues to feel a misfit over long periods, the adaptive mechanism is liable to become chronically and eventually dangerously stimulated. Catabolic arousal continues unchecked, and restorative processes are blocked. Sleeplessness and anxiety continue to increase despite a deepening exhaustion. A breakdown in health becomes progressively more likely. The victim may not appear to others to be overburdened, but there are hidden strains and storms inside which can be far more debilitating than intense emotional arousal with a straightforwardly active purpose in mind.

In animal experiments, a high level of pituitary adreno-cortical arousal has been shown to be linked to unfamiliar or intolerably burdensome challenges and threats. It leads at first to a super-charge of the 'fight or flight' system, and if this fails to resolve the animal's problem, to immobilization – an indication that the animal does not want to struggle further, that it wishes to offer no further threat itself, and that it is throwing itself on the mercy of whatever subjected it to this defeat.

The predominant emotions in people who have become extremely aroused in this way are anxiety, agitation, peaceless-ness, and anger, giving way eventually to dejection, fear, help-lessness, self-reproach and depression. And as in the animals, such defeated individuals are in effect throwing themselves on the mercy of others in the hope that somehow help and support and guidance will be forthcoming and a place will be found for them that permits them to continue to exist. Serious illness becomes increasingly likely when this supercharged state con-tinues for long. Weaknesses may develop, as in a hose subjected to excessive pressure, when internal activity associated with either active or passive responses becomes excessive. The weaknesses may lead to compensatory changes, and then to early signs of illness. If the pressure on the system continues, the changes can cause health to spiral downwards towards a breakdown.

When a patient approaches a doctor in this condition, the

doctor has to do no more than validate the patient's existence – by listening to an account of the illness, and by providing comfort and necessary support – to have an immediate effect on both the mental and the physiological state. Finding at least some token of reassurance of his or her worth through this support, the patient immediately gains a degree of peace, and the 'red alert' can for the time being at least be reduced to a less health-threatening 'yellow alert' state of arousal. This effect, known as the placebo response (from the Latin *placere*, to please), is as real as that induced by any drug, and it is to medical science's shame that it has tended to disregard this as unpredictable and therefore unimportant. In fact, it is usually the most important consequence of the doctor–patient exchange. When the doctor acts correctly, the patient is pleased, and thereby takes a useful step towards becoming well. Recently, endorphin activity has been proved to be associated with the placebo effect, so an understanding of the importance of pleasing the patient ought to find its way back to the centre of the medical stage where it belongs.

The Role of Addictions

When the interaction between an individual and the world is generating too much friction and heat, or has so deteriorated as to threaten his or her continued sense of purpose in living, medical ministrations can give temporary support and relief. But a long-term resolution of the threat to health requires a central contribution from the patient. In essence, he or she has to learn how to fit better into society.

Sometimes, external circumstances change, automatically helping the individual to find his or her feet again. But this is a matter of chance. The more certain way to secure more harmonious relationships with the world is to look at the changes needed in our own selves, and particularly in the ways that we allow ourselves to react to external events. In this respect, human beings are utterly different from the animals on whose example so many mistaken ideas about human behaviour have been formed (the description of the catecholamines in terms of the animal responses of 'fight or flight' is an example of the way we demean ourselves). Whereas animals can only react in stereotyped ways, human beings can become responsible for directing or creating their own responses.

So much depends on outlook. An event that throws one person into anxiety and confusion may elicit a calm and coping response from another. If we can identify why we differ so – what are the qualities which the one possesses and the other lacks – it is perfectly possible to start to bridge the gap. If difficulties which present themselves before us can be seen as entertaining challenges providing opportunities to learn, rather than as exhausting obstacles – that is, as stepping stones rather than stumbling blocks – the physiological changes which accompany our efforts will be far less taxing on the body. Best of all, if we can find the means to replace anger and self-pity with an outlook rich in understanding, happiness, and love, many problems will disappear altogether.

The trouble is, because of adopting what have seemed at various times in the past to be easy solutions to our problems, we have generally lost sight of the 'mind' or 'self' that is capable of deciding how we should think, feel, act and react. As a result, many people do not believe it is possible to change in this way. Returning to our analogy of the emotions and body as a horse and cart, sometimes pulling in different directions, it is as though their owner – who ought to be the driver – has let go of the reins altogether.

The 'easy' solutions take the form of addictions. For example, by keeping endlessly busy in the actively 'doing' frame of mind, limiting the consciousness to clearly achievable tasks, a person can avoid facing up to and making good any deeper insecurities and inadequacies, and hence keep depression and its hormonal accompaniments at bay. In the achievement of these limited tasks, some degree of peace – and protection against distress and illness – is found. People can become addicted to adrenalin arousal just as compulsively as to more obvious forms of chemical addiction like alcohol or nicotine. Behind the workaholic's ceaseless activity there often lies a need to anaesthetize the mind against some underlying pain or feeling of emptiness. Here, work performs a similar arousing function as nicotine – and often, in fact, the two go together. There is no threat to health in any work that the individual is actually fit enough to handle (and nor, for that matter, is there proof that moderate cigarette consumption can seriously harm a fit person). But when the behaviour is addictive, it is uncontrolled and therefore liable to grow. It is a weakness, and there will be an ever-present danger of the addiction getting out of hand.

How can work be both arousing and anaesthetizing? In just the same way as cigarettes can both stimulate and calm the mind. When brain levels of noradrenalin are increased in response either to effort or nicotine, the unquiet mind registers this fact and feels able – for a while – to cease sending out alarm signals demanding effort. A 'worry' circuit is completed, for the time being, and the mind can sit back confident in the knowledge that it has geared up body and brain ready for action to resolve its problems. In the case of the workaholic, it does not realize that the problems are often not the ones that really count, but semi-artificial tasks created to divert awareness from deeper concerns.

The workaholic's addiction to physiological arousal is just as real – just as 'chemical' – as the nicotine addict's. And like the heavy smoker, he or she too may be at risk: mainly of premature illness or death from heart and circulatory disorders, arising from constantly elevated blood-pressure and from having a bloodstream excessively loaded with fats and sugars and other substances harmful to the arteries and veins.

The workaholic does at least get things done (although when motivation is faulty, the end result of the work can sometimes involve more harm than good for others). Another kind of person, too proud or inadequate to be busy and successful in activity, blocks feelings of failure or uselessness by wallowing in negative thought about others. Here we have the seeds of paranoia, and phobic and other neurotic patterns of thought. In such a state, we may worry about the most ridiculous things, uselessly but addictively – such as whether the ash trays are clean enough, and what to eat for supper, and what may happen to us in our old age, and why someone in the street looked at us in that funny way. Like the disturbed child who blots out his mental anguish with physical pain by banging his head repeatedly on the floor, we manufacture or concern ourselves with trivial but 'manageable' anxieties, often keeping our attention directed outwards at the defects and activities of others, to cover up deeper fears and inadequacies in our own being.

As with most addictions, a love–hate relationship develops. We would like to stop becoming so worked up, especially when we see it making us ill; and we may welcome some relief from it, such as alcohol or tranquillizers may provide. But one way or another, the anaesthetizing effect must be sustained. Thus, drinkers who find relaxed comradeship through regular evenings of alcoholic inebriation, or lone alcoholics who block out extremes of pain with a gin bottle at home, will not respond to warnings about what they are doing to their health from friends or professionals who simply condemn their drinking without recognizing the real benefits it brings when no alternative has been found. And in the same way, those who find a seemingly perverse pleasure through wallowing in worry, defeat, frustration and pointless anger will not give up these habits of mind, nor lose the need to have resort to drink or tranquillizers as an alternative, while other people simply tell them to 'pull yourself together'. Condemnatory attitudes are actually more likely to hasten the speed at which they fall apart.

Similarly, smokers are unlikely to give up their cigarettes merely because they are told by propagandists that their habit does them nothing but harm, for they are thus prevented from learning how to find an alternative to the satisfaction and support they know they receive from nicotine; and hard-driving men and women who threaten their own health by making themselves constantly exhausted through excessive effort are unlikely to abandon their lifestyle simply on doctor's orders. They, too, need alternative strategies for living and coping that prove equally, and preferably more, satisfying and effective.

The key that can set us free is a proper knowledge of the self; and that is not something to be acquired through books, but through experience. The disease studies that follow, however, may prompt the reader to start looking for self-knowledge in more promising places than hospitals or a doctor's surgery. They are directed towards obtaining a better understanding of the links between mind – or self – and body, between mental states and physical conditions. It needs to be recognized that as human beings we do at least have the potential to control our thoughts and emotions, and to choose how to react and act in relation to what goes on around us, even though the actual power has temporarily been depleted by many addictive habits of mind. Recognition of the ability to choose, and knowledge of the far-reaching effects that our reactions have on our own bodies, comprise two very big steps towards regaining power, even though practice is needed in order that old, destructive, illness-inducing attitudes and habits should gradually recede.

Part Two

Heart and Circulatory Diseases

4 Heart and Soul

We live in a world that encourages heartlessness, and our hearts suffer as a result. They become the victims of ill-treatment and neglect. External circumstances contribute to this neglect, but the way we think and feel as individuals is paramount in determining the health of the heart. So the principal responsibility for correcting an unhealthy situation lies with ourselves.

The best way of ensuring that our hearts stay healthy is to be kind to ourselves, to think well of ourselves. Then our outlook becomes more kindly, and others in turn are more likely to become benevolently disposed towards us.

To be heartless means not to feel as human beings should. This lack of feeling harms us as surely as it is liable to harm others. It allows normal danger signals to be ignored, and progressive damage to be inflicted on the heart without the owner realizing what is happening.

Many potential heart patients are overconscientious people, who seek the stimulation of constantly being engaged in battles of one sort or another, whether against time, or other people, or themselves. They are often ill equipped for handling failure and will push themselves to the limit – and beyond – to avoid confronting it, blind to the harm they are doing themselves.

Heart patients are not really heartless individuals. If they were, they would not suffer as they do. Their inner motivations are as well meaning as anyone's, and their heightened sense of duty means that they number among their ranks more 'doers' than average. But their seemingly self-sacrificing behaviour is also selfish in a way, because it is directed towards what they consider to be right, rather than what others really need from them. Sometimes these two coincide, and the restless striving yields substantial fruit. But because they often unwittingly lack sensitivity and respect in their attitudes towards others (as well as towards themselves), they are liable to be exploited by those whom they wish to serve, whether family or friends, employer or social institution. Conflict and friction become constant features of their circumstances and relationships. And when failure ultimately looms, chronic tension develops and disaster may swiftly strike.

Whether in success or failure, there is a certain warping of perception and emotion that interferes with the normal flow of information within the individual and between him or her and other people.

The linked ideas of information feedback and physiological arousal are indispensable to an understanding of heart disease. Human beings continuously use feedback circuits running between mind and body, and between the self and the environment, in determining the level of response that needs to be made to challenge and change, and then in returning to a peaceful state when challenge has been faced up to and change accommodated successfully. A simple example is provided by the pedestrian who perceives a threat to his well-being such as a runaway lorry mounting a pavement and careering towards him. Sensory input alerts the mind to the threat, and evasive action is ordered. The brain sends relevant instructions to the muscles via the nervous system, and sensitizes the nervous system itself hormonally. As soon as the sense organs deliver the message that the threat is past, the mind can shut down the emergency arousal system and gradually restore normal functioning.

Many of the events that cause us to become aroused in just the same way do not appear to offer any external threat to our well-being, but demand mental or emotional adjustment. An item of news on the radio that 'makes the blood boil', or a confrontation with a shopkeeper over faulty goods, or difficulty in obtaining a connection on an urgent telephone call, are all liable to take their physiological toll. The reaction may well last longer than a simple physical 'flight or fight' response because when we are aroused by items of news, the limitations of red tape or mechanical devices, we can actually *do* very little in response.

Most demanding of all are those major life developments that uproot us from habitual ways of behaving and belonging, depriving us at least temporarily of the feedback which we all need to confirm that there is some place for us in the world. Major adjustment may well be required before some semblance of meaning in life can return.

Numerous studies have shown how high levels of challenge and change in a society bring increased risks of disease and disorder in the circulatory system. What happens is that some individuals find themselves stirred up so often that their blood chemistry and nervous system function at chronically elevated levels. Sometimes this is beneficial – to others if not to the individuals themselves – as those concerned become used to functioning in a way that allows them to be fully geared up for high-performance tasks. But the heavier the burden of arousal, and the fewer the opportunities for proper rest and relaxation, the greater the risk of disease. For the blood vessels may have to work so hard that they begin to tire or wear out prematurely. As the heart beats faster, and peripheral blood vessels contract in order that the maximum flow of blood should be available for muscles, overall pressure in the system rises. The blood vessels suffer minute tears when the fiercest arousal storms rage, and the blood itself becomes sticky to repair the damage and prevent leaks. It may also become heavy with fats that are released as part of the arousal response, providing a rich fuel for the muscles. When arousal does not lead to physical action – as is so often the case in 'civilized' forms of conflict – blood fats remain high over long periods. Fatty deposits may then stick to vessel walls, narrowing them and making them less elastic. All these developments combine over a period to make the heart work ever harder, as it struggles to shift enough of the sticky, fatty blood through narrowed vessels to meet the needs of body and brain.

One does not have to look to a fatty diet, though this may exacerbate matters by adding to the blood's fat load, or to cigarette smoking, which further stimulates secretion of arousal hormones, to see why cardiovascular disease is common in industrialized countries, but rare in traditional societies. The latter, despite their greater susceptibility to natural disasters such as flood or famine, generally offer more stable, settled lives than those available in developed and developing societies.

Rapid economic change is a feature of high-arousal societies. It causes people to move house and to change their lifestyles, to learn new skills or face unemployment, to worry about the declining value of savings and how to provide for children. Social change can also be physiologically demanding. When people lose their 'place' in the world, as with the breakdown of an out-of-date class system, they may find themselves playing a new game for which they do not know the rules. Indeed, sometimes there *are* no rules. And when family bonds are broken, as in divorce, the burden of adjustment involved in making new friends and finding a new pattern and meaning in life can be great.

However, the level of arousal that results from a stimulus depends not just on the size of the threat or challenge, but even more crucially on how you see it and interpret it; and on how your physiology responds to what you see. (These last two are closely linked: the more you see events as threatening, the greater the level of arousal with which you face each day, and the more reactive to further stimuli your whole body becomes.) Though high levels of unemployment, social change, and family break-down are certainly linked to high levels of cardiovascular troubles, there is no simple cause-and-effect relationship. Unemployment may prove an insupportable strain to one person, but spell liberation from a rut or the spur to success for another. Divorce may impose an intolerable burden of adaptation on one child, leaving him or her emotionally crippled for life; but bring another to maturity, encouraging development of the strength and flexibility needed for survival in a tough world. Furthermore, divorce in a family where people have remained physically together but psychologically poles apart – where the relationship has become a war of attrition rather than mutually supportive – may sometimes relieve tensions more than it adds to them. Some homes are battlegrounds where misunderstandings cause hostilities to last for years, with relatives goading each other through words and actions into feelings ranging from irritation to apoplexy. Because of their unremitting nature, constant pin-pricks in the form of wounding words and attitudes are potentially more debilitating than specific frights or disasters (though the latter are more likely to trigger sudden catastrophe, especially in an already overloaded cardiovascular system).

Although the external features of a society make life highly emotionally demanding for its members and so also tend to push up heart-disease rates, it is the way each individual responds to those features that determines the outcome in individual cases.

For this reason, discussions about 'stress' have sometimes obscured understanding. To talk of cardiovascular diseases as stress conditions is not enough, because life is one long process of response to stress – of adjustment to challenge and change. And too little external challenge can in itself prove to be highly 'stressful' for some, causing them to become more internally aroused than others who are seemingly facing far greater demands.

The key question is: why do some people react hotly to a particular stimulus, while others cope with it coolly and easily? The reader will probably be familiar with the 'Type A' and 'Type B' behaviour classification devised by the American doctors Meyer Friedman and Ray Rosenman. The Type A pattern, which is associated with higher risk of heart disease, involves a readiness to react with anger, haste, hostility, irritation, impatience, anxiety and aggression; while people with predominantly Type B reactions are more easy-going, and are less prone to coronaries. But this classification, while valuable in its time because of the clues it offered the medical profession as to where to look for the genesis of heart disease, is not of much help to the individual patient. For it is really just another way of saying that some people flare up easily in response to life's problems, while others don't. It also tends to overestimate the importance of external behaviour, while it is really the inner feelings that count, whether or not they are expressed overtly. As University of Nebraska stress expert Dr Robert Eliot has graphically put it, 'Many crabby Type As have lived to bury their quiet Type Bs.'

We must ask again, *why* are there these differences? Are they inherited, and inviolable? Are they acquired during childhood and fixed in the personality thereafter? Or are they a product of the level of burdens an individual is carrying at a particular time?

It certainly seems likely that the chemical and electrical reactivity of our cardiovascular systems differs at birth to some degree, but this element can be ignored because there is little we can do about it (apart from the use of drugs, on which more later). It is also true that when someone's ability to handle life's demands is constantly stretched as a result of seemingly intractable troubles or a series of disasters, coping mechanisms such as the level of blood-pressure and the reactivity of heart muscle to arousal hormones and to nervous stimulation may become 'set' at a higher level. But this is a natural adaptational response. In most instances it will not profit us much to try to interfere with the response directly, while ignoring the stimulus that provoked it; though if a practical helping hand can be extended to the individual whom life appears to have been treating particularly harshly, this in itself may help to reduce arousal.

Most people in western countries have 'diseased' hearts. It is unusual for a child even to reach early adulthood without some degree of damage to the coronary arteries, for example, though this is not the case in many so-called 'primitive' societies. One may speculate that the more rigid the infant-rearing programmes adopted by a society, the more lonely, loveless, and perhaps punitively repressive the childhood, and the more fiercely competitive the world the child sees, then the greater the difficulty of knowing and keeping in touch with that essence within us that is loving and cooperative and non-violent, and the greater the risk of that intense friction between the individual and the world that gives rise to heart disease. But such speculations will not change the world, and will certainly do nothing to alter the state of the coronary arteries.

One may also surmise that when deprived by harsh childhood circumstances of the 'licence to feel', to be fully a child, because of having to grow up too fast, a person may be encouraged to develop habits of mind that undervalue, belittle and as far as possible suppress emotions – both positive and negative – from awareness. The result can be a certain blindness to fatigue and strain which interferes with the homeostatic feedback circuits and alarm systems warning the healthy individual to withdraw when life's pressures reach levels harmful to the body. It creates conditions in which the emotions are liable to boil over while the individual is still denying their existence.

I am sure it is no coincidence that those societies where, for example, physical violence against children has long been sanctioned as part of home and school traditions, and where coercion rather than cooperation has been the rule – where a tradition that children should be 'seen and not heard' once held strong and has still not completely disappeared – should have suffered an epidemic of heart disease. Scotland, which even at the time of writing makes widespread use of the tawse and strap in schools, has the highest rate of coronary heart disease in the world; as well as football fans with the most violent reputations, and a fiercely individualistic people known for their solitary whisky drinking and fiery temper. The other side of this coin is that a relatively high proportion of Scots have become high-achievers in the business and scientific worlds (including medical science), where qualities of toughness and self-discipline are at a premium.

But while these speculations may or may not help to explain the prevalence of heart disease in the West, they will still do nothing to reduce the risks we face as we move through life.

The influences on a person's cardiovascular 'temperature' that matter most are the qualities – or lack of them – which they are able to bring to bear in their dealings with the world. This, surely, is the crux of the matter; for whereas there may be little that an individual can do to change deep-seated social ills, the field is wide open when it comes to making good deficiencies in our own ways of responding to the challenges of life. The more adept we become at handling ourselves and other people, the less the strain on mind and heart.

This is not to say that we should become manipulative. That would bring only short-term advantage. The ideal is that we should 'have a heart' in all our dealings, a heart so full that it overflows, even in the face of provocation. In this way we would constantly retain our self-respect and win the love and respect of others too. In such a state of mind it would be impossible for us to harm our hearts.

Everyone has experienced how this works. You receive a good piece of news in the post one morning, and float through the day successfully, untouched by the bad moods and thoughtless actions of others, but instead able to spread some of your cheerfulness around.

The saying 'All you need is love' has much truth behind it, but it begs the question of what you need in order to secure that love. Despite the impressions they sometimes give to the contrary, human beings share a fundamental need for the love and respect of others, sufficient to enable them to feel that they have a place and worth in society. Whether the external influences that can weaken our ability to fit into society – such as unemployment, divorce, or bereavement – will cause disease depends ultimately on our internal reserves of this self-confidence and self-respect. Low self-regard causes us to feel constantly threatened as we move through life, so that arousal stays chronically high; and it will then not take much in the way of external challenge for our coping abilities to be stretched beyond their limits. High self-esteem is protective, not only against heart disease but against many other forms of illness too. It gives us the spare capacity to take knocks and learn from them, rather than to be devastated by them and made vulnerable to exhaustion and physical break-down. It also means that in our relationships with other people we will easily find the strength to think about *their* needs, instead of always looking to them to bolster our own fragile self-respect and becoming angry if they fall short on this service.

Most of us grow up with far too little love in our lives. Love is like a food that allows us to grow emotionally to our full potential as human beings, but being unmeasurable it has become grossly neglected in science-oriented, materialistic societies. Doctors left it right out of their calculations for many years in deciding how best to care for mothers and new-born babies; most teachers, who tend to be used more as child-minders than educators in overcrowded schools, have for decades been unable or unwilling to provide love in the context of education; and adults, having been deprived themselves as children, have increasingly sought a substitute in self-gratification: through overwork and greed for external recognition and material acquisitions, or through excessive indulgence in escapist activities such as television, eating, drinking and sex.

There is a big difference between self-regard and self-gratifica-tion. Self regard develops on the basis of true strength, true qualities and abilities. Self-gratification may arise in the absence of self-regard. It is like a substitute for love: having been unable to find love from other people, the individual finds means of securing it for himself or herself. The false pride obtainable through egotistical thought and behaviour is also self-gratification, not true self-regard. Such falsity feeds on itself, diminishing a society generation by generation, making it less and less fit to rear its young successfully, so that generations of 'misfits' emerge until peacelessness – and, heartlessness, with accompanying heart disease – are rife.

If this account of the dynamics of cardiovascular disease is accurate, one would expect to find that people in 'developed' countries, with high rates of heart disease, have a lower opinion of themselves and a greater capacity for heartless behaviour than those living relatively simple lifestyles. This is surely the case (though it does not mean that overall the underdeveloped societies, most of which have devastating problems of their own, present a superior alternative). One can see beyond the pride which is drawn from affluence, phenomena such as the high levels of violence, actual and as portrayed in films, books and on television; the battering of babies and wives and old people; the widespread use of tranquillizers, alcohol and other drugs; the dehumanization of work; the red tape and traffic jams; the pornography and irreligiousness; and the widespread feeling of having lost meaning and purpose in life, of being out of contact with the 'time and tides of nature'. Within the societies that have become victims of such phenomena, there are many achievements also, but these have tended to be victories *over* nature rather than successful integration *with* nature. And in the long run, nature always wins.

With this in mind, let us look at the dynamics behind some specific cardiovascular conditions, at the way modern medicine has tried to intervene, and at some possible alternative approaches.

5 Angina

Angina is a cry of pain from a heart that is undernourished, or overburdened, or both. It can have a crippling, seizure-like effect, bringing the victim to a halt both physically and emotionally. This can be just what the heart – and its owner – need: a reduction in the demands being put on them. Angina can therefore be seen as an ally, offering a sharp but friendly warning. However, if the warning goes unheeded, and the attacks of pain are permitted to occur too often or to continue for too long, they can become malignant and cause permanent harm.

The cry originates in the heart muscle itself, as the organ's means of letting it be known that it is not receiving enough oxygen and other nutrients for the work it is being asked to do. The heart receives its nourishment in blood that reaches it through two main arteries. These fan out like the streams of a river delta to encircle the heart, forming a crown or corona around it – hence the name coronary arteries.

The main bloodstream, after being oxygenated in the lungs, passes through a one-way valve into a large muscular chamber on the left side of the heart, called the left ventricle. This is the real workhorse of the cardiovascular system, since it has the never-ending task of pumping blood (on average about 7000 litres a day) through another one-way valve and off into the entire network of blood-vessels to serve all the tissues in the body. At the point of exit from the heart the blood enters a single, wide-diameter outflow pipe (the aorta), and the two coronary arteries are the first to branch from this, looping back around the heart. So they take the very best of the blood supplies available. Despite this favoured position, they are not always adequate to their task. The sequence of events described in the last chapter, putting all the blood-vessels at risk in the chronically highly aroused individual, seems to be particularly relevant to the condition of the coronary arteries. Damage in the vessel linings, and the deposit of porridgy fats and other materials at the damage sites, may accumulate to the point where the arteries sometimes cannot keep up with the heart's demands. Over the years the vessels may become narrowed or even blocked completely, and generally less elastic, so that the maximum flow of blood they are capable of allowing past is reduced. This process is called coronary athero-sclerosis (from the Greek *athare*, porridge, and *scleros*, hard, meaning hardening or narrowing of the coronary arteries) and has for the last two decades been held by most cardiologists to be the villain of the piece in angina, and indeed in other heart conditions in which the muscle becomes starved of oxygen. It was a simple, mechanical concept that fitted a mechanistic view of the body's workings, and that seemed to offer hope of mechanical intervention. Recently, however, it has begun to be realized that many other factors have to be considered.

The arteries are lined with smooth muscle, and this has nerves running into it that allow the blood-vessels to be narrowed or widened again as the system requires on direct instructions from the brain (specifically, from the hypothalamus, the switchboard of emotional control). The aorta, the main vessel leading from the heart, seems to be particularly responsive to this nervous control. Narrowing may occur even while the heart itself is demanding more blood, perhaps as a means of protecting the circulatory system in general against excessive rises in blood pressure. Biochemical events also cause the flow of blood to the heart to be reduced. Adrenalin and serotonin, both released when someone becomes emotionally aroused, can both cause constriction of the coronary arteries, and the effects of adrenalin are potentiated by adrenocorticoids. Platelets – minute particles in the blood that play an essential role in the clotting process, and in plugging and repairing damage in vessel walls – clump together far more readily when the blood is loaded with the by-products of arousal. Raised levels of thrombin, collagen, adenosine diphosphate, cholesterol, and in particular the release of throm-boxane, a potent constrictor of the coronary vessels, have all been implicated in a phenomenon called coronary spasm, in which the blood-vessels constrict in a cramp-like paroxysm. (This cascade of events probably only scratches the surface of what really goes on. It illustrates what a very delicate and complicated system of checks and balances is involved. Appreciation of this fact may encourage readers to have more respect for the body's internal workings and powers of recovery, and less for the medical interventions to be described.)

Coronary spasm and platelet clumping are closely associated with each other, because spasm encourages platelets to stick to the wall of an artery, while substances released by the platelets as they clump together stimulate the constriction of blood vessels. This mechanism can drastically reduce the flow of blood to the heart regardless of whether the coronary vessels are already narrowed by atherosclerosis. The mechanism is strikingly similar to one that constricts cerebral arteries in a migraine headache (see Chapter 11). In fact, angina can be regarded as a migraine of the heart, or 'heartache'.

Also as in migraine, the phenomenon of hyperventilation – over-breathing – is often present in angina. Shallow and irregular but rapid breathing causes carbon dioxide to be 'blown out' of the system and the blood to become over-oxygenated. Contrary to what one might expect, this reduces the amount of oxygen available to the tissues, including the heart. (In effect the blood becomes overloaded and cannot make the normal exchange between oxygen and carbon dioxide.) Carbon dioxide is present in blood as carbonic acid, and when this is lost the blood becomes excessively alkaline – a condition that can certainly lead to spasm of brain blood-vessels, and is probably involved in coronary spasm too.

Although the condition is more likely to afflict people with severely narrowed arteries than those relatively free of athero-sclerosis, when these nervous, hormonal and respiratory contributions to angina are recognized, it becomes clearer why many angina patients have normal arteries (including up to fifteen per cent of those referred for arterial surgery). Moreover, many people with coronary arteries in a far worse state than those of angina patients who undergo surgery or take drugs for the condition, stay free of symptoms. And the ability of individual angina 'victims' to cope with their everyday tasks is very variable, so that, for example, on a good day they may be able to walk a hundred times further than on a bad day.

We should also look to the left chamber, or ventricle, of the heart, the 'workhorse' of the system, for further understanding of this variability. When the heart is functioning as it should, the muscles in the wall of the chamber have no difficulty in performing the balancing act of keeping the inflow of blood in line with outflow. As the chamber fills, they resist further intake; and then complete a full, well-timed contraction to send the contents on their way. Problems begin when these muscles become overworked. Gradually their resistance to the inflow of blood may weaken, so that the chamber becomes overdistended; and this causes pressure inside the chamber to rise. The wall becomes stiff because of the raised tension, and the outflow and inflow strokes become incomplete and badly timed. A vicious circle is set up, with the already overworked heart muscle having its efficiency further reduced and therefore its demands for oxygen further increased. It has to run to stand still. It is unable to empty itself adequately and so with the internal pressure remaining elevated, it has to work harder to shift the same or even lesser quantities of blood. Like the drowning man whose lungs feel as though they are bursting, it 'gasps' for oxygen. Hence the angina symptoms of pain and tightness, as though the chest and heart are being gripped by steel hands. Swelling and stiffening of the left ventricle can also cause circulatory back-pressure affecting the lungs, giving rise to a frequent need to stand still and belch. And there may be feelings of great heaviness in the limbs, as output from the stiffening, pressurized heart is reduced. The problems become still more acute if parts of the heart muscle are damaged as a result of prolonged oxygen deprivation, and so even less capable of performing efficiently as the demands on them increase.

It is in this context of the heart being so overburdened that it is 'fit to burst' that angina can be seen especially clearly more as a concerned friend than a hostile agent. (Not all angina patients show obviously struggling hearts, however. The overburdening becomes physically apparent over a period, with the heart actually increasing in size, whereas sudden, acute angina attacks can afflict physiologically normal hearts.) The arterial narrowing brought about by 'spasm', and consequent reduction in blood flow, may provide a means of breaking into the vicious circle described above. It is a feature of angina that the pain *can* usually be cut short: through a reduction in physical effort, or through a refusal to be goaded further into the fury or fear that often lies behind an attack.

Unfortunately, because of their tendency towards emotional insensitivity – including the lack of perception of their own real emotional needs – many heart patients struggle on regardless against mounting pressures; and when confronted with angina, rather than acknowledge having unwittingly brought the condition on themselves, and rather than take responsibility for preventing further attacks, they may prefer to pretend it is a purely physical weakness to be defeated through even more superhuman efforts, aided as necessary by medical technology.

This tendency – allied to the strong predisposition of western medicine to an attitude of suspicion, incomprehension and denial towards emotional as opposed to mechanical weakness – has led to angina being widely regarded as the consequence of irreversible mechanical defects in either the coronary arteries or the heart muscle or both, rather than as an essentially reversible warning sign that the individual's heart and/or emotional resources are becoming overstretched. The results for treatment have been not quite disastrous, perhaps, but tragically wasteful of medical effort and human resources.

The By-pass Operation

The heart operation known as coronary by-pass surgery, introduced in the late 1960s, is now as commonplace in the United States as hysterectomy or removal of the appendix. An unbelievable total of 159,000 Americans had this major operation in 1981 and the figure is still running at well over 100,000 a year. The annual cost of these operations is about three billion dollars. By-pass surgery has become an important industry, with some cardiac surgeons earning a million dollars a year.

And yet the justification for coronary artery surgery is extremely shaky, and certainly not scientifically proven. It has not been shown to extend life. When researchers at fifteen different centres in the USA followed 780 patients between 1973 and 1983 in a government-sponsored study into its effectiveness, they found no difference in survival times between those who had the operation and those treated with drugs.

The operation has also come increasingly into fashion in the United Kingdom and elsewhere in Europe. It received an apparent boost at the end of 1982 with the publication of a report by the European Coronary Surgery Study Group. This presented the results of a multi-national study in which the outcome of surgery in a group of nearly 400 men with mild or moderate angina was compared with a policy of drugs only (with surgery later if the condition worsened) for a similar group of men. The patients were followed for between five and eight years. Although more than three per cent of the surgical group died in hospital at around the time of the operation, surgery did appear to bring some advantage: forty-one of the 394 patients in this group had died at the end of the study period, compared with sixty-nine of 373 patients in the medical group. These results led the authors of the report to suggest, preposterously in my view, that rather than reserve the operation for angina patients whose symptoms cannot be controlled by drugs, 'coronary by-pass grafting is the treatment of choice even when angina pectoris responds adequately to medical management'. Apart from contradicting the conclusions of the American study, this assertion completely ignores possibilities for treating patients that involve neither drugs nor surgery; and it fails to take into account ill-effects that can arise from the operation itself. These can be very severe.

The procedure seems logical enough, when looked at merely from the anatomical and mechanical points of view. The surgeon takes a strip of vein from one leg, and uses three-inch or four-inch lengths of this to by-pass the narrowed or blocked coronary arteries, with one end placed above the obstruction, usually on the aorta, and the other below it. Up to six or seven of these circumventions may be grafted into the heart. While the operation takes place, the heart is stopped and circulation is maintained with a heart-lung machine. When completed successfully, there is no doubt that it can improve the supply of blood to the heart and reduce pain in some patients.

But there is a psychological cost to such major surgery, which can exceed any benefit obtained from an improvement in blood flow. A group of doctors at the University of North Carolina School of Medicine, for example, who interviewed thirty by-pass patients before and two years after surgery, found that eighty-three per cent were unemployed. In addition, more than half were sexually impaired. A high proportion had a damaged view of themselves. This was especially true of patients who had suffered angina for eight months or more before the operation: in such cases the surgery seemed to reinforce rather than make good their loss of self-regard. Other studies on heart-surgery patients have pointed to similar conclusions (though the eighty-three per cent unemployment rate was exceptional). Patients have become less self-reliant and assertive, more socially withdrawn, and more subject to anxiety and depression.

It is not difficult to see why. Open-heart surgery inflicts an enormous scar down the centre of the chest, a permanent reminder of the seriousness of the operation and of the fact that it involves a brush with death. Recovery can entail very great pain, and this may serve as further dramatic warning not to risk coming back for a repeat performance (though re-operations are quite often needed). The patient can end up feeling like a beaten dog, especially if the operation follows months of severe angina pain and unpleasant hospital tests.

Brain damage may also contribute to the poor psychological outcome from the operation in some cases. While major damage happens rarely, a Swedish study has indicated that minor damage is common. It may be reversible, and its importance to the individual's functioning is not known. But as a *Lancet* editorial has pointed out, 'cerebral damage may not be obvious at routine follow-up, showing itself only to spouses and families in changes of mood or personality'. The *Lancet* added that although the origins of brain damage often remain a mystery, 'almost every aspect of the by-pass procedure is unsatisfactory' in this respect. Toxic residues from sterilizing gases and plastic tubes in the heart-lung machinery, debris moved into the circulation from traumatized blood vessels, gas bubbles, and greatly reduced blood-platelet activity, may contribute to the danger.

Several studies have shown that patients usually report a

reduction in their angina pain after the operation. But there are numerous possible explanations for such relief other than improved blood flow. Some may consider themselves such chronic invalids, and be so fearful of going under the surgeon's knife once more, that they never again drive themselves as hard as they had done before. Or the operation, and the recovery period attached to it, may provide an opportunity for patients to change or adjust their role and approach to life in ways that are not necessarily defeatist, but better suited to their personalities. In the 'heartless' individuals whom we have seen to be prone to heart trouble – those who have lost contact with themselves and find it difficult to recognize what their own hearts, and other people, try to tell them – the crisis of major surgery may bring about a better awareness of the intimate links between mind and body. There is also a placebo effect in surgery: patients have so much money and time devoted to them that they tend to believe they *must* feel better, for not to be so would be ungrateful to all those who have helped them, and intolerable to themselves after the ordeal they have been through.

In a sceptical appraisal of by-pass surgery published in 1979, a Harvard professor of medicine, Dr Eugene Braunwald, cited a study which showed that a significant improvement in symptoms occurred in twelve out of twenty-three by-pass patients even though subsequent examination showed that all their grafts had closed up. Indeed in the European group's study, the 'graft patency rate' between nine and eighteen months after surgery was a surprisingly low seventy-seven per cent, with nearly a quarter having failed.

The European report gives little idea as to the quality of life experienced by the 'medical' and 'surgical' groups of patients. The ability of both groups to perform on a hospital exercise bicycle improved only slightly over five years. The surgical group did better than those on drugs at first, but the gap narrowed as the years went by. This is in line with findings from other studies that surgery is only palliative: angina is back in about half the patients within seven years of their operation.

If major surgery is the only way to shock an individual whose heart or coronary arteries are failing into easing himself or herself into less destructive ways of thinking and behaving, perhaps that is in itself an argument for the operation. But the trouble is that shock and fear will not necessarily lead to proper understanding. Some by-pass patients undergo the operation in the belief that it will allow them to carry on just as before. According to a 1981 report in *Science* magazine on the popularity of by-pass surgery, a consensus panel in the US found little objective evidence of improvement after surgery; but that Americans 'want to be seen as men, as husbands, as providers, and they are willing to risk their lives at the time of operation so as not to change their lifestyles.'

Western medicine has a strong prejudice against interfering with patients' lifestyles, almost as though to question the excesses of individualistic, materialistic, competitive and unfeeling behaviour which can overtax the heart – or to give practical help to those who flounder because they are not competitive enough – would be somehow subversive and unmanly. There is certainly a good side to this. It encourages respect for the patient's right to determine his or her own lifestyle, whether healthy or not. But when the prejudice extends against even acknowledging and speaking about emotional life as a factor in disease and health, patients are ill served.

In an article on coronary artery by-pass published in 1981, the *Drug and Therapeutics Bulletin* – written by doctors, but published in Britain by the Consumers' Association – declared that: 'Angina pectoris which has not responded to adequate medical treatment remains the major indication for considering by-pass surgery. Apart from a thorough trial of drugs, medical treatment should involve alteration in the patient's lifestyle so as to avoid the excessive physical and emotional stresses that precipitate pain while encouraging carefully controlled exercise.'

Such 'adequate' treatment is not only very rare, but actively opposed by many leading cardiologists. Thus in a handbook for heart patients published in 1981, a British professor advises: 'If I had angina, I would give medical treatment a reasonable trial, but if pain prevented me from doing what I wanted to do, I would have a coronary vein graft operation, knowing that the risk is small and that the chances of complete pain relief are high.' And for victims of a heart attack – often, as we shall see, the victims of continuing to 'do what you want' in a short-sighted way and failing to heed the warning pain of angina – the professor asserts: 'I would expect to be out of hospital in a week, and I would hope to be back at work a month later. I should then return to my former habits and I should do my best to forget that I had ever been ill. I would certainly not change my job or alter my life in any way that did not appeal to me.' This robust approach springs from a rejection of the 'do-gooding' attitude, but by discouraging the patient from looking to the causes of his illness, it could impair the chances of recovery.

In the European group's study, the claims for making coronary by-pass surgery the 'treatment of choice' are based essentially on a comparison between a policy of offering surgery on the one hand and drugs on the other as the means of treating angina. But I believe the picture would be very different if the comparison had been between surgery and what the London consultant cardiologist Dr Peter Nixon calls 'the ancient therapeutic core' of cardiology: obtaining as much from Hygeia, the Greek goddess of medicine 'who believed that the doctor's main responsibility was to find out where the patient's life went wrong and to teach him how to get back to the good health which was his birthright', as from Aesculapius, who was godsent to 'cure' the illness.

In this therapeutic core Dr Nixon places such major influences as the leadership provided for patients in a crisis, attention to the quality of their sleep, intuitive recognition of their emotional needs and provision of support, and guidance on how to adjust to a new 'career' – a new approach of life – after breakdown brings the realization that they can no longer disregard their health with impunity. This does not necessarily mean a radical change in circumstances, so much as a change of attitude. Through psychological counselling and carefully graduated physical training, Dr Nixon attempts gently to rehabilitate heart patients until they are fit and agile enough both mentally and physically to return as victors to the circumstances that previously defeated them. An important part of their prescription for success is that rather than rely on drugs, they should become sufficiently sensitive to their heart's needs to be able to conduct themselves in such a way as to prevent the return of even a single attack of heart pain.

The Chemical Approach

What was once the 'therapeutic core' is now an extremely unconventional approach, however. At the outset of the European study, three-quarters of all the patients were on beta-blockers: powerful drugs that paralyse parts of the nervous system, so that when blood levels of the arousal hormones increase, the effect on the heart and other muscles is reduced. Beta-blockade has been called a chemical 'straitjacket' or 'wheel-chair' because of the physical restraint it puts on the heart.

Again, one can see the narrow logic of the treatment. Having ill-treated their hearts to the point that angina appears, patients have control partially wrested away from them and put into the hands of their doctor instead. The drugs may impose a kind of compulsory mellowing of the personality, forcing not just their hearts but large sections of the nervous system to become less reactive.

But it is a short-sighted policy because it may leave untouched the internal and external problems and behaviour that caused the patient to develop angina. In fact, his or her ability to resolve those problems will probably be reduced: partly as a result of having a heart that is now less capable than ever of responding to the demands put on it, and partly because the patient is denied some of the physical warning-signs of emotional over-arousal.

Prescription of beta-blockers may also lead to a lifelong dependence on the doctor and the drug company. And as with all drugs taken over long periods, unpleasant side-effects are liable to occur: the adverse-reaction register of the UK's Committee on Safety of Medicines contains more than 10,000 reports of adverse reactions in the beta-blocker class of drugs. They can cause heart failure, respiratory arrest, fatigue, double vision, depression, anxiety, weight gain, insomnia, nightmares, hallucinations, cold extremities, blood-flow insufficiency to the brain, and sclerosing peritonitis (the growth of a membrane constricting the bowels). They have also been reported to affect blood fats adversely, in ways suggesting that they could bring about an increased risk of atherosclerosis. As for an apparent, well-publicized ability to help musicians and similar artists to improve performance by overcoming 'stage fright', this is what one English professional opera singer, David Clyde, wrote to a medical newspaper in response to such claims: 'In my own experience, I have to report that the general lack of strength I and other singers have felt while taking beta-blockers on medical advice can contribute to fatigue and a generally sub-optimal performance.'

In an editorial for the *American Heart Journal* in 1980, Dr Nixon wrote that 'an important feature of the cardiologist's map has always been iatrogenic [doctor-induced] disorder, and in my opinion this has been expanded beyond belief by the beta-blockers. It is now commonplace to encounter the expected and reversible complications of reduced cardiac output such as cerebral vascular insufficiency, intermittent claudication, weakness, tiredness, and inability to cope with tasks.' He believes it essential to stop beta-blockers while preparing heart patients for training at a gymnasium (a carefully monitored training programme that produces incomparably bigger increases in exercise capacity than those recorded in the European by-pass study). The drugs prevent the heart from emptying properly in exercise, so that pressure in the left ventricle rises too high, inviting disorders of rhythm and risk of sudden death. By tethering down the pulse rate, they also remove the patient's simplest means of learning to recognize fatigue, and the effects of training, during rehabilitation.

Another group of drugs on offer for angina patients are the nitrates. These were being taken by similar numbers of patients as beta-blockers in the European study on coronary surgery. They dilate blood-vessels, so increasing the volume of the circulatory system and reducing pressure inside the left ventricle. This relieves tension in the wall of the chamber and thus reduces the heart muscle's work and its demand for oxygen. In the long run, however, the body appears to have means of restoring the 'tone' and contractility of the blood vessels, and although supposedly long-acting nitrate drugs are widely used in trying to reduce the frequency of angina attacks, their effectiveness has long been under question. On the other hand, for quick relief of single attacks of angina, short-acting nitrate drugs such as glyceryl trinitrate often work well. The trap here is that they may allow the patient to battle on through ever-deepening exhaustion and emotional depletion until still more serious heart conditions emerge. Also, when the heart is repeatedly deprived of oxygen so severely as to cause pain, these attacks are liable to cause progressive damage to the heart muscle itself.

The idea that coronary spasm – sudden, intense constriction of the coronary arteries – plays a significant part in angina was popular among doctors half a century ago, but was pushed almost into oblivion by the 'hardening of the arteries' school of thought. Professor Attilio Maseri, professor of cardiovascular medicine at the Royal Postgraduate Medical School, Hammersmith Hospital, London, has recently rehabilitated the spasm theory by showing X-ray film (produced by arteriography, in which the blood-vessels are injected with a radio-opaque dye to make them visible) of the coronary arteries spontaneously narrowing to the point of closure and then relaxing again. This is a useful step forward because it demonstrates the error of the assumption that angina necessarily means there is fixed coronary disease. It is in keeping with the view that attacks of angina result from a breach of the body's mechanisms for keeping chemical and electrical activity within safe limits (homeostasis). When the circulatory and nervous systems are driven into activity that breaks those limits, a downward spiral of exhaustion may become established in which the individual cannot sleep, work, eat or think properly, with the result that behaviour and biochemistry both run out of control. Narrowed coronary arteries reduce the homeostatic safety margins, but rarely present a threat to health in themselves.

Sadly, however, the renewed interest in coronary spasm, rather than leading to a search for better ways of helping patients to help themselves in breaking the grip of this vicious spiral, has simply stimulated new efforts to find an answer through drugs. Growing use of 'calcium blockers', such as nifedipine (Adalat), is one outcome. The drugs block the movement of calcium into the cells of artery walls, producing a long-lasting dilatory effect. Calcium ions play a prominent part in exciting and contracting both the heart muscle and the smooth-muscle lining of arteries.

These drugs may make sense as an emergency measure to relieve spasm-induced angina. But their effects are not confined to the coronary arteries. The dilatation is widespread. Circulation is thus made easier, but in time this can cause the heart to have to work even harder, as blood-flow increases. And in a reflex response to the dilatation of blood-vessels, secretion of arousal hormones with a constricting effect may increase. The end result in some patients can be a throbbing headache, dizziness and vertigo because of lowered blood pressure, followed by a racing heart and worsened angina. If the heart was already tired, these changes can cause it to fail completely.

This all adds up to an extremely sorry story in the conventional medical therapy offered to angina patients. The outlook has recently been acknowledged to be especially bleak in 'unstable' angina (that is, when the pain is not brought on by obvious physical exertion). Within two or three years of the first such attack, nearly a third of victims are likely either to have had a full-scale heart attack, or to be dead; and various studies have shown that forty to seventy per cent of patients treated medically continue to be severely disabled by angina. I am convinced that the situation would be dramatically improved if doctors and patients were to shed their drug-oriented vision and turn their attention instead to the mental and emotional strains that underlie the 'heartache' of angina.

Perhaps the reader will by now be unsurprised at the finding of a review published in *Coronary Medicine and Surgery: Concepts and Controversies* (New York, 1975) that 'a large segment of the patients now being referred for by-pass surgery have had medical care no better, and often worse, than that which prevailed 100 years ago.' In a survey of 200 patients admitted to hospital for the operation, it was found that:

in many instances, ineffectual antianginal preparations had been prescribed or potent agents administered indiscriminately or improperly. Frequently, little effort had been expended by patient or physician to eliminate either precipitating factors for angina pectoris or risk factors for atherosclerosis. In no single instance was the patient returned to the referring physician with a recommendation for more intensive medical management or was surgery deferred on this account . . . From such practices, neither the attending physician nor the cardiovascular surgeon can stand on firm ground in attempting to evaluate the indications or results of operative intervention.

Conclusion

Where does this leave angina patients, and their friends or relatives, concerned to know what to do for the best?

Firstly, if a close examination is made of their recent history, it will almost always be found that they have been inflicting turmoil on the circulatory system. A disaster in the family or business which has left them filled with resentment or anger, for example, or chronic tension at work, may have provided a backcloth of over-arousal against which normal demands on the heart – such as a run for a train or a minor argument – now prove too much to handle. Just to identify that this is so should raise confidence (although the really exhausted individual will often deny it at first) because it indicates that the pain is not an irreversible consequence of damaged arteries but of a *tired* system.

Secondly, there should be recognition that when medical fashions swing and controversies abound as much as they have done and continue to do in angina, a fundamental wrongness and ineffectiveness of approach is indicated. Doctors have been throwing one blunt instrument after another into troubled circulatory systems. The miracle is that these systems, and their owners, often have enough strength and adaptability remaining in them to accommodate the chemical and surgical assaults. The tragedy is that few patients are taught how to look inwards at themselves in order to come to easier terms with habits of fear, rage, worry, or overwork that can lead them into emotional and circulatory exhaustion, and to learn ways of defending themselves against external pressures and burdens that weigh too heavily on their hearts.

Thirdly, while recognizing that drugs of proven value are available that will help them when they fail at a particular hurdle, the patient should be reluctant to acquiesce in long-term drug treatment without trying non-drug approaches to lowering their arousal levels first. The ratio of benefit to long-term risks is uncertain, and the drugs may interfere with the patient's efforts to live free of pain by learning how to recover and preserve sufficient physical, emotional, and psychological fitness for the lives they wish to lead.

Medical science is currently taking a few timid steps in the non-drug direction: an intensive programme of stress management and dietary change undertaken by a group of angina patients attending medical centres in Texas was reported in 1983 in the *Journal of the American Medical Association*. For twenty-four days, living in a rural setting and on a vegetarian diet, they were made to exercise and meditate for five hours a day. The incidence of anginal attacks fell from an average of ten a day to one; exercise capacity improved by forty-four per cent; blood cholesterol fell by twenty per cent; heart muscle function improved; and many patients had either to stop or reduce their dose of blood-pressure pills. Of course, this was short-term treatment and it remained to be seen what would happen to the patients once they returned to 'normal' life. But having tasted such comparative well-being, they could be expected to take steps for themselves at least to try to ensure that they did not once again let their emotions outstrip the competence of their coronary arteries to supply the heart's needs.

Fourthly, by-pass surgery is painful and expensive, carries appreciable risks, and has never been tested for effectiveness against rehabilitative or arousal-reducing programmes along the lines of those employed by Dr Nixon, or cited in the Texas study. Rather than be regarded as a 'treatment of choice' for those with narrowed coronary arteries, it should at best be considered a treatment of last resort.

The heartache of angina can be a forerunner of more serious heart disease, and medical help is needed. With cardiological medicine in such darkness and disarray, the outcome is something of a gamble. The patient may be lucky, and find an accurate guide: one who will 'teach him to sleep well when his mind is oppressed, to harbour reserves of energy and stamina for contingencies, to discipline himself against exhaustion, and to reduce his anger to a level his heart can tolerate', in Dr Nixon's eloquent terms. Or he may find himself thrust into a well-intentioned but relentless and inappropriate regime of drugs and hospital tests that threaten to distance him still further from the heart's real needs. But forewarned is forearmed: a good family doctor, in particular, will welcome a positive lead from patients that they wish to be helped to help themselves.

6   Heart Attack

Many people live in fear of 'dropping dead' with a heart attack. They have the idea that it may arrive without warning, as a bolt from the blue. This is a misconception. Most of the tens of thousands of premature deaths caused by heart attacks each year are the catastrophic end point of a long process of decline, involving emotional deterioration accompanied by physiological turmoil and exhaustion. There are ample warning-signs for those who are able to recognize them as such. But the warnings may be overlooked by patients, because of defective powers of self-perception and judgment; and by doctors, whose training tends to overemphasize reliance on physical and numerical indicators of impending ill-health, such as blood-cholesterol levels or the number of cigarettes smoked, at the expense of the common human ability to detect when another person is nearing the end of his or her emotional and physiological tether.

Other misconceptions about heart attacks include the idea that they are a 'disease of affluence', a kind of punishment for success; and that once stricken, surviving victims are forever after liable to a recurrence and must therefore resign themselves to permanent medical scrutiny, perhaps with prolonged or lifelong medication. Associated with these beliefs are theories highlighting cholesterol-rich foods and cigarettes and exciting but sedentary lifestyles as villains of the piece, each supposedly contributing to a silting-up of the circulatory system until one day a larger than usual piece of debris breaks away from an artery wall and lodges itself at some vital passageway, jamming the entire works.

With such ideas in currency, it is not surprising that there is fear. The overall impression gained is that the more robust our approach to life, the greater the risk that heart disease will strike.

Heart attacks are seen as nature's way of hitting back at us, in a rather haphazard and unpredictable but mean-minded way, if we seem to be enjoying life too much. So we are left with the unenviable choice – it is hardly a choice at all – of either risking our lives, or cutting out the pleasures that for many are what make life worth living.

This conventional view is, I believe, completely topsy-turvy. Heart attacks rarely strike down the truly happy or successful. They hit the lonely and depressed, those who have struggled too hard and for too long, or who are staring failure *in their own terms* in the face. Such isolation and misery can afflict the rich and apparently successful as well as the poor and downtrodden, but wealth in itself is not to blame. It is just that money and achievements pale into insignificance when bought at the expense of healthy relationships.

Similarly, although excessive cigarette smoking, over-indulgence in rich foods, gross physical unfitness, and high blood-pressure are all associated with increased risk of a heart attack, these so-called risk factors should be seen not as causes but as effects. Physical self-indulgence tends to grow in proportion to mental and emotional strain. The strain itself – and the unhappiness implied when the strain is chronic – is the root cause of self-destructive behaviour. It does seem certain that cigarettes, rich food, alcohol and in fact every kind of bodily indulgence can contribute to this process of self-destruction, but to the extent that these indulgences bring positive pleasure in otherwise cheerless or insupportable circumstances they may also enhance and prolong life. To try to prevent heart attacks by exhorting people to cut down or cut out such indulgences without regard to their positive effects and without offering alternative sources of satisfaction and support is worse than useless and bound to fail.

Heart attacks are not a 'disease of affluence', though they may accompany prolonged or unsuccessful striving after affluence when this proves detrimental to the individual's emotional development and relationships. Heart disease is by no means the preserve of business executives: among Britons aged between thirty-five and forty-five, those in social classes four and five are nearly twice as likely to have a heart attack as those in classes one and two. In America, it was prosperous California that first showed a decline in heart attacks (from 1955 onwards) in a trend later to extend to other parts of the USA. Heart-disease death rates among Americans peaked in the mid-1960s and fell by more than twenty per cent in a decade – while affluence continued to increase. Affluence is protective, as long as it is not bought at too high a price. The most likely explanation for the recent falls in coronary mortality (seen in Australia and New Zealand and parts of Europe as well as in the US) is that the long-term effects on the heart of the deprivation and miseries of the 1930s have also passed their peak, and the easier living conditions of the post-depression years are now showing up in the mortality statistics. This turnaround has come rather later in Britain and other western European countries, for whom the 1940s also contained deprivations from which the US was largely spared, but it is just beginning to show itself. In contrast, several eastern European countries, where economic progress has been nothing like that in the West and where the demands of the Soviet military machine have been a drain on national resources, have shown big and in some cases huge increases. Deaths from heart disease rose by sixty-nine per cent in Poland between 1969 and 1977, and by forty-one per cent in Bulgaria, thirty-nine per cent in Romania, and twenty-three per cent in Yugoslavia over the same period. Back in the West, the enormously prosperous and peaceful Swiss people enjoyed a forty-three per cent decline in deaths from heart disease among women and twenty-two per cent decline in men over the twenty-five years up to 1976.

Equally ill-supported is the idea that heart attacks can be prevented through a move towards less rich and fatty diets. Consumption of animal fats rose by twenty per cent in Switzerland over the same period in which the big falls in heart disease deaths were recorded. In Japan, despite a 200 per cent increase in consumption of saturated fats (which tend to be of animal origin, such as those in butter and meat) in recent years, heart disease deaths have fallen. In Scotland, whose people have the highest death rate from coronary heart disease in the world, daily fat intake is lower than in any other part of the United Kingdom.

Numerous well-planned trials of low-fat diets and cholesterol-lowering drugs have been conducted over the past fifteen years. These have been 'uniformly without benefit', according to Sir

John McMichael, Emeritus Professor of Medicine at London University. Urging the withdrawal of official medical endorsement for cholesterol-reducing measures, he has pointed out in the *British Medical Journal* that some vegetable oils and hardened fats have been shown experimentally to be potentially more damaging to arteries than butter.

Several very large and lengthy studies have shown that there is little relationship between levels of cholesterol in the blood and levels in the diet. Most cholesterol is synthesized by the body, in response to day-by-day energy needs. Our bodies will manufacture up to 1800 milligrams of cholesterol a day if none is eaten, and as we eat more, the amount produced internally falls. Cholesterol levels certainly do rise both with physical effort and mental strain, but this is a protecting and coping mechanism; when people are deprived of it artificially through cholesterol-lowering drugs, they can become vulnerable to a variety of health hazards.

A 1984 report from the US National Institutes of Health claimed to provide the first 'irrefutable evidence' that lowering blood-cholesterol levels lessens the risk of heart disease. A group of 3800 middle-aged men with raised blood cholesterol were identified. Half were given the cholesterol-reducing drug cholestyramine; and after seven years, they had had twenty-four per cent fewer heart-disease deaths than the other half who received a placebo. However, the difference all but disappears when one looks at deaths from *all* causes in the two groups. The difference was only three – seventy-one in the placebo group compared with sixty-eight in the drug group – because of an increased death rate in the cholestyramine patients from violence and accidents. Since cholesterol rises in response to effort, it is entirely reasonable to suppose that artificially lowering its secretion may reduce coping ability and thereby be linked with an extra risk of violent or accidental death.

The trial's organizers argued that the results supported the view that cholesterol-lowering by diet would also be beneficial, and this attracted headlines around the world. But the British science journal *Nature* deflated the claim. An editorial, commenting that the trial 'has predictably set off another wave of bad advice from the dietary pundits', pointed out that it contained no evidence that the general population could benefit at all from restricting dietary cholesterol. Such a restriction, it said, 'makes too little difference to those who really need to do something about the cholesterol levels in their blood, and is simply irrelevant to those with average cholesterol levels'.

It has been said that the great tragedy of science is 'the slaying of a beautiful hypothesis by an ugly fact'. In the case of the hypothesis that dietary fats cause heart disease, perhaps the greatest tragedy has been that for many years British and American people have been advised by numerous learned bodies – such as the American Heart Association, the British Cardiac Society, and the Royal College of Physicians – to cut down on fat intake on the basis of an unproven theory that this would reduce heart disease. With the theory now appearing to be unfounded as well as unproven, it means that doctors who pinned their reputations to it with missionary zeal have discredited their profession; health educators who took up the cause have weakened their credibility on other issues also; huge resources have been poured into a false line of inquiry; 'cholesterol neurosis' has been added unnecessarily to the many other hazards of life; and perhaps worst of all, millions of palates have been uselessly deprived of the pleasure and satisfaction of eating in a pattern dictated by taste rather than fear.

The American experience of a forty-year increase in heart deaths, followed by a ten-year fall, has provided a natural 'laboratory' for testing other theories of heart disease with implications for the way we choose to live. Cigarette smoking decreased in the USA over the period of the decline in deaths. But the decrease in the habit was confined to men. The proportion of women Americans who smoke has gone up, yet women's death rates started to fall before the men's, and have fallen further.

Attempts to ascribe the falls in both men and women to increased exercise, such as jogging, seem similarly misplaced. Death rates came down as rapidly among those in their fifties and sixties, both black- and white-skinned, as among the younger age groups among whom the jogging craze was concentrated. This is not to say that smoking and lack of exercise have nothing to do with heart attacks. In the long run, both are liable to render an individual less physically and physiologically fit than he or she would otherwise have been. But the question arises, fit for what?

Cigarette smokers are more likely than non-smokers to suffer damage to the coronary arteries, with fibrous thickening of the walls and increased atheroma. The more heavily they smoke, the greater the damage. This means that the heart becomes progressively less able to respond to demands that it should pump more blood. So certainly, the potential for a highly taxing way of life is eventually lowered. Regular physical exercise can raise that potential. It can strengthen the heart muscle, so that it beats more slowly and efficiently; increase the amount of the oxygen-carrying pigment haemoglobin in the circulation; reduce blood fats, lower blood-pressure, and contribute to an increased feeling of well-being.

In both cases, however, it is misleading and simplistic to blame 'unfitness' factors – cigarette smoking and lack of exercise – for heart attacks. The effect on the individual's coping abilities only becomes noticeable if these are being stretched to the limit. If life is being handled successfully in other respects, those limits should not be reached (at least until old age). It is only when a gap looms between self-inflicted or externally imposed demands on the one hand, and the individual's ability to meet these demands on the other, that such lack of physical fitness may have an effect. Even then, the effect may only be marginal – the gap opens slightly earlier than it would otherwise have done. It is emotional and psychological fitness, including the extent of the individual's self-knowledge, as well as understanding of the external events, that are paramount in protecting against the development of such a gap.

When it occurs, the victim can become so distressed that normal restraints on self-destructive behaviour may disappear. The habitual smoker, previously not at risk, may then increase his consumption to such a level that the sheer burden of coping with the toxic products of tobacco smoke will hasten the decline. Weariness gives way to deep depression and exhaustion, which if still unchecked can slip further into a condition where the individual feels life is no longer worth living; and physiologically, the body 'obligingly' responds to that feeling with the chemical and electrical storms that provoke a cardiac catastrophe.

If, on the other hand, a physically inactive smoker has sufficient psychological skills and emotional adaptability either to recognize danger signs when they occur or avoid them in the first place, his or her reduced level of 'coronary competence' should not interfere with a normal life expectancy.

There is another side to the smoking story which is rarely told. The nicotine in tobacco is a marvellous drug for actually promoting fitness, in the sense of adaptability, in some circumstances. Because of this, those doctors and health educators who indiscriminately advise patients to stop smoking altogether are not necessarily serving their best interests. As a stimulant, nicotine gives a short-term boost to arousal. It aids coping ability when concentration is flagging. If a short-term demand is causing agitation, this effect can not only help to get the task done, but have a soothing effect at the same time. When experimenters ask people to remember long lists of numbers, for example, nicotine has been found to help them screen out irritating or distracting stimuli. Performance has also been shown to be improved in tasks requiring vigilance, such as driving. And smokers will tolerate more demands and show fewer signs of anger and irritability if they are able to take the support of cigarettes during stress-inducing tasks. Research findings suggest that smoking may serve 'multiple regulatory functions', says Dr Howard Leventhal, Professor of Psychology at the University of Wisconsin in Madison, USA. It does more than maintain nicotine levels in those who have become dependent on the drug. It serves 'to maintain or strengthen homeostatic stress-induced swings from a stable "reference level"'

Several studies have shown that people have more difficulty giving up smoking when coping with stressful jobs. If they move into a more stable middle age, where both work and social strains ease off (as in one study among a large group of blue-collar workers), the need to smoke tends to fall away. To the extent that cigarette smoking has fallen in recent years – and it is really remarkably little, considering the amount of propaganda against the habit – this may owe more to general improvements in work and social conditions than to the millions spent on anti-smoking campaigns.

The fall may also reflect to some extent the replacement of one supportive habit by another: the average Briton now consumes twice as much alcohol as twenty-five years ago. Drink is widely recognized to be life-enhancing for many, and in moderation it seems to be life-prolonging as well. When 1400 British civil servants were studied over a period of ten years, it was found that those who took up to three drinks a day (three measures of spirits, three glasses of wine, or about one and a half pints of beer) had a lower death rate than either non-drinkers or heavier drinkers.

But drink-related problems have grown rapidly along with the increased consumption. Drunken-driving offences have doubled in ten years, deaths from alcoholism have trebled, and hundreds of thousands of children are regularly beaten or abused by drunken parents (nearly two-thirds of cases of cruelty to children come from a background of alcoholism). It is also claimed that about fourteen million working days are lost because of drink in Britain each year.

British doctors set a lead in giving up smoking after the links with lung cancer and bronchitis became clear, and deaths among them from tobacco-related conditions, including coronary heart disease, have been falling. But deaths among them from alcohol-related conditions, as well as from causes associated with distress, such as accidents, poisonings and suicides, have been rising, along with a rising tide of alcoholism. One might therefore ask whether the enormous pressures not to smoke which have built up among doctors over the past thirty years have really been either in their own or in the public's best interests. To put it crudely, one would have more confidence entering a consulting room reeking of cigarette smoke than of whisky.

Doctors are particularly prone to 'peer group' pressures, to an extent that the rest of us, mercifully, are usually spared. This may help to explain why despite the emphasis put on smoking and diet in public education campaigns about heart disease, a survey showed that fifty-three per cent of the British public identify 'stress' as a chief cause, compared with only thirty-six per cent blaming smoking or obesity, twenty per cent a bad diet, and five per cent high blood-pressure. Yet to the extent that 'stress' is acknowledged by doctors, it tends to be considered medically intangible. When this survey was published, it was greeted by the then director of the Health Education Council – which in its

'Look After Yourself' campaign had urged regular exercise, sensible eating and not smoking as the key routes to health – as indicating widespread public ignorance. But where does the ignorance really lie?

'Risk Factor' Trials Flop

To try to strengthen the case for tackling heart disease by interfering with people's smoking and eating habits, and by drugging them if their blood pressure was raised, a hugely expensive and ambitious experiment involving thousands of people's lives was set up during the 1970s. A number of large trials were started to prove that when doctors intervened with advice, encouragement, and, where necessary, treatment related to these risk factors, the heart-disease toll could be reduced. Unfortunately for the theory, and millions of pounds later, the trials have proved nothing of the sort.

Perhaps the most spectacularly unsuccessful was the UK Heart Disease Prevention Project. A total of 18,210 men, aged forty to fifty-nine, employed in twenty-four factories, took part in a study lasting six years. Nearly 10,000 of them were given quite intensive advice – through factory medical departments and a visiting central team, and involving personal interviews and letters, booklets, posters, and film shows – on cholesterol-lowering diets, smoking, weight control, exercise, and treatment for high blood-pressure, while the remainder acted as a control group for purposes of comparison.

The programme of medical examinations and preventive advice was popular, the researchers reported in the *Lancet* (14 May 1983), reflecting a widespread concern among men (and their wives) supposedly at risk of a heart attack. Most men claimed to have made some change as a result of the advice, though objective testing showed the changes to have been generally small. Nevertheless, in the intervention group the trial achieved a considerable reduction in smoking, an increased intake of polyunsaturated fats (in accordance with the advice) and an increase in drug treatment for those workers identified as having high blood-pressure.

But when the figures for deaths in the two groups were examined at the end of the study period, the outcome was an embarrassing failure, to say the least. Among the workers given the advice, 402 died – compared with only 282 in the control group. The number of deaths from heart disease was also higher: 173 compared with 129. After taking into account the different numbers in the two groups, the intervention group had an eleven per cent higher death rate than the control group.

This UK trial was part of a collaborative venture held under World Health Organization auspices in four different countries, involving a total of 49,731 men. Despite seemingly more encouraging results elsewhere, there was no difference overall between death rates from heart disease in the two groups. In the USA, a similarly vast trial – costing 115 million dollars – produced similarly negative results. It was ambitiously called MR FIT – Multiple Risk Factor Intervention Trial. It screened 360,000 men, aged thirty-five to fifty-seven, to find more than 12,000 at high risk of coronary heart disease. Half of these (6436) were then returned to the 'usual care' of their own doctors, and half (6420) to a special intervention group. The latter were subjected to an intensive effort to modify their smoking, cholesterol and blood-pressure, with weekly discussion groups followed by four-monthly or 'more often if necessary' interviews by a team consisting of a behavioural psychologist, a scientist, nutrition-ists, nurses, physicians and general health counsellors. High blood-pressure was controlled with drugs, radical dietary changes were pressed on the subjects, and anti-smoking measures included aversion techniques and hypnosis. All patients were followed for an average of seven years, to see what dif-ferences emerged between the two groups. The result: despite a supposedly favourable shift in risk factors in the intervention group, death rates were virtually the same. There were 265 deaths (including 115 from heart conditions) in the special group, and 260 (124 heart cases) in the 'usual care' group. There were more cancer deaths – including lung cancer – in the special group: eighty-one compared with sixty-nine.

A number of arguments have been put forward to try to explain away the results of these studies, and to salvage from them some remnants of support for the policy of risk factor intervention. In the UK project, it is said that the intervention was not powerful enough, so that changes in risk factors were too limited. On the basis that in some sections of the WHO project, and in a trial conducted in Norway among a high-risk group, bigger risk factor changes did appear to bring deaths from heart attacks down, the researchers concluded rather lamely:

The implication for public health policy in the UK is that a preventive programme such as we evaluated in this trial is probably effective, to the extent that it is accepted; the problem is how to improve its acceptance.

As for the immensely expensive MR FIT trial, it has been pointed out that men in the 'usual care' group also showed reductions in smoking, blood-pressure, and cholesterol, perhaps by virtue of being volunteers in a trial of heart-disease prevention. It is also speculated that the drugs used to control blood-pressure may have caused more deaths than they saved in the special group, thus concealing possible benefit from other measures.

A *Lancet* editorial commented: 'One can only offer sympathy to the investigators, who have so painstakingly conducted and analysed this vast effort to so little scientific profit. The results prove nothing, and we must turn elsewhere to answer the question, Does prevention work?' But these studies do surely prove something: that if medical interference on a mass scale with the *symptoms* of pressured or distressed lives such as smoking, raised cholesterol, and high blood-pressure have any beneficial effects at all, they are so small as to be very hard to prove.

Furthermore, both the UK and MR FIT trials lend support to the argument that to interfere with drugs in a routine way can be dangerous. In the first year of the UK study, the death rate from heart disease in the intervention group was double that in the usual care group. The excess may reflect the effect of giving people whose hearts are already struggling the additional burden of coping with anti-hypertensive drugs. The effect could be expected to decline as the study continued, as patients adapted to the changes induced by the drugs.

In June 1983, at the inaugural conference in London of the International Society for Humanism in Cardiology (ISHC), one of the world's leading experts on drugs and the heart called for a new medical definition of 'risk factor'. At present the concept considers in blanket fashion those factors identified statistically as being associated with increased risk of disease, and this has been considered grounds enough to intervene. But a safer and more useful definition would be 'the degree of deviation from normal where it is certain that both detection and treatment will do more good than harm', said Professor Michael Oliver, the Duke of Edinburgh Professor of Cardiology at Edinburgh University, who is also president of the British Cardiac Society.

Professor Oliver played a key part in devising and directing an immensely useful and important international trial involving the cholesterol-reducing drug clofibrate. Financed by the WHO it took several years, and at today's (1984) prices it would cost £25 – £50 million. But it revealed quite unexpectedly that this drug, widely used in the 1960s and 1970s, while successful in reducing cholesterol levels and heart attacks, caused an increase in deaths from cancer and other conditions that outweighed the benefit gained.

When the trial was conceived, the organizers had in mind that it would test effectiveness rather than safety. There had been no suggestion from the normal tests and trials required during the drug's development, or from its use in practice, that safety was in question. After all, clofibrate had seemed to be doing its job, and any deaths that occurred would have seemed to individual doctors to be from completely unrelated causes. But when looked at from the commanding heights of a multi-centre study involving thousands of patients, a thirty-two per cent increase in non-cardiovascular deaths emerged; and the overall death rate of those treated with clofibrate was twenty-five per cent higher than in those who did not receive the drug.

Professor Oliver believes that the use of such drugs – and an enormous number are available, most of which have not been subjected to long-term, controlled testing – should be confined to patients at high risk of death from an evident disorder. They should no longer be used among people who are healthy, and who merely face some relatively low statistical risk because of raised blood-pressure or blood fats. He left no doubt as to his concern at the conference. 'What are we doing to these healthy people?' he asked as he listed the side-effects of diuretics, beta-blockers, anti-clotting and cholesterol-lowering drugs. He also urged that 'since drugs are here to stay', prolonged clinical trials for safety as much as effectiveness should be insisted upon, particularly when the drugs are profered to healthy people to free them from a supposed risk of heart attack or stroke.

It would certainly be much better to put more emphasis on watching what happens in human beings who take these drugs, and less on the currently stringent requirements for testing in animals. Such tests are often a poor guide as to what will happen in people, and many find it repugnant to ill-treat fellow creatures in this way. But even if such a change takes place, it will be many years before the benefits start to be felt.

If one accepts that 'drugs are here to stay' – and in our drug-dependent society this certainly seems likely for the time being – then so are the dangers. But for *individuals*, both patients and doctors, there is an alternative. It is to take heed of the failure of the drugs, diet, and anti-smoking approaches to the prevention of heart attacks, and instead to face up to and examine ways of changing those patterns of thought and feeling that generate internal responses conducive to cardiac degeneration and disease.

Going over the Hump

The mechanisms whereby loss of internal order can put the victim at risk of a heart attack are fairly well established. We have seen that, essentially, the catabolic (energy-release) body processes become too strong or go on for too long, and anabolic (build-up) processes necessary for restoration and recovery are not given enough room to do their work. Blood-pressure and blood-flow become highly variable as booster arousal mechanisms are brought into operation in a tired system – there are sudden, uncontrolled surges; blood cholesterol and uric acid concentrations rise steeply in response to emergency output of catabolic hormones such as adrenalin, noradrenalin and cortisol; and so also do blood platelets and plasma fibrinogen, thickening the blood and making it ready to form clots. In time, coronary arteries become damaged as a result of repeated assaults, and the heart muscle, perhaps enlarged because of having to pump so hard against a circulatory system repeatedly put under high pressure, may suffer infarction: a wasting away or scarring of tissue caused by an insufficiency of oxygen arising from reduced blood-flow.

Depending on the severity of the attack, this may have only transient effects, or leave the victim permanently crippled, or prove fatal. Final disaster may also strike in the form of a process described medically as sudden coronary death, which is usually caused by nervous/electrical disturbance in the heart muscle leading to fatal loss of rhythm. The disturbance can be triggered directly by the brain, but is most likely to kill when it happens in a heart already damaged or struggling as a result of a long period of effort unrelieved by the positive feedback that promotes anabolic rest and repair.

To understand these mechanisms, whereby the heart can become increasingly incapacitated, and ultimately stop work altogether, is still only to look at the surface signs of trouble, however. We need to know much more about why as well as how these self-destructive processes occur, and what governs their intensity of impact.

The International Society for Humanism in Cardiology was founded specifically to promote a closer examination of pro-longed stress, mental exhaustion and the effort of coping with modern life as factors in the development of heart disease. Despite the common-sense view that intense mental strains can lead to serious illness if they are too unremitting, and despite the cascade of physiological changes accompanying such strains which so clearly predispose people to heart trouble, mainstream medicine has been reluctant to consider the contribution of psychological and social factors to coronary illness.

One reason for this reluctance has been the difficulty of measuring people's feelings, as opposed to their behaviour, in a scientific way. A study that tried to circumvent this difficulty through the use of a psychological questionnaire was described at the ISHC's inaugural conference by Dr Ad Appels, Professor of Medical Psychology at the University of Limburg, Holland. The questionnaire was answered by 3570 male civil servants in Rotterdam. It was found that 562 of them – fifteen per cent – met the description of being exhausted and depressed. Over a period of just three months, six of the men had a heart attack – and five of these six were in the 'exhausted and depressed' group, compared with only one out of the remaining 3000. On the face of it, this gives the 'exhausted' group a heart-attack rate twenty-seven times that of the others, said Professor Appels. Even after taking into account the small numbers involved, the relative risk remains strikingly high, much more so than in the case of any of the 'traditional' risk factors of smoking, cholesterol, and high blood-pressure. The study indicates that the drained, helpless state often noted in (and by) heart-attack victims – 'You want to hide yourself from it, just sleep and put yourself in their hands,' said the comedian Eric Morecambe after the first of a series of attacks that finally proved fatal – is a cause as well as an effect of coronary illness. Those most at risk will tend to answer 'yes' to questions like, 'Do you have a feeling that you have come to a dead end?' Professor Appels said that one victim, an obsessive worker who had to give up his job at fifty-nine after an accident, said he felt the power leaving his body 'like the air leaves a bicycle tyre when it has been ridden over a nail'.

But we all become exhausted and depressed at times. So why don't we all have heart attacks? What were the differences between the 557 civil servants who did not have a heart attack despite their exhaustion and depression, and the five who did? A concept developed by the London cardiologist Dr Peter Nixon, also presented at the ISHC conference, throws light on these questions. He calls it the human function curve (see diagram).

At first the curve rises rapidly from the commencement of a given task or job, indicating ample physical and mental coping resources. As it nears its peak, fatigue sets in and relatively big increases in arousal are required to squeeze out a still higher level of performance. Then there comes a point of decreasing returns: the individual is exhausted, and further effort only deepens the exhaustion and worsens performance. To outsiders he or she may appear to be running round in circles, endlessly active but achieving less and less, worried but not capable of showing the calm concern that removes problems. Ill health may set in if this over-aroused state continues for too long; if the individual still does not spot the danger signs, and the ill health does not force a withdrawal from effort, breakdown may result. A heart attack is one such breakdown.

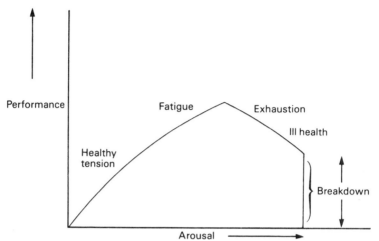

Arousal signifies the extent to which an individual is activated by the sum of demands faced, and performance is the ability to cope or contend successfully with those demands.

Some people, one suspects, live 'over the hump' as a matter of habit, constantly courting exhaustion and ill health. Curiously, however, their very familiarity with this territory may be protective. They go on for years feeling 'below par', and worrying about themselves, but know how to avoid sliding into the deepest trouble. Others enjoy living dangerously near the top of their curve, and make occasional forays into exhaustion and ill health, but they keep their sense of self-protection intact and know how and when to pull back into healthy function.

Others again may spend all their life on the upslope of their curve, but are caught out by a big emotional blow or series of blows that plunge them into a highly aroused state with which they have never had to contend before. In such cases they may go careering into a breakdown almost by accident, insisting that the increased effort that has always resolved their problems in the past will surely do so again. Such people, if they survive the breakdown physically intact, stand a very good chance of making a complete recovery, once they understand how the crisis occurred.

With less favourable prospects for recovery are those who at a certain point discover themselves to be for whatever reasons so ill-equipped for satisfying roles or relationships in life that illness and ultimately 'Just death, kind umpire of men's miseries' seems to beckon enticingly. It is distress accompanied by hopelessness, a giving up rather than a continued coping effort, that carry them towards the final curtain.

Shelley wrote in *Queen Mab*, 'How wonderful is Death, Death and his brother Sleep' and it is significant that Peter Nixon identifies poor sleep as a feature often accompanying his heart patients' exhaustion. His treatment programme makes use where necessary of drug-induced sleep as a means of pulling patients back from a debilitatingly high level of arousal into a state in which they may become receptive to advice on what has happened to them, and to guidance on facing the future as health 'winners' rather than 'losers'. He believes that after such counselling, health can often be restored by natural methods – whereas the present preoccupation with controlling the symptoms of heart disease with diet, drugs and surgery obscures the possibility of restoring healthy function.

Present at the ISHC's inaugural conference in London was an American doctor closely associated with the Framingham project: a pioneering epidemiological experiment in which 5000 inhabitants of a small town in Massachusetts have been watched and questioned for many years in the hope that their experience might cast light on the causes of heart attacks. It was from the results of this study that high blood-pressure, high cholesterol and animal fat intake, and cigarette smoking were shown to be related to increased risk of heart attack. On the basis of this statistical association, the theory that these risk factors were causes of heart attacks emerged and grew until it came to be accepted almost as fact.

The doctor was disturbed by the challenges to this theory that he had heard during the conference, and at its close he asked, 'If you are not going to talk to patients about diet, smoking and blood pressure, what are you going to say to them? What can you do to help prevent heart attacks?'

No answer was offered, wisely, I think, and the conference was allowed to end on that note of dissent. For there is no glib solution. In so far as there is an answer, it was implicit in the tenor of the day's contributions, and in the 'humanistic' aim expressed in the society's title. It lies more in the area of human relationships than in numbers, in the art rather than the science of medicine. The risk factor concept is useful as a means of building up a generalized understanding of heart-disease processes, but even when widened to include the warning signs provided by patients' feelings (an aspect for the most part neglected by the Framingham investigators), it does not give valid grounds for interference in individual cases.

The doctor has to form what is in the end an essentially subjective judgment: 'This person is ill, or is likely to become ill soon, and needs help.' The ideal strategy is a double one: to take measures to relieve the distressed and exhausted *state*, such as by trying to ensure comfort, rest and relaxation; and then to attend to the *trait* that may have helped to lead up to the exhaustion, by trying to improve the patient's understanding of the self and of the way our responses to circumstances and events determine their impact upon us. As Hippocrates put it, it is more important for a doctor to know what sort of person has a disease than what sort of disease a person has.

For the reader as a prospective patient, freedom from risk of a heart attack lies in learning to become an 'easy effort-maker': handling oneself smoothly in relation to the turbulence of external events, so that these are coped with successfully. This involves a positive commitment to making the most of life rather than the negative approach of, 'I mustn't smoke, drink, eat too much or let my blood pressure go up.' As and when our level of well-being permits, 'not smoking', for example, then becomes a natural part of staying well, along with moderate eating and drinking habits, rather than an end in itself.

Similarly, rather than trying to stay alive by withdrawing from struggle through the alluring option of letting ourselves be labelled as 'diseased' (because of high blood-pressure, angina, or even a heart attack itself), we can protect ourselves while continuing to take part in the fray by transforming our attitudes towards ourselves and our responses to events. Anger, irritability, self-pity, self-reproach, hopelessness, are all cardiopathic – they put the heart at risk – especially in combination. Respect for the self and for others, contentment even in adversity, and love for life, are cardioprotective.

After a Heart Attack

Lack of recognition that a heart attack represents an emotional and mental as well as a physical crisis has led to some unfortunate developments in what may happen to a patient after an attack has occurred. Sophisticated monitoring equipment was introduced in the 1960s and 1970s, and special 'coronary care units' established in hospitals, in the hope that these would help to reduce the risk of death in the early stages after an attack. But the machinery has tended to intrude too much, coming between patients and the human care and concern for which they yearn. Any benefits arising from these specialized units appear to have been counterbalanced and even outweighed by the increased fear and alienation caused by them. Admission to ordinary medical wards has been seen to carry no higher a risk of death; and studies have indicated that most heart-attack patients are better off not being taken to hospital at all, but being treated at home, where family and friends and GP can provide the reassurance and comfort that appear to save more lives than banks of instruments monitoring heart-beat, blood-pressure, and fluid balance.

In his book *The Diseases of Civilisation* (Hodder and Stoughton, 1981), Brian Inglis recounts a story told by the epidemiologist Professor Archibald Cochrane that illustrates poignantly the double-think that pervades these matters. When one survey showed that patients treated at home did a little better than patients treated in coronary units, the figures were deliberately transposed before being shown to a cardiologist. He promptly denounced the trial as unethical: it had condemned people to die at home who might otherwise have lived. But he could not be persuaded to declare the coronary unit unethical when the table was shown to him the right way round.

The story illustrates a bias that is deep rooted not only in medical science, but in what most westerners expect and demand from their medical systems. How many people, confronted with a close relative undergoing a heart attack, would not feel uneasy if the family doctor advised that rest at home would be the safest form of care? And if the relative died, how many would not chide themselves – and even sue the doctor – for having failed to insist on hospital treatment? But if the patient died in hospital – albeit alone and friendless, and wired into defibrillator and electro-cardiograph rather than human company – we would comfort ourselves that 'everything possible was done'.

This bias towards 'doing', and a neglect of the health-promoting value of letting a patient 'be' (where circumstances permit), lie behind decades of enormously expensive but futile medical efforts to find drugs to fight the risk of death in the months or years subsequent to a heart attack. Trial after trial of agents with an anti-coagulant action on the blood, for example, not only failed in the end to show benefit, but put many thousands of people at unnecessary risk of serious bleeding caused by the drugs, as well as imposing on them the debilitating inconvenience of frequent hospital attendance in order that this risk could be monitored. As long as such treatment lasts, it prevents the recipient from putting a heart attack into the past and getting on with the business of living more successfully and enjoyably. Aspirin, which reduces blood coagulability through an effect on platelets, has also been the subject of several huge studies in heart-attack patients in Europe and the USA, some of which are still continuing. But it causes an increase in gastro-intestinal bleeding and pain, and no benefit has been shown; it may even be causing a marginal increase in cardiac deaths.

How frustrating it must have been for those involved in such work when their repeated efforts to provide life-saving measures for heart-attack patients have led monotonously to failure. One may feel critical of the culturally shared bias towards 'doing' that has led them into making so many mistakes, but the medical profession has become increasingly self-critical, aware of the pitfalls, and vigorous in its assessment of new claims. British doctors have had a particularly good record in this, and Britons have been spared some of the gross treatment excesses inflicted on the American people in areas such as heart surgery (see Chapter 5) and anti-hypertensive treatment (see Chapter 7).

Conclusion

The comic Mel Brooks has remarked that 'people let their hearts attack them'. This insight is supported by the failure of attempts to prevent heart attacks through attention to physical signs of intense effort such as raised blood-pressure, cholesterol, and smoking, and through drug treatment to modify blood-pressure and blood constituents.

People let their hearts attack them when they feel so trapped by exhaustion arising from prolonged struggle with seemingly insoluble problems, and so wracked with inner misery arising from life having lost colour, flavour, spice and meaning, that a desperate self-inflicted injury of this kind seems to be the only way out. As with suicide attempts, there may sometimes be a real determination to end it all; but the attack can also be a means of focusing dramatically on the victim's plight in the hope that the mould can be broken and that help may bring change.

Patients and their relatives, as well as doctors, often prefer to concentrate their attention on the physical events surrounding the attack, rather than the faulty dynamics in the victim's life that led up to it. This seems simpler and in the short run has the advantage of being less painful than facing past mistakes and learning from them, but it will not truly strengthen the patient. To prevent life's problems from becoming overwhelming again, and inviting another coronary, the individual needs increased knowledge of the self, with a better understanding of such arts of living as knowing when to fight and when to 'flow', and the strength of character to find contentment in circumstances that might previously have made the heart sad. The writer and former coronary patient Rex Edwards described this, direct from experience, in his book *Coronary Case* (Faber and Faber, 1964):

I know for a certainty that I shall never have another heart attack unless in some way it is brought about by me, either by allowing my physical condition to degenerate, my mind and body to become overtaxed, or by permitting a too personal and too subjective reaction to some situation of stress. This conviction has relieved my mind of its most potent weapon for destruction; worry . . .

Stage two on my road back to health was the ability at last to learn to 'box clever' – that is, to deal with all stressful situations, whatever their nature, intelligently and constructively, or else calmly to refuse to have anything to do with them. This implies a degree of mental awareness and self-control which is difficult to cultivate but which, with per-severance, will always come. Instead of reacting to a situation with emotion – one reacts with reason. In matters involving personalities one comes to understand other people better, to see more of them, as it were. Situations which contain the seeds of hostility undergo a subtle and significant change: in fact, life itself takes on altogether more significance.

Postscript

In July 1978, I received a letter from the manufacturers of Anturan, a drug originally developed as a treatment for gout, announcing that it was now available on prescription in the United Kingdom and Republic of Ireland for preventing death following a recent heart attack. The letter declared that the results of a major trial in the US and Canada 'suggest that the lives of as many as eighty to 100 patients in the UK could be saved each week by treatment with Anturan following a myocardial infarction'. A copy of a preliminary report on the trial, from a recent issue of the *New England Journal of Medicine*, was enclosed. It claimed to show a forty-nine per cent reduction in total cardiac deaths amongst those treated with Anturan, compared with an identical group of patients receiving a placebo drug; and a fifty-seven per cent reduction in sudden death.

Also enclosed was a commentary from the *NEJM* by Dr Arnold Relman, the editor, describing the results as important and highly promising, congratulating the group of ninety-six researchers on their 'heartening success', and raising the question: 'Can one ethically continue a double-blind trial of this sort when the drug under study has already been shown to reduce mortality by more than half?' In January 1980, a final report from the research group was published in the journal indicating that Anturan had caused an astonishing seventy-four per cent reduction in sudden death during the critical period of two to seven months after a heart attack. The manufacturers, Ciba-Geigy, reinforced further publicity with a press conference in New York.

But the following spring, the US Food and Drug Administration turned down the company's request for permission to label and advertise Anturan as a prescription drug for preventing death after a heart attack, saying that the reduction in sudden deaths had been exaggerated. Some patients who died, according to Dr Robert Temple, director of the FDA's cardio-renal drug products division, had been excluded for 'minor protocol violations' – and most of the excluded patients turned out to have been taking Anturan. Furthermore, there were misclassifications of deaths, which nearly all also turned out to favour Anturan. Some suggestion of beneficial effect from the drug remained, but it did not approach statistical significance and could well have been due to chance.

Reporting on this 'abrupt turndown', the US correspondent for the *Lancet* referred to speculation that unconscious bias could have found its way into the Anturan study's conclusions.

The reason for these doubts is that Ciba-Geigy, which had a stake in the outcome, not only paid the bills (around four million dollars), but also was deeply involved in the daily processing and collection of data before turning over the information to an independent policy committee. The controversy has a direct impact on medical practice in the treatment of heart-attack victims. Ciba-Geigy says physicians in 32 countries – including the UK, Canada, France, South Africa, and New Zealand – are prescribing Anturan or its equivalents for patients in this category. Even in the United States, despite restrictions against company claims, the Government cannot forbid physicians to prescribe it.

Two successive chairmen of the trial's operations committee had both been full-time employees of Ciba-Geigy, the *Lancet* reported, although neither was identified as being affiliated with the company in the final report in the *NEJM*. Dr Relman said he did not think it necessary to identify Ciba-Geigy since the company's interest had been noted in the preliminary report two years earlier. This was true; but in the accompanying editorial at that time Dr Relman wrote as follows:

The study was organized and financed by a private pharmaceutical firm, but the design and conduct of the study, as well as all policy decisions, were fully in the hands of an independent outside group of consultants expert in the fields of thrombosis, epidemiology and biometrics. This was, of course, a calculated entrepreneurial gamble by a company that stood to gain much from a successful outcome. What is admirable, and probably unique in the annals of the United States pharmaceutical industry, is that a private firm was willing to undertake a large-scale, rigorously controlled study of this sort while delegating scientific direction entirely outside the company.

Pharmaceutical companies have been much maligned of late, so it is particularly gratifying to be able to note here that capitalistic self-interest can sometimes be enlightened, and perfectly compatible with the most scrupulous kind of clinical testing. Not all large-scale clinical trials need to be funded by the National Institutes of Health. Firms standing to profit from the sale of safe and effective pharmaceuticals have a responsibility to share in the sponsorship of the expensive large-scale trials that are sometimes required. And to assure objectivity and rigorousness, such trials ought to be designed and controlled by independent consultants. Let the present case serve as a model of what can be achieved by this means.

Perhaps we should let it do just that, though not in the sense that Dr Relman meant at the time. The story is certainly instructive. The fact that a study involving ninety-six researchers, backed in such glowing terms by the editor of so prestigious a medical journal, can still reach conclusions so utterly full of holes, illustrates how elusive 'objective' science can be.

There is nothing to suggest that any of the researchers acted other than in good faith; but even leaving aside the company's interest, the very existence of the trial betrays bias, towards the belief that intervention with drugs is the right and proper way, the 'ethical' way, to approach the treatment of patients recovering after a heart attack. One feels that the jubilant tone of Dr Relman's words also indicates how much he had been 'willing' it to succeed. Yet I do not know of a single, well-controlled, long-term study proving significant benefit from drugs either in the general prevention or treatment of attacks. My own bias is towards the view that it may in the end be impossible ever to prove such general benefit, and the best that can be hoped of these trials is that they will show whether or not a drug is dangerous in general use. Objective scientific methods cannot be used to determine a set treatment regime for struggling human individuals.

This is not to say that drugs should have no part in the treatment of heart disease. As Professor Oliver declared, they are here to stay, and in individual cases, as part of the interaction between doctor and patient, they can help. Nor should the failure of the risk factor intervention trials aimed at preventing heart attacks cause doctors never to tell patients to cut down on fatty foods or cigarettes or to take more exercise. It is the search for mass solutions to the problems of individuals, and the attempt to find scientific backing for such mass treatment approaches, that has proved so unfruitful.

Doctors can best judge what to advise individual patients on the basis of a personal assessment of each individual's needs – and on the basis of those needs at the time of consultation, not next month or next year or for the rest of the patient's life. Far from being a negation of science, this is the only way that a doctor can exercise either true science or art in medicine. As William Blake wrote in *Jerusalem*:

> He who would do good to another must do it in
>   Minute Particulars.
> General Good is the plea of the scoundrel,
>   hypocrite, and flatterer;
> For Art and Science cannot exist but in minutely
>   organized Particulars.

7 Hypertension

If a doctor nods sagely after wrapping a sphygmomanometer around your arm to measure your blood-pressure, little do you know what scientific uncertainty that apparent confidence conceals! And while ignorance is sometimes bliss in medical matters, if the reading is judged to be high there is such a strong possibility of your being offered inappropriate and potentially harmful treatment that it makes sense to examine for yourself the pros and cons of accepting a diagnosis of hypertensive disease (i.e. high blood-pressure).

Orthodox medical opinion holds that high blood-pressure is the biggest treatable medical killer, responsible for thousands of deaths each year from heart attacks, strokes and kidney failure. Drugs are very widely used to try to reduce it to a 'normal' level, and general practitioners are regularly urged to seek out hypertensive patients, even those who consider themselves to be fit and well, in order to let them know that they have a serious condition which, so it is said, could silently destroy them unless they submit to lifelong medication.

Yet one of the first difficulties with this approach is fundamental: no one knows how to define 'high' or 'normal' pressures. In western society it is considered normal for blood pressure to rise with increasing age, but there are other societies – usually leading simple, low-pressure lives – where this does not happen.

Life insurance records show that, statistically, each upwards step in pressure is associated with an increased risk of dying from failure of the circulatory system at some point, whether in the heart, kidneys, or brain. But blood-pressure rises as a normal physiological response to exacting or worrying circumstances. So which should we regard as abnormal, the circumstances or the elevated pressure? To lower people's blood-pressure with drugs, while leaving them struggling with jobs and situations and lifestyles that demand 'high-pressure' responses, may be to interfere with normality rather than restore it.

Blood-pressure is not a physiological constant, but a condition that varies widely from minute to minute and hour to hour. Pressure falls when an individual is relaxed, and rises when he or she becomes aroused. These changes are part of the broader patterns of bodily adaptation coordinated by the brain in response to life's demands. Readings can treble in the course of twenty-four hours, and pressure changes of twenty to thirty per cent happen throughout an average person's day. Yet an astonishingly large number of family doctors seems unaware of this variability, judging from the results of a survey reported in the *Journal of the Royal College of General Practitioners*. It was found that among a group of patients on pills for their blood-pressure, more than a third received their prescription on the basis of only one reading.

This finding alone could mean that very large numbers are taking blood-pressure pills unnecessarily, because a single reading is highly likely to show an unrepresentatively high figure. People are usually anxious about undergoing any procedure at the hands of a figure of authority such as the doctor, and this nervousness may well cause a temporary rise in pressure. They may also be anxious about the outcome of the test, since it is no joke to be told you have a condition generally considered irreversible. And they probably visited the doctor in the first place because of some other anxiety or illness, which may also have pushed up their blood-pressure. People often go to the doctor because a general unease about their health, arising from the feeling of having too much to handle, makes them conscious of some minor complaint that normally does not trouble them.

Often a second reading taken only minutes after the first will show a considerably lower figure. This was brought home to me in a dramatic way when I tested a few years ago an automatic blood-pressure measuring device installed in a big London department store – the first to reach Britain. An early-morning press conference had been called at the store, and I had rushed there from the Underground to write an article about the machine for my newspaper. There were television cameras, hot lights, photographers, and a lot of anxious people, including myself, milling around. I could feel my heart racing when my turn on the machine came, and the readings were 155 systolic (the pressure, measured in millimetres of mercury, reached in the arteries as the pulse comes through) and 103 diastolic (the eased pressure while the heart's main chamber refills ready for its next beat). These figures would be enough to qualify me for lifelong medication, by some doctors' reckonings. But a few minutes later, when a nurse on hand for the press launch repeated the test with a manual device, both figures had dropped by more than twenty points, well into the 'normal' range.

When blood-pressure soars in a malignant, uncontrolled way, intervention with drugs can very definitely save lives. But the balance of advantage becomes much less clear cut with the middling range of pressures into which fall the great majority of patients currently receiving treatment. While in some cases the drugs may help to postpone cardiovascular breakdown, for many others they do no such thing; and for all, there are risks of physical and psychological side-effects. These can be deeply distressing, and even life-threatening. But many doctors, probably the great majority, are unaware of what damage the drugs can cause. Reservations tend to be confined to certain researchers and academics. The pressures and trends at the level of the family doctor and the patient have been towards ever more aggressive treatment. The drug 'solution' is the norm.

These pressures increased as a result of a recent US study of anti-hypertensive treatment, in which 10,500 patients were followed for five years. The researchers (the Hypertension Detection and Follow-up Program Cooperative Group) concluded that systematic, effective management of hypertension, using drugs, had great potential for saving lives among the large numbers of people with high blood-pressure, including those with only 'mild' forms of the condition. The comparison was not between 'drugs' and 'no drugs', however, but between on the one hand free and carefully supervised all-round therapy, including drugs but with frequent consultations at special centres, and on the other the patient's usual source of medical care. The special-care group received extensive psychological and social attention and support. They were encouraged to attend clinics frequently – five times a year was the minimum – not just for drug treatment follow-up, but for general medical treatment, health education, and help from 'social support groups' for reducing risks to cardiovascular health such as obesity and smoking. All these services were free, including transport to the clinic. And a large team of field workers went out to persuade absentees (often the most worn-out and most at risk in studies of this kind) to change their minds.

Most of the differences in outcome – benefit in the form of fewer deaths in the special care group – occurred in black patients, even though they comprised less than half the total. Since black Americans are more likely to be socially, financially, and medically deprived, this strongly suggests that the benefit being received was psychological and social in character rather than pharmaceutical. The free care and attention received by the special-care group may also have helped to save lives from conditions unrelated to hypertension. An overall reduction of nearly seventeen per cent in deaths from all causes was achieved, but within this, the fall in deaths fron non-cardiovascular causes (a benefit unlikely to be attributable to blood-pressure pills) was almost as much as the fall in cardiovascular deaths.

At present, academic medical opinion in Britain appears to favour a policy of treating patients with a diastolic blood-pressure of 100 or more (while in America diastolic readings of ninety plus and even eighty have long been considered grounds for drug therapy). But according to a survey among doctors and nurses in a large British hospital, there is widespread disagreement both on the level of hypertension requiring treatment and even on the method of reading diastolic blood-pressures. 'Diastolic anarchy' was how the authors of a report in the *British Medical Journal* described it. Most of the doctors treated 'mild' hypertension – between eighty and 100 diastolic – although as the authors of the report said, 'no proof exists that such treatment is beneficial'.

Drug trials in this territory of mildly raised blood-pressure have proved contradictory or inconclusive. A Medical Research Council study, involving the biggest drug trial ever mounted in Britain, is looking at the effects of treating patients with initial pressures of ninety to 100, and its results are anxiously awaited around the world; not least by the drug companies, who stand to add about three million middle-aged people in Britain alone to their market of potential lifelong customers. But at the time of writing the trial has been under way for six years, without any clear interim indications of benefit being reported; while on the other hand there have been definite suggestions that serious physical disorders, including impotence and diabetes, are associated with long-term use of some anti-hypertensive drugs. Even for those with blood-pressures at levels now considered the undisputed territory of drug therapy – diastolic pressure over 100 – the grounds for treatment seem to me to be nothing like as clear-cut as doctors believe.

Apart from the uncertainties over measurement, and the physical side-effects (on which more later), pharmaceutical trials have for the most part failed to consider the effects of pressure-lowering drugs on the quality as opposed to the length of patients' lives. There are strong indications that these are almost always of an adverse kind.

Medical assessments are usually hopelessly inadequate in detecting such ill-effects, and the patients' own reports are also unreliable. This was illustrated dramatically by research conducted in Newcastle upon Tyne, reported in the *Journal of the Royal College of General Practitioners* in 1982. Seventy-five patients with diastolic pressures above 100 – forty-one women and thirty-four men, with an average age of about fifty – were questioned about their progress on anti-hypertensive drugs. Their doctors, and a relative or close companion, also completed questionnaires. The doctors registered 100 per cent improvement. Blood-pressure was under control in all their patients; none had deteriorated clinically, and there had been no complaints about the effects of the treatment. However, only forty-eight per cent of the patients said that they felt improved on the treatment (twenty-six of the women and ten of the men), and eight per cent said they felt worse.

In contrast to both these assessments, nearly 100 per cent of the relatives (seventy-four out of seventy-five) judged the patients to have deteriorated overall while on the drug treatment. On a life-impairment scale, nearly a third of the patients were said to have suffered severely, forty-five per cent to have shown moderate adverse changes, and twenty-five per cent only mild or negligible changes. Even in this least impaired group, 'energy' was judged to have been adversely affected in sixty-eight per cent. In the severely impaired group, 100 per cent of the patients had suffered losses of energy, in their relatives' eyes. A large proportion had also suffered deteriorations in memory, mood, interest, initiative, and activity; increased worry and irritability; and hypochondria. Reduction of sexual interest (where the patient had a husband or wife available for comment) was reported in all groups, increasing with the level of overall deterioration. There were no differences between men and women in this regard. The drugs being taken were mainly beta-blockers, diuretics, and methyldopa.

This was a modest research project, using a comparatively small number of patients, headed by a GP who is an honorary research associate at the University of Newcastle upon Tyne (aided by a consultant psychologist at Newcastle General Hospital and two research associates at the Medical Research Centre, Newcastle). But I regard it as worth more than the numerous big-finance, multi-centre mega-studies of the effect of anti-hypertensive drugs that have failed to ask the right questions (of the right people).

A few years ago an article appeared in *The Times* concluding that the National Health Service should introduce more screening for hypertension. Questioning this, Professor Thomas McKeown, of Birmingham University's Department of Social Medicine, and author of *The Role of Medicine* (Blackwell, Oxford, 1979), wrote in reply:

When people are identified as hypertensives by mass screening, because of the unreliability of the measurement some are incorrectly diagnosed; some who are correctly diagnosed do not follow the prescribed treatment; in some who follow the treatment, control of pressure is not achieved; and some are treated unnecessarily, for there are people whose raised pressure appears to be compatible with a life of normal duration and quality.

But perhaps the most serious consideration is that quality of life is gravely prejudiced for many people when they are told that they have a life-threatening condition of which previously they were unaware. (A recent investigation in industry has shown that absentee rates are doubled among workers when they are informed that they have raised blood-pressure.)

Professor McKeown concluded reasonably that 'the suffering and costs from screening need to be weighed against the expected benefits'. We may equally reasonably substitute for 'screening' the word 'treatment', and perform a similar weighing operation as to whether or not to allow ourselves to be categorized as suffering from the sickness of hypertension, should a doctor wish to give us this label and the drugs to go with it, at some present or future date.

Blood-pressure is relatively low in the resting, 'anabolic' state, but it rises, along with cardiac output, when the individual is required to cope with internally generated or externally imposed demands. In arousal, extra blood-flow speeds extra energy to vital tissues such as muscle, heart and brain, while at the same time the flow to areas of anabolic activity such as the gut, kidneys and skin is reduced and cell-renewal and other repair processes are postponed. So it is not at all surprising that when a drug is taken that interferes with this natural adaptive process, a deficiency of energy should result. That deficiency might be a price worth paying if the alternative was rampant energy expenditure in an individual so highly aroused as to be on a rapidly self-destructive course. But the situation is very different for people whose blood-pressure is up as part of their strategy for *survival*, not just physically, but as a reasonably successful and happy human being in a demanding world.

In the case of married people, especially bread-winners, more than individual well-being is at stake: spouses and other relatives may also be adversely affected if the ability to cope with life is reduced by drugs. In drug trials which look for reductions in death and illness rates among people treated for high blood-pressure, perhaps the fate of relatives should be included. If faced with extra problems because of a husband or wife's drug-induced incapacity, the burden of illness might simply be transferred to their shoulders. This would never show up in present studies.

Perhaps it is just as well that the internal blood-pressure control systems at the individual's disposal are complex and adaptable enough to render many drug attempts at interference relatively ineffective in the long run.

Three natural bodily mechanisms contribute to the *raising* of pressure. One is the ability to increase the contents of the cardiovascular system – the volume of blood – through water retention. Another is to decrease the volume of the system itself, through narrowing the blood-vessels. With more blood in smaller vessels, the pressure has to rise. The third is for the force and rate at which blood is pumped through the system to be increased, as the heart works faster. In order that pressure should neither rise nor plummet wildly, two automatic controls operate these three mechanisms.

One involves the kidneys. A *fall* in blood-pressure prompts them to produce the hormone renin, which stimulates the formation of angiotensin. This is a vasoconstrictor – it tightens blood-vessels – and it also causes the adrenal gland to secrete aldosterone, which in turn causes the kidney to excrete less sodium and water. Thus the volume of blood is increased, and blood-vessels are narrowed, so that pressure will tend to be restored and the stimulus for the production of renin removed. Sodium retention also promotes vasoconstriction because it tends to increase the 'tone' of the muscles lining the blood-vessels. A *rise* in blood-pressure, conversely, suppresses this renin-angiotensin cycle, and stimulates the transfer of sodium and water from the blood to the urine.

The second automatic control involves the autonomic nervous system. The walls of many parts of the cardiovascular system contain receptors that are wired to the brain and are sensitive to blood-pressure. Stimulation of these receptors caused by a rise in blood-pressure brings about reflex responses in which the heart is encouraged to slow down and the blood-vessels to widen, thus holding blood-pressure to whatever 'steady state' the system is set.

If these automatic regulatory mechanisms were to have the last word, blood-pressure would stay so constant that increases and decreases in physiological arousal and relaxation could not properly be expressed. Flexibility is ensured by the provision of override mechanisms under the control of the brain. It is the brain, in fact, that determines what blood-pressure is to be, minute by minute and hour by hour. Short-term elevations are achieved mainly through nerve signals to the heart, spurring it into beating faster and more strongly. The aorta, the main outflow pipe from the heart, is also very responsive to nerve stimulation from the brain and appears able to narrow greatly so as to increase the pressure of blood leaving the heart, like water spurting from the tight nozzle of a hose.

Secondly, the brain can order coordinated shifts of total hormone patterns. The pituitary gland at the base of the brain secretes the hormone vasopressin, which has an anti-diuretic effect on the kidney, stimulating water uptake and thus increasing blood volume. It shares this task with the adrenal hormone aldosterone. Aldosterone and vasopressin also act directly on the brain to stimulate thirst, and an appetite for sodium (in the form of salty foods).

Raised levels of sodium in the circulatory system contribute to a third line of control through which the brain can raise blood-pressure, this time using the mechanism of arterial constriction. Sodium increases the readiness of blood-vessels to tighten in response to nervous stimulation, and in response to raised levels of the adrenal gland arousal hormones noradrenalin and cortisol.

If the brain registers chronic arousal, with blood-pressure remaining high over long periods, these three mechanisms between them allow the whole system to become set at a higher level of activity. The heart grows bigger and stronger and can pump harder. The adrenals also increase in size when habitually asked to work overtime through direct nervous stimulation from the brain and in response to hormones released by the brain. The kidneys are also under direct neural control by the brain, and the pressure threshold for switching on and off the renin–aldosterone mechanism causing water and sodium retention is raised. Blood-vessels thicken and become more 'muscular' so as to be able to withstand the high-pressure flow. This thickening and increased resistance means that even in relaxation, blood-pressure remains higher than when the arteries were more flexible. And when the vessels constrict in response to nerve or hormone stimulation, resistance to blood-flow – and hence sustainment of pressure – is high.

Furthermore, there is alteration in the pressure-sensitive

receptors (baroreceptors) in the walls of the cardiovascular system that have lines through to the brain to help it to monitor what is happening. They become 'blunted': the pressure at which they will fire is raised, so that they do not discharge their nervous impulses to the brain until higher than 'normal' pressures are reached.

These changes are adaptive to life at high pressure, and as 'natural' as the short-term changes that accompany acute arousal. However, just as a car 'souped up' for racing is more prone to mechanical breakdown, so also is the individual with a high-pressure cardiovascular system. The blood-vessels – particularly the arteries, which take the full force of the high-pressure blood-flow – may develop small cracks and tears in their linings. These damage sites often become the focus for deposition of fats, such as cholesterol, which circulates at high levels in the fuel-rich system required to sustain chronic arousal. As time goes on, arteries serving the heart, kidneys and brain, all of which work overtime when serving the needs of a high-pressure life, may begin to fail. The blood-vessels may rupture, and cause damage by bleeding into surrounding tissues; or their damaged state may make them progressively inadequate at supplying enough blood to vital organs. Heart failure, kidney damage (sometimes leading to malignant hypertension in which blood-pressure races right out of control), stroke, and more gradual deterioration of mental function such as in senility – all endemic ailments in the high-pressure societies of the West – are all frequently associated with chronic hypertension.

These undoubted links between chronically elevated blood-pressure and cardiovascular disease have been thought to provide a firm rationale for taking drugs to bring the pressure down, when it appears to be both relatively high and 'fixed'. But many hazards and uncertainties still arise.

Diagnosis remains difficult. While it is certainly bad medical practice to prescribe blood-pressure pills on the basis of only one reading, even a series of elevated readings should not be interpreted as necessarily signifying the presence of disease; but rather that the individual is chronically highly aroused. If arousal is reduced for long enough, some of the changes that led to pressure being 'set' high can be reversed. Vessel walls can become thinner and less resistant to blood-flow; baroreceptor sensitivity can return to what it was; the enlarged adrenal gland will shrink again, and become less reactive, when demands on it are reduced; as also will the enlarged heart; the brain will cease to call up high levels of arousal hormones; arousal hormone receptor sites throughout the body will fall in number when the pressure is off, making the entire system less reactive; and the blood, now carrying less oxygen and fat, becomes thinner and flows more easily again.

It is true that long periods at high pressures, or often repeated sudden bursts of pressure, are likely to have raised the base pressure in the system, the minimum to which the individual's blood-pressure can fall. But drugs are not going to change that either. To the extent that they have an effect, it is to interfere with the individual's ability to make the most of whatever flexibility of response still remains in the cardiovascular system.

Another difficulty is that when a drug is used to block one of the body's three mechanisms for raising blood-pressure – water retention, vasoconstriction, or increased heart action – compensatory responses take place. For example, when a diuretic is prescribed to stimulate salt and water excretion and thus lower blood volume and pressure, the brain detects this change and sets about reversing it. Compensatory increases in renin, angiotensin, aldosterone, and vasopressin stimulate the kidney into trying to save sodium and water, induce an increased appetite for salt and water and stimulate blood-vessel constriction. And nervous system responses may include further vasoconstriction and an increase in the rate of the heartbeat. Drugs such as methyldopa or hydralazine can be given to block the vasoconstriction, but these tend to stimulate still more compensatory responses, particularly in cardiac output.

When the patient's blood-pressure is seen to be back up again, another increasingly popular line of pharmaceutical attack has been to add a beta-blocking drug (or to use a beta-blocker as 'first-line' treatment). The molecules of this drug occupy the beta-receptors in heart tissue, blocking nervous system excitation of the heart (and also impeding activation of the renin-angiotensin-aldosterone system). Originally introduced for angina, beta-blockers are certainly a potent addition to the anti-hypertensive armament, and in conjunction with other drugs they have made it possible for doctors to bring about relatively sustained reductions in blood-pressure.

However, each of the drugs has undesirable effects, not occurring unpredictably as rare events, but intrinsic to the fact that they are interfering with rather than aiding the achievement of the internal balance towards which the individual's physiology is striving. Thus, diuretics, the most commonly prescribed anti-hypertensives, cause partial dehydration on a chronic basis (or until compensatory changes render them useless anyway). This thickens the blood, tending to decrease its flow, especially where vessels are damaged; so diuretics can contribute to oxygen starvation in a struggling heart. The artificial reduction of salt and water stimulates compensatory increases in renin production by the kidneys, aldosterone production by the adrenals, and vasopressin production by the brain, and these hormonal changes commonly alter the balance of various vital blood constituents: potassium and magnesium tend to fall, while calcium, uric acid, and glucose often rise. The changes are not of theoretical interest only, but may cause dangerous disorders when the drugs are taken for years on end.

A recent study from the Royal Postgraduate Medical School at London's Hammersmith Hospital showed 'quite pronounced' diabetes-like alterations in blood chemistry in a group of thirty-four patients who had taken thiazide diuretics for fourteen years. None had diabetes when examined fourteen years previously; but six were now diabetic, and a further seven had the pre-diabetic condition of glucose intolerance. (Of a further thirty patients involved in the earlier tests but who were no longer available for study, eleven had died, and eleven had given up their thiazide drugs – in eight cases because their doctor had detected the side-effects of either potassium deficiency or elevated blood sugar.) The researchers pointed out in their *Lancet* report that glucose intolerance is associated with raised risks of death from coronary heart disease. Development of this abnormality during long-term thiazide treatment for raised blood-pressure, they concluded, 'suggests that we may be substituting one long-term cardiovascular risk factor for another'. On a more cheerful note – for the millions currently taking thiazides – they found that the glucose intolerance quickly lessened when the drugs were stopped.

The magnesium and potassium falls often seen in patients taking diuretics should also give rise to concern. Loss of potassium can cause fatal disruption of the heart's rhythm. Loss of magnesium can cause spasm of the coronary arteries and has been implicated in some of those cases where people suddenly drop dead through heart failure, without any warning. A study in Norway found that the incidence of sudden death among patients with mild hypertension who were treated with the diuretic hydrochlorothiazide was three times that of an untreated group.

When drugs are being tested for safety, patients' biochemistry is monitored and deficiencies or excesses can be corrected. But this leads to underestimation of the dangers, because such monitoring is rare when the drug is used generally. In one study of a group of patients whose hearts were failing because of ventricular fibrillation (rapid, uncoordinated muscular spasm in the heart's main chamber), eighty-seven per cent of those receiving thiazide diuretics had potassium depletion, compared with only just over two per cent of those not receiving these drugs.

The rise in uric acid accompanying diuretic treatment can cause gout. The rise in calcium, along with the fall in magnesium, is associated with excitation and constriction of artery walls, sometimes uncontrolled and dangerous.

Recognition of the role of calcium in blood-vessel spasm has led to the introduction of calcium antagonists – drugs which reduce the entry of calcium into blood-vessel cells (as well as other tissues, including the heart) – as a new treatment for hypertension. But a principal side-effect of this treatment is . . . fluid retention. So we come full circle: tackle one feature of the system to try to reduce blood-pressure, and another pressure-elevating device immediately takes its place.

A *Lancet* editorial on calcium antagonists concluded that their future seemed promising, but added: 'Inevitably, for some time cautious monitoring of patients is necessary, particularly bearing in mind the novelty of the pharmacological effect and the need for life-long treatment of hypertension. If experience with diuretics is to be repeated, we may still be learning about the calcium antagonists in another quarter of a century.' And patients are the guinea pigs in the meantime.

A longer-established drug for treating high blood-pressure by relaxing the blood-vessels is hydralazine. But this produces compensatory increases in the renin-angiotensin-aldosterone system, and also in heart output. There is evidence that when the heart is already working near the limits of its energy reserves because of damaged coronary arteries (very common in hypertensive patients), the increased workload caused by the drug can trigger angina and cause damage to the heart muscle through oxygen starvation. Hydralazine can also cause fever, skin eruptions, numbness in the extremities, flushing, nasal congestion, dizziness, headache, palpitation, and arthritis.

Finally, the beta-blockers. These drugs appear to come nearest to the root of the problem in hypertension. By occupying the beta-receptor sites at which adrenalin and noradrenalin produce their effects, they frustrate the arousal process at many different levels. The receptors exist not only on the muscle cells of the heart and blood vessels, but also on renin, insulin, liver and fat cells, and in the respiratory system. However, this depth of action is accompanied by a corresponding depth of unwanted reaction. Patients with struggling hearts may experience fatal heart failure when a beta-blocker interferes with cardiac stimulation. Similarly, by blocking adrenalin-induced release of sugars from the liver, the drug can cause serious hypoglycaemia – shortage of blood sugar – in the acutely aroused individual. Beta-blockers can also cause respiratory arrest (because of a loss of stimulation to the muscles that dilate the respiratory passages), deterioration of kidney function, and blood-flow insufficiency in the brain. There can also be alterations in fat metabolism, with an increase in blood levels of triglycerides, worrying from the point of view of atherosclerotic damage to the arteries.

Little is known about the long-term effects of the beta-blockers. They have not been around long enough for these to become clear. But the galaxy of short-term effects, and the far-reaching consequences of beta-blockade on physiological systems, ought to arouse the most profound caution. Furthermore, one consequence of prolonged use that has emerged is that the actual structure of the heart muscle undergoes striking changes. Like wheelchair-bound legs, the drug-restrained heart may begin to shrink. In rare instances this has already been seen to lead to heart failure.

I find this possibility of a withered heart most frightening. Not just because of the risk of heart failure – which might be offset by the benefits that may accrue to other parts of the body when an overactive heart is put in chemical chains – but because heart function is so intimately connected with brain function and personality. A review in the *Journal of the American Medical Association* found that in several groups of patients who were interviewed before and after a course of a beta-blocker drug, there were marked personality changes. 'Type A' behaviour – aggressive, restless, impatient, striving – was altered by the drug, and in one group most patients acquired characteristics more appropriate to 'Type B', tending, according to the researchers, to become unhurried and easygoing, yet constructive in outlook. This led 'Onlooker', a witty and acerbic columnist in the *Pharmaceutical Journal*, to comment:

Having worked with one or two 'Type A' colleagues, I am sorry I did not know enough at the time to slip a slug of propranolol [a beta-blocker] into their morning coffee, and so save myself endless stress. And I can think of a few prominent you-know-whos whose reaction to a course of beta-blocker might change the shape of society and the course of history. The great virtue of such drugs is that they do not render 'Type A' people drowsy; they just appear to mellow their outlook.

Not drowsy, perhaps; but according to those relatives questioned about the effects of anti-hypertensive drugs (including beta-blockers) on their husbands and wives in the Newcastle study cited earlier, certainly not improved for the better. Cardiologists, and other doctors with sufficient perception to see past the brave front that patients often put on to mask their deterioration, report weakness, tiredness, and inability to cope with tasks, especially ones requiring sustained concentration and effort, as common side-effects of beta-blockers. Unexplained central nervous system effects that can be accompanied by sleeplessness, night-mares, hallucinations and depression suggest that the psychological arousal that has been denied physiological expression will not just go away, and bear witness to the fact that in accepting these drugs, patients are taking a huge step into the unknown. (For further discussion on beta-blockers, see Chapter 5.)

The potential for harm is probably lessened by the fact that beta-receptors multiply in response to beta-blockade, demonstrating once again the complexity and ingenuity of the body's compensatory mechanisms. But to the extent that this occurs, it may be reducing the effectiveness of the drug in lowering blood-pressure. It also explains a withdrawal syndrome that has been found when beta-blockers are suddenly stopped: the cardio-vascular system may become more sensitive than ever to the action of the arousal hormones, so that heart-rate and blood-pressure both shoot up. The effect only seems to last a few days, but it is obviously important that patients should rest during this time, or the rebound effect could be dangerous.

According to an editorial in the *Lancet* (December 1982) discussing the pros and cons of diuretics and beta-blockers for hypertension, beta-blockers 'are no longer believed to be more effective anti-hypertensive agents than diuretics'. The editorial concluded that there was not much to choose between the two groups of drugs. So beta-blockers seem to be going the way of so many other drugs: causing great excitement at first because of their evident impact, but with the effects only lasting as long as it takes the body to circumvent them. If the individual continues in an aroused state, bigger doses will then be felt to be needed; but as the dose grows, so does the risk from side-effects.

Yet patients are rarely given even a partial picture of the hazards and shortcomings of anti-hypertensive drugs. Indeed, doctors themselves are generally not aware of them. If a patient taking a diuretic drops dead suddenly from heart failure, his death will probably be attributed to his hypertension rather than the drug. If a patient on beta-blockers seizes up at the wheel of a car and causes a fatal accident, how can an individual GP be expected to suspect that the drug was to blame? Besides, if patients were told the full risks they were taking by accepting the pills, their blood-pressure might go through the roof. Especially if they had only been diagnosed as mildly hypertensive, and therefore not shown to benefit from medication even by the short-sighted and deficient logic of drug trials.

Why, then, expose the illogicalities and uncertainties here?

Because control of blood-pressure should not be considered the exclusive or even the predominant terrain of doctors, but rests very largely in the patient's hands – or, rather, in his or her mind. It is the mind that reacts to the flow of events with which we are confronted and which determines, through the brain, the level of bodily arousal required to cope with this flow. When the flow is fast, as in industrialized, highly technological societies, high-pressure existence will encourage a high-arousal lifestyle and a high-pressure cardiovascular system. This is a valid strategy for living in such circumstances. To interfere with it through drugs, as thousands of doctors are doing, without providing advice or support of a psychological or social kind that would help to ease the pressures and therefore the need for hypertensive responses, is an act of deprivation and cruelty.

Moreover, to impose a chemical handicap on physiological function just at the time when the individual may need his or her wits to be working at maximum efficiency is to *increase* the chances of the problem becoming chronic and unsolved, a permanent irritant. Failure to cope means that the mind lacks the signal that it is coping effectively, so that it has to continue to maintain a physiological 'red alert'. Success resolves arousal, allowing effective sleep, deep relaxation, and energy renewal. Thus, another report in the *Lancet* has shown that when a group of forty men with so-called 'established' hypertension were watched over six to seven years without being given drugs or any other kind of intervention, blood-pressure returned to normal in one third of them. The rises and falls observed were associated with 'stressful and less stressful' periods in the men's lives.

Intervention *of the right kind* can help. A three-week programme of exercise, relaxation through meditation, and vegetarian diet devised by a group of Texas doctors caused eighteen of forty-six heart patients either to stop or reduce their dose of anti-hypertensives. Other studies have shown that falls in blood-pressure induced by meditation can be accompanied by falls in noradrenalin, renin and cholesterol (and no doubt much else besides). Reduction of blood-pressure through relaxation, in contrast to drug treatment, does not bring about compensatory increases in other arousal mechanisms.

We need to be able to face challenges with fully free and flexible physiological responses, untrammelled by drugs. But there can come a point where further increases in arousal are counter-productive. Hyperaroused people can find themselves on a slippery slope in which problems seem so overwhelming that the greater the efforts to solve them, the more intractable they seem to become. Attempts to extract still greater efforts only increase exhaustion, inefficiency and incapacity. At London's Charing Cross Hospital, the cardiological team led by Dr Peter Nixon has helped numerous hypertensive patients to break through this vicious circle with a short programme of sleep and rest, aided by sedative drugs as necessary, accompanied by advice on how healthy tension and fatigue can give way to exhaustion, ill health and breakdown if arousal is allowed to climb too high. He has reported that this simple regimen alone allows about half of patients to go forwards into their particular circumstances without the hypertension recurring during the next year. Forty per cent need further counselling or training to enable them to cope without re-exhausting themselves over and over again, while fewer than ten per cent appear to have a permanently established condition requiring drugs.

It is rare, however, for Britain's tax-funded health service to provide 'humanistic' care of this kind. Billions of pounds are spent uncritically on pharmaceutically or surgically oriented treatment for 'disease', but there is great suspicion and discomfort over strategies such as Dr Nixon's, in which the individual is spared the energy-sapping burden of being designated as suffering from a chronic illness. Such strategies recognize that patients may be functioning healthily at some times, but endangering their health at others, when arousal is high and prolonged and brings on exhaustion.

This approach, although in line with ancient medical principles, bears little relation to that of the current medical orthodoxy, not just in Britain but in most countries with western-style medical systems. A 1978 brochure issued by the National Institutes of Health in the USA illustrates a view that has prevailed for many years, even though there are signs that it is beginning to change:

Most people who have high blood-pressure . . . have difficulty in adjusting to the fact that they will have the disease for the rest of their lives . . . you can help inform them. You can tell them about the disease and emphasize that they can still have an active life if they stay on their medication.

Such advice, by grossly misinforming people about the complex relationships between mind and physiological function, distorts their self-perception and increases rather than reduces the chances of ill health.

Understanding is one of the keys to self-control, and thereby to the effective control of blood-pressure. To accept responsibility for your own blood-pressure, rather than to hand the task of trying to keep it within safe bounds to a doctor, is the first step towards making sure that you only allow it to rise when really necessary.

Relaxation techniques do help by providing a breathing space for the system, an artificial break during which your cardio-vascular 'temperature' can be allowed to cool. Even more important in the longer term is the fact that this breathing space may also help you to restore your sense of perspective and discriminate better between what is or is not worthy of your concern, a faculty that easily disappears in the severely pressed, emotionally drained individual. People on the brink of a health breakdown arising from prolonged over-arousal often insist that every item on their schedule of responsibilities and activities is an absolute must; while others see them as expending enormous amounts of energy running round in circles.

An interesting explanation as to one of the possible mechanisms by which this loss of discrimination occurs concerns the baroreceptors, the sensors in heart and blood-vessel walls that slow the heart when they detect a rise in pressure. These can also have an effect on the brain, blunting its response to stimuli. It is as though the human organism is able to protect itself from too much distress when problems and pressures become acute. Discovery of this mechanism has led to speculation that chronically distressed people may develop the habit of high blood-pressure deliberately to keep their baroreceptors stimulated and their brain semi-anaesthetized. Attention is concentrated on the problem immediately at hand – regardless of its importance – at the expense of a loss of wider vision and sensitivity.

Patients are often more ready to take a drug to lower their blood-pressure than to tackle the problem of overarousal at its roots. This may be because the drugs also 'anaesthetize', so that one dulling effect is substituted for another, leaving the real source or sources of distress unacknowledged and undisturbed.

Stimuli so painful that they become buried in this way may concern not just temporary circumstances, but a deep dissatisfaction with the direction in which the individual's life has evolved; with feelings of loss of control, loneliness, lack of role, and lack of worth. Such feelings of impending failure and displacement are common in rapidly changing technological societies, and help to explain why the mere act of attention from the doctor can so often be therapeutic. By validating our existence through the administration of treatment, the doctor automatically eases distress, lowers arousal, and provides an opportunity for natural recuperative processes to regain their footing. This is the well-known placebo effect, which is recognized as contributing greatly to the apparent benefit seen when a patient starts taking anti-hypertensive drugs, since patients given chemically inactive pills often respond with falls in blood-pressure of similar magnitude. But when treatment is confined to chemical intervention rather than human care, benefit is likely to be short-lived, and may soon be outweighed by the added physiological burden of adjusting to the effects of the drug.

The deepest causes of discontent, hardest to confront, concern ourselves and our failings. The more virtues we have – such as tolerance, consideration, equanimity, discrimination, judgment – the smoother our path through life and the lower the friction we engender. Such low-friction lives are also low in arousal and therefore conducive to low blood-pressure. We need to feel that we belong, and our social assets – friends, relatives, educational skills, success at work – provide vital confirmation of this belonging. This is why upheavals such as retirement, redundancy, bereavement, family break-ups, and emigration, can prove threatening to health, though they do not necessarily do so. The individual who is rich in self-esteem, who feels confident of his or her place in the world, can take one or more of these blows and adapt to it positively. But the person who feels an underlying sense of inadequacy and loneliness and apartness will be put at risk.

In one long-range American study, two researchers looked specifically for common factors linking the personalities of women who were later to develop 'essential' hypertension. They found that they were more likely to experience hostile, tense, abrasive interactions with other people; were less attractive; accepted the feminine role less readily; and showed less social poise and ease. They had a provocative 'chip on the shoulder' attitude. Yet they tried to hide their emotions, so that when these became aroused they lasted unduly long.

This description, although confined to one sex, is partly reminiscent of those 'Type A' personality characteristics in 'Onlooker's' colleagues that caused him such discomfort, and for which he felt a 'slug of propranolol' in the morning coffee would be appropriate. But I can't believe drugs really change personality. The 'mellowing' noted with beta-blockers is superficial. Suffering goes on underneath. Besides, the 'Type A' classification is also an oversimplification, overlooking the fact that many chronically 'heated' and overaroused people do not show their feelings externally. Keeping feelings bottled up is one of the factors that can contribute to hypertension.

A World Health Organization briefing document on hypertension refers favourably to two modes of treatment long practised in India, though recently spread to other countries: yoga and meditation. Yoga is a system of self-culture, aiming at harmonious development of body, mind and soul. Its purpose is to try to make good gaps in the development of our personalities that leave us unfulfilled or discontented, and consequently liable to abrasiveness and insensitivity to the needs of others; and thus to allow us to move through life more smoothly. Meditation in its highest forms is a part of yoga: it involves taking conscious control of the thoughts in order to develop habits of positive instead of negative thinking, habits of cheerfulness and ease in the face of obstacles, for example, instead of irritability and depression. It is strategies such as these that really go to the heart of the matter. Religious contemplation, long practised in the West, has had similar beneficial purposes and aims. It has largely fallen into disuse in this secular age, but is, I am sure, due for a revival; propranolol is no substitute for effective prayer.

Conclusion

In the meantime, it may help to remember these points:

1   The mind has overall control of the mechanisms for raising and lowering blood-pressure. By altering your perception of events, you can gradually lose the habit of letting your pressure soar. If someone is abusive, for example, you can tell yourself that he or she must be feeling bad and you are not going to add to the sum of suffering by feeling angry or miserable yourself.

2   A habit of regularly counting your blessings, and adding to them, calms the mind and thus protects against overarousal. If you discount your weaknesses and take quiet pride in your genuine qualities, you will induce good feelings in yourself. These will be catching and others will like to be with you. This way you will develop social strengths that help to sustain you through hard times.

3   The mind has an inbuilt ability to elicit a sense of deep calm. Relaxation techniques may help break a vicious circle of over-arousal; and then beyond that, silent contemplation of natural beauty, whether in ideas or objects, can provide deep physiological refreshment.

4   If beauty is not evident externally, it can be conjured up in the mind at times of need through the visualization of scenes that have previously struck harmonious chords.

5   Circumstances with pressure-raising potential can be identified in advance. For many people the telephone, for example, is an extremely hypertensive agent, especially when calls concern work. A sticker on it could remind you to take a mental grip on your feelings as you take or make difficult calls. And in driving a car, the hotly reactive individual often uselessly expends much energy by going too fast or fretting over other drivers' performances.

6   Overoxygenating the blood through rapid, shallow breathing causes it to become overalkaline. This promotes blood vessel constriction, with a consequent rise in pressure. Slow, abdominal breathing reduces physiological arousal and can help you to stay in control of your feelings.

7   Salt (sodium chloride) promotes water retention and increases the reactivity of blood-vessels, thus having a double potential for raising blood-pressure. It is vital to the body, but can be harmful in excess. The brain has a hormonal mechanism that encourages high salt consumption in people leading high-pressure lives or facing threatening or frustrating circumstances.

8   When carnivorous people switch to a vegetarian diet, their blood-pressure has been shown to fall significantly, especially if it was high in the first place. Eating more fruit and vegetables increases the intake of potassium, which helps to counteract the effects on blood-pressure of a salty diet.

9   Losing weight helps to reduce blood-pressure: the cardio-vascular system has less bulk to serve.

10   Cigarette smoking raises heart-rate and blood-pressure. The smoker whose reserves of health are good welcomes this stimulation, but it can drive an already overburdened and hypertensive cardiovascular system over the precipice to disaster.

11   Aerobic exercise, such as twenty to thirty minutes of running or jogging, brings about falls in blood-pressure afterwards that can last for several hours. This is apparently known to airline pilots, some of whom avoid being grounded for hypertension by going for a run before their annual medical. However, pressure rises at first during the exercise, before blood-vessels serving the muscles have had a chance to dilate, so the hypertensive individual should be particularly careful to warm up slowly.

12   Many doctors mistakenly regard hypertension as an illness unrelated to the circumstances of the individual, to be treated with drugs, perhaps for a lifetime. This approach has numerous drawbacks and hazards. Far better, in the light of the information offered here, to seek to regain control over your own body's functioning rather than hand the reins over to outsiders. If you

can enlist your doctor's cooperation in this, you will be aiding your own self-recovery.

13   Do not suddenly stop taking anti-hypertensive drugs as this can cause a potentially dangerous rebound effect.

14   Providing they are correctly interpreted, regular checks on blood-pressure can provide a useful insight for people who otherwise have a tendency to be insensitive to their body's needs. Temporary rises can be expected as you move through life with varying levels of emotional intensity and at different speeds. Semi-permanent rises can also be sustained as the accompaniment of a high-pressure life without loss of normal life expectancy, providing care is taken not to push the cardiovascular system to breaking point. But if blood-pressure becomes chronically and uncomfortably high – and particularly if you have other body signals of exhaustion or impending breakdown, such as chest pains, chronic tiredness, or depression – then a stocktaking review of your aims and living strategies might prove both life-prolonging and life-enhancing.

Part Three

Medical 'Mysteries'

Introduction

The studies that follow are of conditions that in the recent past have generally been held to strike 'out of the blue'. Doctors have been so utterly in the dark as to possible causes that they have not even known where to begin in the search for preventive measures, so that very little work to this end has been done. Once again, the reason for this lack of illumination has been medicine's overly materialistic and narrowly scientific focus: searching for proof and certainty, it has concentrated its attention too strongly on physical states that can be measured and controlled. The subtle influences arising at the level of mind or 'self' – the thoughts and feelings that can have such devastating physiological consequences – have largely been ignored.

Although gross physical influences taken into the body from the external environment can and do play a causative part in illness, they are rarely central and never solely responsible for a person's disease. The word 'disease' implies a process of suffering, experienced at the level of mind – the person no longer has mental 'ease', or peace. Just as a person horribly handicapped by an external event such as a road accident can come to terms with their disability in such a way that they do not suffer, so it is with the handicaps involved in the following series of conditions. In every case there may have been genetic or environmental factors predisposing the individual to some specific physiological weakness. But the weakness only develops into disease with the victim's compliance. It is able to grow and blossom into a chronic source of suffering only for as long as the individual provides it with nourishment.

Actually, disease flourishes on a *lack* of true nutrition. Sometimes this lack is an obvious physical one, in the form of dietary inadequacies; far more commonly, the problem lies in mental malnutrition. Disease is a negative state, and an excess of the negative emotions – such as anger, greed, self-pity, anxiety, depression – produce favourable physiological conditions in which it may take root and grow.

8 Arthritis

American writer Norman Cousins, in his book *Anatomy of an Illness*, tells of meeting Pablo Casals at the cellist's home in Puerto Rico a few weeks before his ninetieth birthday. Don Pablo was an evident victim of rheumatoid arthritis: he entered the living room on his wife's arm, badly stooped, walking with a shuffle, his hands swollen and his fingers clenched. Before sitting down at the breakfast table, however, he went to the piano and with obvious effort arranged himself on the stool. Norman Cousins' story continued:

I was not prepared for the miracle that was about to happen. The fingers slowly unlocked and reached towards the keys like the buds of a plant toward the sunlight. His back straightened. He seemed to breathe more freely. Now his fingers settled on the keys. Then came the opening bars of Bach's 'Wohltemperierte Klavier', played with great sensitivity and control. I had forgotten that Don Pablo had achieved proficiency on several musical instruments before he took up the cello. He hummed as he played, then said that Bach spoke to him here – and he placed his hand over his heart.

Then he plunged into a Brahms concerto and his fingers, now agile and powerful, raced across the keyboard with dazzling speed. His entire body seemed fused with the music; it was no longer stiff and shrunken but supple and graceful, and completely freed of its arthritic coils.

There was no mystery about this miracle, which happened every day.

Creativity for Pablo Casals was the source of his own cortisone. It is doubtful whether any anti-inflammatory medication he would have taken would have been as powerful or as safe as the substances produced by the interaction of his mind and body . . . He was caught up in his own creativity, in his own desire to accomplish a specific purpose, and the effect was both genuine and observable. And the effects on his body chemistry were no less pronounced – albeit in a positive way – than they would have been if he had been through an emotional wringer.

This story raises an intriguing question. Cortisone, made by the outer part (cortex) of the adrenal glands, is an arousal hormone. It is one of a group of corticosteroid hormones involved in a bodily 'red alert': mobilizing energy reserves, preventing the take-up of carbohydrate by tissues, and inhibiting inflammatory responses to injury and immunity defences against infection. In many studies, raised levels of cortisone and its close relative cortisol are shown to be associated with a distressed state – the consequence, as Norman Cousins puts it, of going 'through an emotional wringer'. Yet in Pablo Casals the arousal process appeared to have a wholly positive, beneficial outcome. How can this difference be explained?

A similar question arises in relation to Norman Cousins's own remarkable story. With his adrenal glands exhausted after an intensely frustrating and demanding visit to the Soviet Union as chairman of an American delegation considering problems of cultural exchange, he was immobilized by an illness in which the connective tissue – collagen – in many parts of his body began to come 'unstuck'. (All arthritic and rheumatic diseases are in this category; the term rheumatoid arthritis describes the more generalized condition, and osteoarthritis more localized damage.) At the low point of his illness, Cousins's jaws were almost locked. He had difficulty in moving his limbs and even turning over in bed. One specialist declared that he had only one chance in 500 of making a full recovery. But he rejected that verdict, and with the cooperation of his own physician set about restoring his body's capacity to halt the continuing breakdown of connective tissue. He moved from hospital, where he had been subject to seemingly endless tests, to a hotel room, 'a place somewhat more conducive to a positive outlook on life'. He stopped taking the painkillers and other drugs prescribed at the hospital and put in their place a systematic programme for making himself laugh: old Marx brothers films, 'Candid Camera' recordings and humorous books. He also received large blood infusions of vitamin C. Somewhere in this unconventional package he stumbled upon a healing mechanism that had eluded the hospital doctors. Ten minutes of genuine belly laughter, he found, would give him two hours of pain-free sleep. And gradually the fever receded, the pulse stopped racing, and the agonizing pain disappeared. A few months later he was back at work.

Was he cured by laughter? Scientists in Sweden and London have tested the blood chemistry of people exposed to funny films, and found that they bring about similar increases in 'stress' or arousal hormones as anger-provoking or agitating films. But if Norman Cousins's illness developed in the first place because of undue stress, as he maintains, how could he be helped by a renewed upsurge of the arousal hormones?

These stories indicate that the chemical messengers which our bodies use as part of the process of adapting to changing needs and circumstances should not be regarded as specific to negative feelings, as some commentators have tended to believe on the basis of tests in animals. Countless experiments with rats and mice have shown that when the animals become distressed (because of what the experimenters do to them), corticosteroid production greatly increases. The very term 'stress hormone' has an unpleasant connotation. Yet for Pablo Casals and Norman Cousins, the arousal process was employed in a positive way, directly improving their well-being.

The factor that makes all the difference between a positive or a negative outcome is the way one perceives the event. When the arousal hormones are involved in a process that satisfies and pleases the self, the demands on the body are short-lived, and a relaxed, restorative state ensues. Satisfy the mind and it no longer demands satisfaction from the body. Hence the overriding importance of pleasing the self in order to stay well, restore health, or minimize infirmity.

In Norman Cousins's case, the medical treatment he received before moving himself from hospital seemed calculated to displease, and therefore to impede recovery. Panic and depression – both high-arousal states – often accompany the mere diagnosis of a supposedly incurable illness. Had he not rejected the 'incurable' verdict, it would have done him disservice in itself. Furthermore, the hospital routine, which involved frequent tests and examinations, and being awoken for bed baths and meals and sheet changes, was not at all 'productive of serenity', as Cousins puts it. Finally, his drugs – mainly aspirin and phenylbutazone, in maximum dosages – were proving toxic, actually causing discomfort, and adding to the body's inability to marshal its defences against the illness. By distancing himself from the medically induced discomforts, and by pleasing himself with the challenging notion of 'laughing' himself well, Cousins overcame what might otherwise have proved to be a chronically disabling illness.

In the case of Pablo Casals, the arthritis was probably more due to weariness than disease: to the tiredness in an old man's blood and bones. But in requiring those bones to perform what he loved most to hear, his mind found the means to summon up internal medicaments powerful enough to suppress the aches and pains.

If the anti-inflammatory steroid cortisone, or some related hormone or hormones, played a part in the natural recovery process in these two cases, why shouldn't it do the same when provided artificially to victims of arthritis? It has been tried; indeed, corticosteroids were for many years the mainstay of treatment. But the results were often disastrous. What happens is that after brief suppression of the inflammation and pain, the body adjusts to an artificial influx of corticosteroids by reducing its own output, and in time this can cause the adrenal glands to shrink and cease to function. Alternatively, overdosing with corticosteroids may cause hypertension, muscle weakness, diabetes, fragile bones, and vulnerability to infection.

When Pablo Casals needed extra cortisone in his joints, the complex nerve and hormone links between mind and body could provide just the right amount, taking effect in just the right places, to allow him to play for a short while, and then stop in order that healing should take place (reflected in renewed stiffness and pain a few hours later). But no doctor can fine-tune the external administration of steroid drugs in the same delicate manner. On the contrary, using them to suppress arthritic symptoms is liable to interfere drastically with the individual's own fine-tuning systems and mind–body communication channels.

The difficulties seen to arise with steroid treatments in arthritis have been such that these are now rarely started on a long-term basis. Instead, a class of substances rather pretentiously called Non-Steroidal Anti-Inflammatory Drugs (NSAIDs) dominate present treatment regimes. Aspirin is the best-known of these. All drugs in this category are able to provide some degree of relief: as well as reducing swelling and inflammation, they interfere with the pain-producing processes at diseased joints. But they do nothing to halt or reverse the disease process itself, merely suppress symptoms. In fact, there are good grounds for believing that they interfere with natural healing mechanisms in such a way as to make the development of a chronic condition more likely, as we shall see.

Use and Repair: a Question of Balance

As joints are used, damage occurs. There is constant wear, which has to be made good. Cells have to be renewed and debris carried away. Arthritic pain occurs when this repair process is not taking place fast enough to keep up with the damage caused. The mechanism makes sense: pain and inflammation help to slow the body down, so that healing and waste disposal can catch up with the rate at which damage is inflicted.

In osteoarthritis, simple physical demands on the joints, when repeated for long enough, can cause the repair mechanisms to begin to fail. But other factors are almost certainly involved as well. Bone and cartilage cells are constantly being replaced, and if for some reason there is interference in this process, even a low level of wear and tear may put the repair systems under strain. There are several points at which interference can occur. One involves the linking and assembling of collagen, the biological rope that gives bone and cartilage their wear-resistant properties. Various cooperating systems are involved in this, and each depends on having the right nutrients available. So diet is important. Dietary deficiencies can weaken the rope and prevent adequate repairs being made.

Copper, for example, plays an essential part in the activity of enzymes needed for collagen formation. Enzymes which contain copper also have a fundamental role in protecting body cells from damage caused by the presence of oxidizing agents. Such poisons are constantly being produced during normal body reactions, but are usually swept away before they can do any harm (such as by interfering with oxygen transfer between cells). If the levels of toxicity build up, as when lack of copper prevents adequate detoxification, joint tissues are liable to 'choke' into premature decay and death. Copper is also believed to be essential for the incorporation of iron into haemoglobin, the oxygen-carrying pigment of the blood. So in this respect, too, a copper deficiency could contribute to tissue starvation, premature wear, and ineffective repair.

Outlining these mechanisms in *Minerals and Your Health* (Allen and Unwin, London, 1980), Dr Len Mervyn notes that traditional remedies for rheumatoid arthritis include shellfish, nuts, mushrooms, and cider vinegar, all of which are rich in copper. There may be substance, he says, in the old wives' tale that a copper bracelet can cure rheumatic pains. Since the skin is slightly acid, the bracelet may slowly dissolve, producing soluble copper salts that are then taken up by the body.

Deficiencies of selenium, zinc, magnesium and manganese are also cited by Dr Mervyn as being among the many factors which contribute to the development of arthritis. Zinc, for example, is an essential component of more than eighty body enzymes and hormones. When zinc is deficient, for such reasons as food refining, drug treatment, physical injury, or too much alcohol, so is protein synthesis, and body growth and repair. Manganese, needed in the maintenance of normal connective tissue, is also removed during the refining and processing of foods. Selenium suffers the same fate, and in addition many soils have been drained of it through unbalanced use of fertilizers. Yet it is essential to the efficient action of a cleansing enzyme widely distributed in the blood and tissues, glutathione peroxidase (GTP). A lack of GTP delays the removal from the body of pollutants, such as lead, as well as the by-products of normal metabolic processes. It may also make the red cells of the blood prone to excessive breakdown.

In prosperous countries, nutritionists have tended to maintain that the average diet provides us with more than enough in the way of minerals and other essential body components. But when an individual is highly aroused, he or she has radically different needs from those of an average person. The body has much more work to do in tracking down, detoxifying and removing waste products of arousal, and repairing and replacing tissues and blood components. Furthermore, chronic arousal often interferes with digestion, hindering the absorption of nutrients. In such circumstances greater attention to diet and eating habits could make a vital difference between a system that copes and one that becomes diseased.

Even when the body is absorbing ample supplies of the materials it needs for repairing joint wear, problems can arise in the transport of repair equipment to damage sites. Constant tension in a particular limb or limbs can produce a local blood deficiency, for example, and this may trigger degenerative changes which go beyond normal wear and tear.

A healthy body maintains and repairs tissues discreetly, without the drama of pain and inflammation. But if this maintenance work does not proceed satisfactorily, emergency services come to the scene. These emergency procedures constitute the nub of arthritic pain and inflammation. They include the release of prostaglandins, messenger chemicals which cause blood-vessels to become engorged and throbbing, and which greatly enhance the activity of pain-inducing chemicals such as histamine and bradykinin. At the same time, prostaglandin action eases the passage to the danger site of a variety of white blood cells, which break down harmful waste products and carry them into the bloodstream for safe disposal. The white blood cell (leucocyte) army is normally between 5000 and 10,000 strong to every cubic millimetre of blood, but this can double as a result of emotional turbulence or vigorous physical exercise. It includes monocytes, which play a part in maintaining the turnover of normal body constituents as well as breaking down unwanted materials; lymphocytes, which produce protective antibodies against infective and other unwanted agents in the body; and macrophages, which congregate in chronically inflamed tissue and secrete collagenase, an enzyme that destroys both collagen and the organic part of bone in what seems like an attempt by the body to remodel the badly damaged joint.

The logic of the system is quite beautiful. In arousal – when the body is being called upon to perform actions – prostaglandin production is inhibited, blood-flow to potentially painful sites is reduced, and natural steroids reduce migration of leucocytes from the bloodstream. When the period of activity is over, the restraint on these healing mechanisms is lifted and instead they are spurred into action to make good any wear and tear resulting from previous efforts.

What, then, goes wrong?

In chronic arthritis, something happens to upset the natural balance between catabolic, energy-releasing activity and the anabolic, healing processes. Bodily mechanisms whose purpose is clearly beneficial seem instead to turn on their owner and cause more harm than good. Current theory favours the idea that damaged tissue can become 'foreign' to the body and thus the target of an immunological reaction that gets out of hand. Yet the body even seems to be prepared for this eventuality: it has 'suppressor' lymphocytes which can turn off the production of antibodies when this becomes excessive, countering the effect of other white cells.

Drugs Suppress Symptoms, Induce Disease

The seemingly humble aspirin and other anti-inflammatory drugs, which are swallowed in vast quantities in order to obtain short-term relief from arthritic symptoms, have extremely far-reaching effects on these regulatory systems. Aspirin irreversibly immobilizes a crucial enzyme, cyclo-oxygenase, involved in the formation of prostaglandins. It thus interferes in a most fundamental way with the healing process by which extra blood is sent to body sites needing rest and repair. The prostaglandins also increase the action of other inflammatory agents such as histamine and bradykinin. The short-term reduction in pain and inflammation may be a big price to pay for the longer-term changes caused.

These include direct effects on the white blood cells, as well as interference with their passage to trouble spots. The drugs inhibit the ability of lymphocytes, for example, to synthesize chemicals that allow them to take action against unwanted wastes and poisons. A consequence of such interference could be to bring about 'rebound' immunological activity, this time of a more violent, less controlled nature.

Prostaglandins regulate the early stages through which lymphocytes and macrophages become 'activated' – that is, receive instructions on how far they should go in their 'policing' work of modifying bone and cartilage. Prostaglandins released by activated cells are also believed to serve as signals telling 'suppressor' cells when to switch off the work of reconstruction or repair. So to swallow a drug that blocks prostaglandin formation is to throw a large spanner into the entire regulatory works. In blocking the enzymes that give rise to prostaglandins, the drugs may allow other enzymes – such as collagenase, which destroys collagen and bone – to become dangerously active.

Aspirin also interferes with the clotting function of platelets, the smallest cells in the bloodstream, whose main job is to prevent bleeding in the event of either internal micro-injury or an external wound. Aspirin damages the lining of the stomach, causing loss of blood there, and preventing proper utilization of food. It also blocks the uptake of vitamin C, which improves the blood's capacity to carry oxygen. People suffering from arthritis are often deficient in vitamin C, possibly because large amounts are used up in combating tissue damage. Aspirin adds to this deficiency. The drug also affects the kidney and liver, which play central roles in monitoring and balancing blood components. Even a single dose of aspirin can damage the stomach lining and cause bleeding. Horrifying to contemplate, then, what Norman Cousins's hospital treatment was doing to him: twenty-six aspirin tablets and twelve phenylbutazone a day. 'No wonder I had hives all over my body and felt as though my skin were being chewed up by millions of red ants,' he wrote.

With an estimated 2000 tons of aspirin being consumed every year by the British population, it is often argued that the drug must be remarkably safe. Yet it has also been calculated that in the UK the annual blood loss resulting from its use is about 90,000 litres. It has to be taken in relatively large doses to relieve arthritic pain, and while rarely fatal in normal use, these 'therapeutic' doses unquestionably send shock waves through the system. The damage it is causing may be missed by doctors. For example, although serious kidney damage is found in twenty to sixty per cent of patients with rheumatoid arthritis on examination after death, screening in arthritis clinics has revealed little evidence of drug-induced kidney damage – a discrepancy hard to explain, as a recent *Lancet* editorial commented.

By swallowing aspirin and similar drugs to suppress bodily mechanisms of inflammation, pain, detoxification and repair, patients with an arthritic state would seem to be encouraging the development in themselves of chronic arthritic disease. A natural bodily adaptation aimed at enforcing rest and repair is blocked by these drugs, and a chronic disease process takes hold. But the link is not made in doctors' minds because on the basis of patients' aches and pains they have already made a diagnosis of arthritis, confusing symptoms with disease. When that 'disease' gets worse, it is labelled 'progressive'. This is considered an adequate explanation of the patient's worsening condition, and the drugs remain free of suspicion.

It is sometimes argued that by reducing inflammation, drugs used in arthritis not only relieve pain but may also reduce the damage to the joints which results from the inflammatory process. This claim turns upside down nature's purpose in providing the inflammatory response, and overlooks the disruptive effects of anti-inflammatory drugs on the protective system of prostaglandin checks and balances. If the claim had any validity, one would expect to have seen a reduction in arthritic conditions as aggressive drug treatments became the norm. But this is not the case. Arthritis is one of the most prevalent disorders in the West, and has become worse over the past forty years. It is the greatest cause of disability and impairment in the UK. It affects at least fifty million people in the USA, with many experiencing chronic pain and receiving continuous medical attention.

The pain is very real, often excruciating, as the disease progresses because of the body continuously being prevented from healing itself. So patients come to depend on their drugs for the temporary relief they provide, as heroin addicts depend on renewed injections to keep the horrors of withdrawal at bay.

With such huge captive markets, the drug industry has, not surprisingly, devoted much effort over the past ten to twenty years to developing variations on the aspirin theme. There are twenty-five different NSAIDs listed in the British National Formulary, and many of these are available in a variety of different formulations. But this proliferation, accompanied by lavish promotion, has confused rather than helped doctors and patients, because there has been no substantial advance in treatment; just an attempt by different companies to make sure that they retain a substantial slice of the growing anti-inflammatory trade.

In the wake of the Opren (benoxaprofen) affair in 1982, when a new anti-arthritic drug was withdrawn after two years following the deaths of more than sixty patients, rheumatologist Dr Derrick Brewerton, of Westminster Medical School, asked the *Lancet*:

Why must the NHS make available drugs which we do not need? Ten years ago we had an adequate supply of non-steroidal anti-inflammatory drugs which gave modest relief of symptoms. Why has there been an avalanche of new such drugs since then, all of them little better or little worse than their predecessors – and each quickly declining in popularity or found to have side-effects that outweighed its benefits? Who decided? Even benoxaprofen was described (before the recent dramatic events) as being simply 'something slightly different in a sea of similarity'. Despite the immense cost to the NHS in providing these new drugs, it is arguable that overall, rheumatic patients have not gained. Certainly, they would have benefited far more if the equivalent money had been available for improving services, for developing rehabilitation, for cutting orthopaedic waiting lists, and for much greater investment in research to reveal the root causes of arthritis. Personally, I doubt whether there will be important advances in the therapy of most rheumatic diseases before we understand more clearly what we are treating. When there are truly effective methods of prevention and treatment, we will all look back with shame at this period when we wasted resources and used drugs for ends which they could not be expected to achieve.

One other drug approach in arthritis deserves mention: chemical suppression of the immune system (based on the idea that antibody reactions in the joints have got out of hand, so that the body has begun to attack itself). A study of the immunosuppressive drug cyclophosphamide by rheumatologists at Rotterdam's

Erasmus University has illustrated the hazards of such an approach. It was found that out of eighty-one patients with rheumatoid arthritis who had received the drug, fifteen developed cancer – an incidence four times higher than in a comparable group of patients with the same disease who did not receive it. The rheumatologists now reserve it 'for the fully informed patient in whom all other therapy has failed and who clearly announces that a life with pain and disablement is not worthwhile living'.

But does 'fully informed' include knowing about the healing powers of 'Candid Camera' films, nutritional strengthening, and a completely drug-free hotel stay?

The Mind Factor

It is not open to everyone to obtain the help and the facilities with which Norman Cousins conquered his arthritic illness (though his hotel bed, he tells us, cost a third of a bed in hospital). It is possible, however, to take heed of his experience – and that of numerous others who, by taking their treatment into their own hands, seem to show that even widespread and crippling arthritic conditions can be conquered.

The positive emotions to which Cousins attributed a large part of his cure – 'love, hope, faith, laughter, confidence, and the will to live' – counter the negative feelings and accompanying prolonged arousal states that oppose healing. The physical disability that afflicts victims of severe arthritis can be an external reflection of an inner immobilization and pain, made worse by the appalling effects of large doses of drugs. The patient becomes trapped in a vicious circle of suffering.

Research in Manchester among a group of 100 child victims of arthritis, and their parents, showed that those who thought their lives to be a disaster experienced aggravated distress and more joint pain. Counselling helped to reduce distress and pain. 'In a busy clinic there is a tendency to overlook psychology and go for the pragmatic,' said a group consultant connected with the research. 'We have been surprised by the extent of the psychological problem.'

Sometimes this problem is made worse by the pronounce-
ments of those purporting to help. 'To the lay public rheumatoid
arthritis is incurable and universally crippling,' wrote consultant
rheumatologist Dr Anthony Hicklin in the medical newspaper
General Practitioner:

This impression is reinforced by organizations collecting money for
research. They concentrate on images of the most severe and heart-
rending cases. The truth is very different. Rheumatoid arthritis is an
enormously variable disease whose clinical course may range from a
rapidly progressive disease – destroying joints and involving arteries,
lungs, heart, liver and kidneys – to a transient episode of joint-swelling
lasting only a few months followed by decades of spontaneous
remission.

When arthritis, especially osteoarthritis, develops in older
people, physical causes may predominate. Their bodies may have
been damaged in the past by prolonged, violent exercise, by
circulatory deficiencies arising from a lack of exercise, or by
trauma such as being involved in a road accident. But even so, the
body's ability to keep the condition under control will depend on
the extent to which other burdens are being carried by the
individual. If the circulatory system is preoccupied with removing the waste products of chronic emotional disturbance affecting
vital organs, it may not have enough maintenance and repair
'staff' available – enzyme and blood cell systems – to attend to
relatively unimportant areas such as knee or shoulder joints. If the
problem is then made worse by taking drugs, which permit
further use of the affected joint by suppressing pain and which
add to the burdens of toxicity in the blood, permanent damage
may result.

In rheumatoid arthritis – the more generalized inflammatory
condition in which fever, weight loss, depression, and anaemia
are also commonly seen, arising from a major breakdown in
central repair and waste-disposal mechanisms – emotional distress and its accompaniment of prolonged physiological arousal
seem more likely to be a main cause. Gross physical factors such
as breathing polluted air, or eating too much food contaminated
with chemical poisons, or simply coping with an exhausting
schedule of physical activity will then contribute to the likelihood
of such a breakdown.

Two doctors at Westminster Hospital in London interviewed a group of women with rheumatoid arthritis about events in their lives during the year preceding the start of their illness. Most had suffered a distressing and disorientating loss of some kind: the husband's firm going bankrupt, an important relationship broken, a severely depressed mother coming to live in the family home, an only daughter getting married abroad. The rate at which such events were reported was double that in a group of women used for purposes of comparison. It was also found that twice as many of the arthritis victims reported having had a bad relationship with their mother in childhood – a deprivation that would make them more sensitive to loss in their adult years.

Other studies confirm the picture that people who 'freeze' emotionally in response to excessive strains, becoming locked into a passive, self-pitying or self-reproachful frame of mind, are more at risk of developing rheumatoid arthritis than those with a lighter or more self-assertive disposition.

Conclusion: What You Can Do

1   Check whether the mind has become locked into a distressed pattern of thought, causing arousal hormones from the adrenal cortex to be circulating continuously, gradually pushing body-maintenance systems towards breakdown. Among the negative emotions, fear and self-pity are probably particularly likely to lead to arthritic illness – more so than anger, for example – because they encourage a high-arousal, low-activity state. The blood circulates sluggishly as well as being depleted of detoxifying and healing enzymes and other agents.

2   Snap your attention into activities that can bring immediate, positive results. Writing to or spending time with loved ones, helping others, finding laughter, completing new challenges – these all give a sense of movement and purpose in life that first stimulate but then also bring a measure of peace to the careworn. Albert Schweitzer, a tireless worker, once said that disease tended to leave him rather rapidly because it found so little hospitality inside his body.

3   Don't put unnecessary physical demands on aching limbs and painful joints. They need external physical rest as well as the internal rejuvenation encouraged by mental serenity.

4   Take gentle exercise if possible, to promote circulation. Walking and warm-water swimming are ideal.

5   Eat wholesome food. Vitamin C, trace minerals such as copper, zinc, selenium, magnesium and manganese, and unsaturated fatty acids of the kind found in vegetables, nuts and fish, are essential to the processes by which the body destroys damaged tissues and toxins and forms new collagen. Meat is nutritionally rich, but contains amino-acid complexes which can be a burden on the bloodstream, particularly if they enter it partially digested – as they are prone to do when there is inflammation in the digestive organs. For this reason also, eat methodically and in a calm state of mind. The digestive process is affected by the mind: observations on a middle-aged teacher of anatomy showed that the mere prospect of having to lecture to medical students after a meal slowed down the rate at which fat particles disappeared from his bloodstream. Avoid 'junk' processed foods low in nutritional content and high in additives.

6   Keep affected parts of the body warm. Cold constricts the blood vessels and delays healing.

7   Avoid drugs, including aspirin. Anti-rheumatoid drugs kill hundreds of people every year in the UK – they account for about a quarter of all recorded 'therapeutic' drug deaths – and may be worsening the condition of millions. By suppressing pain they allow you to cause more damage to yourself. By interfering with the inflammatory process and with blood cell activity, they may convert a temporary crisis into the chronic, degenerative disease that forms the familiar picture in rheumatoid arthritis. Have no truck with such a fate. It does not have to happen, as many have shown. Instead of taking drugs, take plenty of rest – 'the safest and most effective anti-inflammatory which we have', as one rheumatologist has put it.

9 Diabetes

This is not simply a disease involving too much sugar in the blood, correctable by insulin injections, as so many have come to believe. It is a condition in which the body's ability to use food for energy, growth and repair becomes generally impaired. The handling of proteins and fats, as well as carbohydrates (sugars and starches), is profoundly disrupted.

What causes this disruption? Medical science, sixty years after the discovery of insulin, will tell you that still no one knows. Heredity, obesity, malnutrition and infection have been observed to play a part and because they are measurable influences have lent themselves to study, but they have failed to provide anything like a complete picture.

Some very useful clues are available, however, pointing to the patient's mind – the thoughts and emotional reactions – as playing a leading role in many cases. Perceptive doctors have noted from time to time that their diabetic patients may have been afflicted by some deep sorrow or overwhelming strain before the onset of their illness, but since sorrow is a subjective affair such evidence is generally dismissed as 'anecdotal'. However, with new techniques such as electron microscopy, it has become possible to demonstrate the existence of intricate mechanisms linking brain and body, whereby it becomes much clearer how the dictates of the mind are put into physical effect.

Insulin is an anabolic hormone: it promotes the storage of chemical energy derived from food in the muscles and liver and promotes the utilization of glucose by cells. The insulin-producing pancreas gland, just behind the stomach, is in direct contact with the brain through two sets of nerves: one of these suppresses, and the other stimulates, insulin secretion. The brain also has a chemical line through to the pancreas: the chemical messenger is somatostatin, produced by the hypothalamus, which acts directly to suppress insulin production. So, here already are two very powerful mechanisms through which the individual 'self' can be seen to be intimately involved in the behaviour of the pancreas. Although the gland does monitor and regulate blood sugar levels automatically as well, it is by no means an independent agent. The brain is able to switch off insulin production so as to preserve glucose in the blood *in anticipation* of the extra energy being needed for coping with strenuous activity.

We have seen that when someone faces a challenge or threat to which an immediate response must be given, the 'doing' hormones adrenalin and noradrenalin are sparked into action. These prepare the body for physical activity by removing from storage the two fuels used by the muscles, glucose and fatty acids, making them available in the blood. So their effect is the very opposite to that of insulin.

Sugar is called up first, mainly through the action of adrenalin, from its chief storage place in the liver. But the diabetic, because of his insulin deficiency or defective sugar-handling mechanisms, may not have much to spare. If the body's demands for energy continue, fat is withdrawn from storage instead, through the action of adrenalin and more especially noradrenalin. But fat is a more hazardous fuel than sugar. If the fatty acids that are freed into the bloodstream are not used up by the muscles, their accumulation can cause acidosis. In extreme cases this can lead to circulatory collapse, diabetic coma, and death.

Fat demands more oxygen than sugar when being burned as a fuel, so a high level of free fatty acids in the blood can put the heart under severe strain. The fatty acids also thicken the blood, making it harder to pump. And those not used by the muscles can be converted back into neutral fat and cholesterol, both of which are linked with progressive damage to the arteries when constantly present in the bloodstream.

These dangers are greatly increased when the brain orders the alarm reaction into overdrive by calling up hormones from the adrenal cortex – the corticosteroids. The main representative of these (in relation to metabolic activity) is cortisol, which promotes the synthesis of blood sugars from other body substances as well as further stimulating the release of fatty acids, intensifying the effects of adrenalin and noradrenalin. So the role of insulin is opposed by all the arousal hormones.

I hope the description of these mechanisms is helping to make it clear that the excessive sugar in the blood and urine that is the first sign of diabetes is far from being attributable to a straightforward shortage of insulin. In fact, recently it has been discovered that many so-called diabetic patients have nothing wrong with their pancreas at all. Instead they appear to suffer from a shortage of special receptors in their body cells where insulin performs its role of metabolizing blood sugars.

How much of a success story, then, has insulin treatment really been?

The sad experience of patients shows that although life-saving in certain rare circumstances, it is far from being anything like a cure for their condition.

Diabetes remains a leading cause of death in most developed countries. It ranks third in the United States, after heart disease and cancer, with about 300,000 deaths a year from the disease and its complications (including heart attacks, strokes, and kidney failure). Britain's 600,000 diagnosed diabetics are similarly at risk. About a quarter of these receive insulin, while others take drugs to stimulate their own insulin production. Drugs are also taken to lower blood sugar chemically. Yet world-wide, millions of diabetics suffer from high blood-pressure, blindness, impotence, gangrene and chronic infections linked with their diabetes.

There is a growing suspicion, which I share, that this catalogue of ailments associated with the condition may have been lengthened rather than reduced by medical advice and treatment based on the oversimple view of it as a mechanical defect in the body's ability to handle sugar.

Dietary advice to diabetics, for example, has for decades been to eat a low carbohydrate diet. But the result has been a higher consumption of fat – whose combustion is, as we have seen, more of a strain on the body than the utilization of sugars from carbohydrates. Fat actually impairs sugar metabolism, while carbohydrates advance it. Moreover, the body adapts to a high-carbohydrate diet, increasing the number of insulin receptors.

And carbohydrates include foods high in fibre (wholemeal bread, vegetables, cereals) which are absorbed more slowly from the intestine and therefore provoke less of a sudden burst of blood sugar than the low-fibre foods such as milk and cornflour and other dairy products which diabetics have been encouraged to consume.

In 1982, I am glad to say, the British Diabetic Association issued a new set of dietary recommendations from doctors which turns previous advice on its head. Described by a doctor in *Medical News* as 'one of the most remarkable turnabouts in the history of medicine', the new guidelines indicate that the previous standard low-carbohydrate diet for diabetics was probably the worst conceivable dietary advice that could be given. Less fat and normal carbohydrate consumption – in high fibre form – is the new orthodoxy.

Actually, I believe the role of diet as a means of controlling the diabetic condition has been exaggerated. Overemphasis of this aspect of the diabetic life has contributed to the neglect of what I am sure is the crucial role played by the mind–body arousal mechanisms. As we have seen, the brain can both switch off insulin production with a direct order to the pancreas, and promote the release of arousal hormones which counter the influence of insulin and boost blood levels of sugars and fats. If these fuels are not then burned up in activity – as is so often the case in sedentary but stressful lives – they burden the blood excessively to produce the sugar overload and other disorders which are liable to attract a diagnosis of diabetes.

But how helpful is that diagnosis to the patient? If it were simply to serve as a warning, and persuade him or her to conduct an examination of the self and the lifestyle that produced these symptoms, well and good. But doctors are not trained to think of disease as a dynamic process intimately connected with a patient's thoughts and actions. They tend to take a 'snapshot' of the condition at the time the patient comes to them, and assume it will be present for the rest of the patient's life. There is a very great need for patients to be ultra-careful, then, not to accept a disease label and the treatment that will go with it unless they are quite sure they have done all they can to heal themselves.

Insulin injections or drugs may achieve short-term benefit in relieving symptoms, perhaps saving a life in a crisis. But regular use carries severe risks. Excesses of insulin arising from injections may cause the pancreas to reduce its own production of this vital hormone, so that the patient is actually made dependent on life-long treatment.

A second major problem is the development of hypoglycaemia (as opposed to hyperglycaemia), in which there is weakness and dizziness as a result of blood sugar falling too low (the brain depends almost totally on sugar, in the form of glucose, for its energy needs). A third problem is that the sudden fluctuations in body chemistry caused by injections put the eyes and kidneys at risk. One in ten insulin-dependent diabetics loses his or her sight after twenty years of conventional treatment; and half those diagnosed as diabetic before the age of fifteen are dead before they reach forty, often from kidney failure. Insulin injections are a very blunt tool indeed to be thrown into the body's beautiful and intricate systems for maintaining energy flows appropriate to the individual's needs. The sensible person will do all they can to give an abused system a chance to recover before succumbing to long-term medical treatment.

In some patients (a small minority, usually children) the insulin-producing cells in the pancreas simply stop working in a catastrophic collapse. For them, external administration of the hormone is essential – though I do not believe enough effort is made in such cases to see if they can be weaned off the injections once the immediate crisis is over. Though there is usually a genetic basis for the weakness that culminates in such a collapse, severe emotional stress is often also present.

Conclusion

In general, patients should resist the diabetic label when it is based on only a few blood tests showing elevated sugar, especially if they know they have reason to be feeling strained. They should bear in mind:

1   That those levels may have risen as a natural response to challenge.

2   That they can reduce the levels themselves without insulin by burning some of the sugar off through exercise.

3   That they can further reduce their blood sugar by eating sensibly, avoiding animal fats and rapidly absorbed carbohydrate foods such as milk, cornflour, and sugary drinks, especially on an empty stomach.

4   That rushing meals is liable to hinder the utilization of the newly absorbed sugars and fats – insulin release is triggered if you contemplate your food for a while before eating, as part of a pattern of digestive reflexes, so that the rise in blood sugar afterwards is relatively modest. If rapidly absorbed foods are gobbled down greedily in a rush, the sudden surge of sugar in the blood catches the pancreas unawares. It then tries to catch up through hyperproduction of insulin, but if this happens repeatedly the body responds by cutting back on insulin receptors, setting up a vicious circle that can end in metabolic exhaustion and chaos.

5   That if their blood sugar still stays high on a chronic basis, they should look into their hearts and minds to try to identify any distress that may be causing the constant high arousal underlying the condition, and take steps to sort themselves out.

If that last piece of advice sounds too glib for those who feel their burdens to be overwhelming, I will simply remind them that nobody else is likely to tackle their living problems for them. The alternative is to let the metabolic system fail through being overburdened by the combined chemical effects of chronic stress, poor eating habits, and lack of exercise, eventually to develop a life-long dependency on doctors and their well-meant administrations.

10 Kidney Disease

The advent of machinery and surgical techniques capable of saving patients with 'end stage' kidney disease from their apparently remorseless decline towards death has provided a rich source of drama. Hundreds of articles have appeared about shortages of kidney machines, and of kidneys for transplant. In Britain's cash-restricted National Health Service, a London surgeon had to halt his transplant programme after overspending his budget – a not inconsiderable £300,000 – less than half way through the financial year. Fund-raising organizations have claimed that patients are being left to die because of a chronic gap between demand and supply, a gap which even at the time of writing is still the subject of television documentaries and newspaper stories. Thousands of good-hearted souls have contributed towards efforts aimed at improving the availability of the extremely expensive facilities involved, while in the United States a multi-billion-dollar blood dialysis industry has grown up, including networks of centres operating kidney machines two shifts a day on a profit-making basis.

While reporting on these developments myself, there has been a constant nagging doubt at the back of my mind about some of the claims being made. So many vested interests are involved. Hospital specialists like to see their empires expand, as also do fund-raisers. Politicians naturally like to be seen to be active where emotive issues are concerned: I remember with embarrassment seeing one Secretary of State pose for photographers at London Zoo amid giraffes as well as child beneficiaries of kidney treatment, in the wake of a decision to make extra funds available for new machines (subsequently an embarrassment in themselves, as there were not the staff to run them). Hospital equipment manufacturers and drug companies are naturally gleeful and unquestioning as they see new areas of demand for their goods appearing and rapidly expanding. And the media welcome a new source of good 'life or death' stories.

But what about the patients, supposed beneficiaries of all the activity? Doubtless some have received a new lease of life as a result of a transplant, and kidney machines can certainly save the lives of those patients actually dying of acute renal failure. But puzzles remain. For example, I was assured at one time by the British Kidney Patient Association that children with kidney failure were being allowed to die because of the shortage of treatment facilities, but despite repeated appeals for specific examples I never succeeded in locating any such case. Later, when the overspent London surgeon claimed that lives were at stake because of his budget restrictions, this was denied by the same association, which said there were at least two other London hospitals with spare capacity for transplants. Facts seem to change to suit the circumstances, and solid information can be very hard to come by.

One discernible trend seems to be that demand for treatment has constantly expanded to meet the supply. Evidently, patients who might formerly have received other forms of care – or no care at all – are now being put forward by their doctors as candidates for the new technology. This is a natural enough process – if the need is real. But what if the new technology, at least in some cases, were *creating* a need in the minds of doctors and patients? After all, according to European figures, only two-thirds of patients receiving hospital dialysis, and followed over the period 1976 to 1978, were still alive after three years; would such patients have done any better, or worse, without a kidney machine? Benefit is assumed, but not proven. Clearly, much will depend on whether 'end stage' patients have really reached the end of the line, or whether recovery is still possible, either spontaneously or as a result of non-technological forms of help.

If survival on a machine or as a result of a transplant were without hazard or complications, unnecessary treatment would perhaps give no great reason for concern (other than on grounds of cost). But life on a kidney machine can be very unpleasant:

many patients feel permanently ill. If treatment is in hospital, the victim can become distressingly dependent on and tied to the nursing team; if a machine is installed in the home, where survival rates are better than for hospital, relatives can be driven to breaking point with the effort of coping.

Patients often only feel able to continue on a machine in the hope that a transplant will soon become available, but there is a chronic shortage of kidneys, and even if a suitable one is found success is not at all assured: a third of grafts fail within three months of the operation. Furthermore, the transplant business, while saving some lives, has often been a source of added distress to the bereaved relatives of the donor. For technical reasons, kidneys are best removed from a body in which the heart and lungs are still functioning, and this causes hopeless accident victims to be put on respirators purely with the needs of the transplant teams in mind.

The case of a man in his early twenties who went missing for three weeks, during which he failed to attend his usual thrice-weekly, eight-hour sessions on a dialysis machine, increased my doubts. This should have been fatal – treatment is supposedly only undertaken as a last-ditch, life-saving procedure, when the patient's own kidneys are irreversibly diseased and can no longer perform their essential job of removing poisonous waste from the bloodstream. Yet the young man concerned, who I think had been suffering from amnesia, was otherwise in perfectly good health when found. His doctors said that he was extremely lucky and would inevitably have died if he had missed treatment for much longer. He was put straight back on the machine.

It occurred to me at the time that another response might have been preferable: to see if he could continue to do without the dialysis treatment, in case his kidneys had somehow recovered sufficient function to liberate him from the machine. Such a strategy would call into question, however, the original diagnosis of irreversible kidney failure. And that in turn might challenge the *raison d'être* for drastic treatments given to thousands of other patients, for these usually rest on the belief that such a diagnosis and prognosis can be made with certainty.

The kidney has great regenerative powers, after injury resulting from acute poisoning or physical trauma. Why, then, is chronic renal disease usually regarded by doctors as bound to become progressively worse? I believe the answer is that the most important influences contributing to this degeneration have been neglected, if not ignored completely.

One of these influences is diet. The biggest waste that the kidney has to eliminate is urea, the end product of protein digestion. It was suggested more than thirty years ago that people with diseased kidneys should restrict their protein intake, so that the filtering units (nephrons) still in good order should not become overworked. The idea was almost forgotten, however, with the arrival of dialysis machines and transplantation. 'Until lately,' said the *Lancet* in December 1982, 'dietary protein restriction has generally been reserved for the management of uraemic symptoms [urea building up in the blood], and has been regarded as merely palliative in the management of renal failure.' Sometimes kidney patients have even been advised to eat plenty of meat protein, in order to build up their strength.

Dietary factors are now belatedly receiving attention. Dr Barry Brenner, of the Laboratory of Kidney and Electrolyte Physiology at Harvard Medical School, has marshalled a wide body of evidence from both animal and human studies in support of the idea that unlimited intake of protein-rich food, now generally regarded as normal in most western countries, has dramatic effects on renal function which could be contributing to kidney disease.

Immediately after a large meal there is a surge in the kidney's throughput of blood, and consequent excretory work; while between meals this activity falls to relatively low levels. It is the kidney's task to conserve wanted substances – fluids, minerals, vitamins, amino-acids, glucose, hormones – as well as to get rid of those that are unwanted or present in excess, and different populations of nephrons specialize in these two tasks. 'Superficial' nephrons, which have smaller filters and reside in the outer part of the kidney, serve as a rapid transit system for urgent disposal of waste, while 'deep' nephrons, which have a longer filtering and absorbing tube, play more of a part in conservation.

Brenner and his team of researchers believe that a continuous diet of rich foods can cause both sets of nephrons to become continuously occupied, leaving no room to spare for handling exceptional loads, and thereby rendering them vulnerable to damage. The first part of the nephron – the glomerulus, a capsule containing a tuft of blood capillaries – becomes 'sclerosed', or scarred, and may stop working. Most people have some degree of glomerular sclerosis as they grow old. There are more than a million nephrons in each kidney, and a considerable percentage can be lost without threat to well-being. But beyond a certain limit, if overall demands on the kidneys stay high, remaining nephrons have to work so hard that the disease becomes progressive: one by one they give up under the strain, and the burdens on the rest are further increased. The original cause of severe loss, such as an infection or poisoning incident, could long since have disappeared, but in the absence of countermeasures to reduce vulnerability to disease the damage continues to grow. According to Brenner this downward spiral may be initiated by the loss of one kidney – a fact that should be taken into account when surgeons consider transplanting a healthy kidney from a patient's living relative. Other causes of severe nephron loss include the metabolic disruption that accompanies diabetes, and very high blood-pressure.

Dr John Moorhead, director of the department of nephrology and transplantation at London's Royal Free Hospital, offers a refinement of Brenner's theory. He suggests that progressive kidney disease is associated with problems in handling blood lipids rather than protein products in general in the failing kidney, and that restriction of dietary fat may play a part in preventing kidney failure.

The implications of these theories are enormous, as a *Lancet* editorial in December 1982 recognized. If the burden of waste sent to the damaged kidney can be tailored so as to stay within the limits of its reduced processing capacity, it may be possible to disprove the dogma that chronic kidney disease inevitably progresses to ultimate failure and the need for dialysis or transplant. This dogma becomes vastly more questionable still, if we look at kidney trouble from the point of view of the dynamics of physiological arousal.

The Arousal Factor

The kidneys play a central part in blood-pressure control mechanisms. They produce the hormone renin, which starts a chemical chain reaction which results in blood-vessels becoming constricted, fluids retained, and the volume of the blood increased, with the result that pressure in the system rises. Short-term pressure increases of this kind gear the brain and body up for intensive effort.

Beyond a certain point, a safety cut-out should come into effect, halting renin production. But as well as functioning according to the dictates of automatic feedback circuits of this kind, the kidney is under nervous control from the brain. Thus the mind, via the brain, can override the cut-out effect and order the kidney to continue producing renin. This may happen as part of a generalized hyperarousal response if the individual is facing chronic life difficulties for which he or she feels unremitting struggle is not only appropriate but essential. Blood pressure stays high, and so does the supply of blood that the kidneys have to process. This increases the workload of the nephrons. If the extra demands continue for too long, especially in a kidney with pre-existing damage or some other susceptibility, there will be a risk of a vicious circle of effort and ever-increasing damage becoming established.

Similarly, the effects of chronic arousal on blood viscosity – the stickiness and thickness of the blood – must play a big part in determining kidney wear and tear. Prolonged secretion of arousal hormones causes the release from storage and increased absorption from the diet of high-energy fats, whose breakdown leaves more toxic wastes to be disposed of than when energy is obtained from carbohydrates. Furthermore, when unburned fats circulate in the blood, and blood 'stickiness' is further elevated by the increased platelet cell activity that accompanies turbulent circulatory conditions, the scene is set for blood clots to form. These may reach the kidneys, damaging the nephrons and renal arteries.

Angiotensin, another hormone involved in the energy-releasing processes that accompany arousal, includes among its actions constriction of the renal arteries, thus restricting the flow of blood to the kidneys (in order to divert it to the muscles). This is a two-edged sword: reducing renal blood flow reduces the stream of wastes to be disposed of, thus providing temporary relief in the workload, but may damage an already overworked kidney by starving it of oxygen.

This multitude of potential ill-effects on the kidney probably just scratches the surface of the renal burdens imposed by overarousal. Yet as we have seen again and again, arousal is not a notion that the modern doctor with his technologically oriented education has been happy with. It involves people's thoughts and feelings and emotions, which are considered for the most part intangible and unmeasurable and therefore 'unscientific' and best ignored; especially as patients also often prefer to conceal their pain and worries and resist attempts at interference with their life strategies.

The omission is a tragedy, made worse by the fact that telling patients that their kidney trouble is inevitably progressing towards ultimate failure, and sentencing them at some point to life on a kidney machine, must add a great deal to the chronic distress that may have caused or accelerated their deterioration in the first place. Not surprisingly, doctors report that an appreciable number of their dialysis patients are depressed, hypochondriacal, and even suicidal. In the USA, patients on kidney machines have a suicide rate seven times the national average.

Even those who receive a transplant continue to live with uncertainty over the future in addition to their pre-existing worries, because of the ever-present risk that their body will reject the graft. And drugs taken to counter rejection can have both mental and physical ill-effects. One study from Denver, analysing the cause of death after kidney transplantation, found that fifteen per cent of deaths were due to suicide; while a study from the Cornell Medical Center in New York, which was described in 1983 in the *Journal of the American Medical Association*, found that forty-eight per cent of dialysis patients and forty-six per cent of transplant patients were 'psychiatrically impaired'. There was an extremely high prevalence of emotional illness in both groups, which, as the authors pointed out, challenges the assumption that the approximation of a normal life that a transplant offers necessarily makes it a better treatment than dialysis.

However, the study did not tackle the question of how much of the emotional illness *pre-dated* the patients' chronic renal failure. The similar level of emotional illness in both groups suggests to me that perhaps only a small part of their distress is directly caused by the treatment. If the arousal theory is right, one would expect such distress to be a common feature of patients with failing kidneys, merely made worse in such cases by the orthodox medical responses to their illness.

Either way, the arousal factor is being almost totally ignored at present, either in the prevention or treatment of disease.

Drugs that Kill

Pitifully little attention has been paid to the prevention of kidney failure compared with the resources poured into its treatment. Ironically, perhaps the most effective preventive measure to date has been the banning of a medicine, the painkiller phenacetin, which was almost certainly harmful to kidneys. Some specialists, however, say the kidney is put at risk by all painkilling drugs, especially when taken over long periods. Dr L. F. Prescott, for example, consultant physician to Edinburgh regional poisoning treatment centre, told the *Pharmaceutical Journal* recently that he does not believe 'analgesic nephropathy' (kidney disease induced by painkillers) declined after phenacetin's withdrawal. On the contrary, he maintains that excessive use, or abuse, of aspirin or other acidic anti-inflammatory drugs is probably more of a problem than phenacetin ever was. (Such excessive use and abuse of painkillers is sometimes a feature of the behaviour of people who are finding life too much for them, and is linked to a general syndrome of distress.)

Attempts to treat failing kidneys with therapeutic drugs have focused on the kidney itself, rather than the patient's general physiological state, and have been unsuccessful. For years, doctors have pursued the theory that chronic kidney degeneration results from an immunological reaction, and that it is inexorable; and they have discounted suggestions that diet, or other lifestyle modifications affecting blood composition and dynamics, could have any appreciable effect.

Aggressive drug treatment directed against the immune system has been a widespread form of treatment in early kidney disease, the idea being that the body's defences against unwanted invaders were somehow mistakenly attacking the nephrons. Yet there has been a 'conspicuous failure' to provide scientific support for this orthodox clinical practice, according to Italian kidney specialists Tullio Bertani and Giuseppe Remuzzi, of the division of nephrology and dialysis, Ospedali Riuniti di Bergama, and the Mario Negri Institute for Pharmacological Research, Milan. Despite there being no shortage of pointers to new therapeutic approaches, 'the old drug-based approach continues to rule', they wrote in The *Lancet* (9 July 1983). Occasional and temporary gains might justify the use of drugs if they were harmless, they said; but in two controlled studies, deaths were among the treated patients, not in the control group. 'Why is this not mentioned in surveys and reviews that focus so clearly on the benefits of such treatments?' they asked. 'It is true that patients and their families nowadays demand treatment with drugs. It is also true that for doctors to watch impotently the inexorable progress of a disease is deeply distressing. But does this justify doing harm?'

Machine Madness

That word 'impotently' gives a further clue to why medical treatment of kidney disease has perhaps done as much harm as good. While doctors seek to exercise 'power' over disease processes, albeit with the interests of patients in mind – and while patients and society look to doctors to exercise such power – true healing, which comes from within the patient, is discouraged.

Kidney machines were originally devised to help people through an acute crisis, giving their own kidneys the breathing space to recover their function. As such, they were a wonderful invention. Then they began to be used to sustain life in people whose kidneys had irreversibly failed because of some catastrophic injury – but only rarely, in cases judged to be most deserving, where the patient was young and productive and well-motivated. Such patients tended not to be diseased as such, but rather to have suffered sudden and severe injury to their kidneys. In other respects, they were well.

As time went on, the seeming miracles that the machines worked allowed them to grow in importance in our minds to such an extent that they became the subjects of a kind of idol worship, a monument to technological power, to be made available to all who might conceivably benefit from their use. The pressures on politicians and administrators to increase spending on 'end stage' renal disease became irresistible, while efforts to find means of helping patients to keep out of kidney failure, or to recover lost function, have been minimal. The result is that many patients have been condemned to life tied to this false idol without good cause. In such cases, when the victims discover that the machine sustains life while leaving untouched the inner turmoil that constitutes their true illness, they cry out in agony – or add their voices to the clamour for kidneys for transplant.

Those patients who manage best on a machine, I believe, are those whose kidneys were damaged through predominantly external causes, such as drug side-effects or infection or trauma. Those who suffer most are the ones whose kidneys failed mainly because of *internal* distress, in whom storms of bodily arousal, accompanied perhaps by an over-rich diet, overwhelmed their kidneys' capacity to cope. This latter group, which I suspect are now in the majority, would stand to gain much more from help with their thoughts, feelings, and circumstances, aimed at reducing the friction between them and their environment that lies behind the overaroused state. If this friction continues unabated, the dependence on the kidney machine, coming on top of all the other burdens, must be absolute torture.

In the USA, where legislation was introduced in 1973 under which the federal government pays most of the costs of dialysis or transplantation for ninety-five per cent of the population, the number of beneficiaries had by 1980 reached double the total predicted when the scheme was devised. The cost, at over 1000 million dollars, was four times the original estimate for that stage of the programme. Some recipients of treatment – according to an article in the *British Medical Journal* by Wallace K. Waterfall, of the Institute of Medicine, National Academy of Sciences – are so old or chronically ill that the dialysis machine 'begins to take on the complexion of a respirator, sustaining life irrespective of flagging sentience'; in others, 'their machine-dependence is a psychological burden rather than the joyous reprieve of the chosen patients in the earlier days'.

The provision of dialysis machines has not grown as fast in the UK as in richer countries elsewhere in Europe and in North America. There is a very close relationship between national income per head and the number of patients on treatment for chronic renal failure: in 1978, the rate of intake of new patients in the UK was nineteen per million population, compared with more than sixty per million in the USA, and thirty per million in France and West Germany. But even with this relatively low level of provision in Britain, there are still good grounds for believing that the same principle of supply creating demand, rather than meeting true need, is at work.

Just as there are large differences between countries in the numbers treated, so there are major differences between regions within the UK that cannot possibly be explained by uneven distribution of disease or by transfer of patients. An Office of Health Economics report published in 1980 showed that the Wessex and north-western regions, for example, were treating less than half the number of patients per million population than the northern, Oxford, and London Metropolitan regions. Yet when directors of nine renal centres were interviewed, covering nine of the fourteen National Health Service regions, five said that they were not rejecting *any* patients referred to them whom they felt to be medically suitable for treatment. In only one region – the West Midlands – did the director report rejecting good as opposed to borderline cases.

The *Lancet*, commenting on these findings, correctly interpreted them as indicating 'a process of rationalization . . . in which medical indications were unconsciously determined by medical resources'. But it does not necessarily follow, as the *Lancet* implied, that the true need is at the higher levels of treatment, and that the directors who were satisfied with less were wrong. On the contrary, those who were forced to be more discriminating because of having fewer resources may thereby actually have reduced suffering, and even saved lives.

Some patients are finding their way onto kidney machines for the same reason that men climb mountains: because they are there! The 'rationalizations' for treatment can be random and unpredictable, as a survey by two doctors from London's King's College Hospital showed. Kidney specialists in twenty-five units were presented with medical and social details of forty patients with renal failure who had been treated at King's and asked to select ten who were to be rejected for dialysis. Big differences between units emerged in those chosen: only one-third of the forty patients would have been accepted by all units – in other words, two-thirds were rejected for one reason or another. Yet no patient was rejected by all units.

The idea that people become kidney-machine patients for clear-cut, obviously life-saving and life-enhancing reasons is clearly exposed as a myth. One is forced to conclude that doctors and patients are groping around in a thick fog of uncertainty.

That is not to say that this analysis makes matters any easier. In fact, should it reach those struggling to do what is right for patients in these difficult areas, to whatever extent the arguments are accepted it may weaken their faith in what they are doing and make their lives even more difficult. The root of the problem is a social one, in which medical technology is elevated to a holy status at the expense of human considerations.

But surely it is wrong that we should continue as at present. Patients are being treated unnecessarily. At the time of writing, a report appeared in the *British Medical Journal* about three transplant patients in whom function unexpectedly returned in their own, supposedly irreversibly failed kidneys. This was only detected as a result of radio-isotope scanning, months or years after their operation. Furthermore, the scan showed that the transplanted kidneys had stopped functioning – making it necessary, as the authors comment, to question the validity of long-term transplant survival statistics. (It also makes highly questionable the readiness of some surgeons to remove the patients' own kidneys at the time of operation.) The study, by doctors at St Thomas's Hospital in London, also showed recovery of function in four patients on kidney machines.

In all, recovery was seen in nearly three per cent of a series of 250 patients examined – a considerably higher proportion than had previously been believed possible. And this was spontaneous recovery; many more patients might be spared the indignity of dialysis or the trauma of transplant surgery if they were first encouraged to take steps to relieve the pressure on their kidneys through dietary measures, and through being given support and advice aimed at reducing internal arousal.

Those who argue that the health service cannot afford to interest itself in patients' emotional burdens, however these may arise, might reflect on the costs of treating 'end stage' renal disease: about £12,000 a year per patient for hospital dialysis, £8000 a year for a kidney machine at home, and between £7,000 and £10,000 for the first year's treatment in a transplant patient.

Self Help

What can patients do for themselves? The following guidelines are based on the information and arguments advanced in this chapter:

1 Be alert to early signs that your kidneys are failing, but don't accept doom-laden medical predictions about their future without at least trying to do something to reverse the trouble. Symptoms include puffiness in the face especially around the eyes, and in the ankles, as fluids that ought to have been cleared start to accumulate in the tissues. The abdomen may also swell up. There may be pain in the kidneys, which are situated on either side of the spine just above the small of the back. Breathlessness, exhaustion, and anaemia are likely. Nausea, vomiting, and diarrhoea are common as wastes normally disposed of in urine build up in the blood. Headache, sleeplessness, and irritability often accompany a rise in blood-pressure. Urine may be cloudy and spotted with blood. The breath may start to smell of urine.

2 If chronic renal failure is diagnosed, try to establish with your doctor that the primary aim to be pursued is to help the kidneys recover, whether they are considered to be failing or failed. He may assert that this is obviously so, and yet the specialist may already have marked you down in his mind as a future candidate for dialysis or transplant, because until very recently doctors have

believed that chronic renal failure inevitably progresses from bad to worse to 'end stage'.

3   Take pity on your kidneys, and reduce the amount of work you require of them. A simple measure is to eat much less protein, and in particular to reduce consumption of fatty meats. A well balanced vegetarian diet is probably ideal although it might not be sufficient for your needs unless you also:

4   Identify those areas of your life that cause you to become tense or distressed, and try to find countermeasures. Relaxation techniques, massage, biofeedback methods for learning bodily control, autogenic training, yoga, meditation, all help to provide respite from arousal; more fundamental self-examination and life change may be necessary to remove the causes of chronic over-arousal, and the accompanying physiological burdens which in your case appear to have proved too much for your kidneys to handle.

5   Remember that drug treatments for deteriorating kidneys have not worked, and may hasten death.

6   Be wary of painkillers such as aspirin, which can cause kidney damage. Avoid regular or large doses.

7   Remember that even if your kidneys appear to have failed completely, so that machine treatment is essential, the development of a calm and positive outlook will not only minimize the discomforts of living tied to a kidney machine, but may lead to restoration, in time, of sufficient renal function to allow you to break free from the dialysis regime.

11 Migraine

Migraine sufferers have headaches. But there is so much more to their condition than that! In fact, a headache is not even a necessary feature of a migraine, and never the only one. The migraine attack is, in the words of the British neurologist Dr Oliver Sacks, 'a wonderland of nature'. Its origins, course, and resolution may involve almost every body system. So it is not surprising that intensive research efforts have failed to produce either a complete explanation for the mechanism of the illness, or anything approaching a certain cure. To many, migraines remain an utter mystery.

However, there are at least three good reasons why migraine victims, and perhaps their close relatives, should make a study of what *is* known about the condition. The first is that there is a positive side to migraine attacks, and to understand this may make them easier to bear. Secondly, while a migraine attack is in itself very unlikely to cause long-term harm to the patient, this cannot be said for some of the treatments on offer from the drug industry and doctors. As Dr Sacks, a world authority on the subject, writes in his book *Migraine: Evolution of a Common Disorder* (Pan Books, 1981): 'The history of "treatments" for migraine is largely a story of medical "overkill" and patient exploitation.' Thirdly – if the victim chooses – there is much that he or she can do to modify the likelihood of an attack, and the intensity of the attacks that do occur.

Enough of the pieces in the jigsaw can be assembled to assert, first of all, that a migraine is a defensive strategy. It comes in two principal forms, each countering a different threat to the system. In one, the bloodstream is the primary battleground, and the migraine appears to be a by-product of automatic bodily mechanisms for removing various kinds of chemical excess or physical strain. In the other, though the bloodstream still plays a crucial part, the imbalance appears to lie instead deep within the nervous and emotional system, and in this case it is within this system that the defensive manoeuvres which lead to a migraine attack are initiated.

Both blood-chemical and nerve mechanisms are involved in every migraine attack, and almost always some degree of prior imbalance, making an individual vulnerable to an attack, is also present in both the circulatory and nervous system. But the course of events differs, it seems, depending on which direction the stimuli that actually trigger the attack come from. So for convenience and simplicity we can refer to 'chemical' or 'nerve' migraines. A helpful way to view the migraine attack in both cases is to see it as a cleansing process for an overloaded system.

In chemical migraines, the factors that push the system into a migraine response are often external – that is, they have entered the system from outside. Constituents from cigarette smoke are an example: at one London migraine clinic it was found that half of all the women attending with an acute attack were smokers, and sixty-eight per cent of the men. Certain foods are notorious for bringing on attacks in susceptible people: chocolate, cheese, citrus fruit, and alcohol, for example. Petrol, diesel and household gas fumes can also poison the blood sufficiently to cause an attack. And the toxins released by certain bacteria in cases of food poisoning can cause some of the most painful migraines of all.

Features of an attack are:

1   Widespread constriction of the net of minute blood-vessels serving brain tissues, reducing the throughput of blood inside the brain by up to fifty per cent. In the case of 'chemical' migraines, this may be in order to protect the tissues against excesses of psychoactive agents in the bloodstream. Cheese, for example, contains various amines which can give rise to substances capable of disturbing the chemical control-systems of the brain.

2   Exaggerated *widening* of arteries and veins in the temples and scalp. It is as though the minute muscles in the walls of these blood-vessels are instructed to swing open the floodgates, so relieving pressure inside the brain itself, and hastening the flow of

blood towards the cleansing organs that will ultimately remove the threatening substances.

3 Nausea – to prevent further intake of food – perhaps leading to vomiting; and apathy and tiredness, to promote rest and protect the system against further stimulation.

A central part in this drama is played by the platelets, minute particles in the blood which carry round with them a number of components, including histamine, serotonin, and ATP (adenosine triphosphate), which help to deal with internal injury or threat. The platelets themselves can influence blood-flow by clumping together, and this may contribute to the big reduction in the amounts of blood reaching the brain that often marks the onset of a migraine attack. When they stick together, the platelets release serotonin, which in big enough quantities seems able to cause paroxysmal constriction and then dilatation of blood-vessel walls. It also has neurotransmitter properties and plays a leading part in producing pain in the traumatized and throbbing cranial blood-vessels of the migraine victim. ATP also has a role: it is a powerful agent for widening blood-vessels; it stimulates synthesis of prostaglandins, which regulate blood-flow and help to repair damaged tissue through the inflammatory response; and it too produces pain.

Here, then, are the beginnings of an explanatory picture of the migraine attack: as a kind of log-jam in the blood-vessels in and surrounding the brain, followed by emergency action to break this up, along with the production of tenderness, pain, and inflammation in some vessel walls as a means of promoting rest and repair.

But this is only to scratch the surface of the 'wonderland of nature' we are exploring. Migraine attacks are estimated to afflict at least one in ten of the population. Are we to assume that nature has been so inefficient as to make such large numbers vulnerable merely as a response to a piece of cheese, or too much chocolate or banana?

It is true that some victims have been helped through the identification and avoidance of offending foods such as these. What is more, many of those same sufferers appear to have antibodies to the food, indicating an allergic reaction in the gut, though that might be a consequence of the migraine-inducing tendencies of the food rather than a cause. However, even in those cases where food plays a significant part, other mechanisms are undoubtedly involved too. The body has specific enzymes for breaking down the amine group of substances that can cause trouble; and these enzymes – notably monoamine oxidase (MAO) and catechol-o-methyl transferase – can have their work impeded or disrupted by cigarette smoking; by hormone changes associated with the contraceptive pill, and the menstrual cycle; and by a host of changes in blood chemistry arising in response to effort and emotional arousal.

For example, MAO activity is greatly increased in the ovaries and womb during ovulation, and is known to be depressed during a migraine attack. There seems to be only so much to go round. 'It is as if the mopping-up system is rationed,' says Dr Ellen Grant, a British migraine researcher. 'A woman may be able to drink alcohol, eat cheese, breathe cigarette smoke for three weeks, but not in the week of the period without getting a migraine.'

Especially not if she has a bitter argument with her daughter and a near-accident in the car. The catecholamines adrenalin and noradrenalin, which flood the bloodstream in response to such challenges and threats, mobilize fat reserves ready for action, and raised levels of free fatty acids are a cue for the clumping together of platelets, which, as we have seen, can play a central part in the generation of migraine. The catecholamines also cause the heart to pound and the blood-pressure to rise, with consequent risk of damage to the micro-arteries serving the brain – and of a defensive migraine reaction – if the emergency lasts long enough.

Noradrenalin itself is a very powerful constrictor of blood-vessels, and is central to the drastic reduction in blood-flow to the brain that is usually the first phase of a migraine attack. When there is an acute upsurge of this self-administered chemical in the blood, it is as though the individual is being told: there is no time to think – just let instinct take over, and act! But the catecholamines, which have been described (not altogether appropriately) as 'fragile flowers of feeling', produce effects lasting only a few minutes. Then, reaction sets in. The smooth muscle linings of the blood-vessels serving the brain collapse, freed from the influence that drove them into spasm, and in conjunction with other aspects of the mechanisms described above, the head-splitting pain of a migraine headache begins.

We are now approaching the category of reaction artificially classified as a 'nerve' migraine, to distinguish it from those migraines that appear to be triggered by external chemical influences. The distinction is artificial because there is so much overlap between the two. It is likely that nervous, emotional mechanisms of arousal often sensitize the system first, while the dietary or other external chemical factor or factors are the straw that breaks the camel's back, setting off the sudden, paroxysmal reaction in an already charged nervous system. There are some migraines, however – perhaps a majority, if they are clearly distinguished from straightforward headaches – in which both the trigger and the prime driving-force behind the attack seem very definitely to come from within, and these are often the most perplexing and intractable of all.

Edward Liveing, the nineteenth-century author of *On Megrim, Sick-Headache, and Some Allied Disorders*, described the general picture of the classical migraine attack as a kind of nerve storm, starting with a seizure deep in the brainstem, and then slowly projecting upwards on to the cerebral cortex and outwards and downwards to nerve structures surrounding blood-vessels, glands, intestines and other vital parts. The visual and other sense distortions associated with the migraine 'aura' preceding an attack are consequences of the nerve activity in the cortex, and this is followed by throbbing and sensitivity in the temporal arteries, and perhaps shock, noises in the ears, pallor, distension of the gut, and nausea as the storm spreads through the body.

Another vital piece in the jigsaw which helps to support this picture is the recent discovery that some fibres from a part of the brain called the locus coeruleus, in the lower brainstem, extend directly to the walls of the cerebral blood-vessels. Noradrenalin, which is a neurotransmitter as well as a blood hormone, is secreted at the ends of these fibres. So there is a direct mechanism by which one part of the brain can order noradrenalin release in the cerebrum, with consequent immediate constriction of the blood-vessels and a dramatic fall in cerebral blood-flow – the paroxysm that brings in its wake the full migraine response of blood-vessel engorgement and throbbing pain.

Why should the brain – or rather the brain's controller, the mind or self – wish to do such a thing? Very rarely, there may be some innate defect, like a nervous tic, that triggers the crisis for little or no reason. There is an element of habit in these matters, too: having once found such a reaction useful in certain circumstances, the reaction may be triggered subsequently without good reason, like an oversensitive burglar alarm that responds to the vibrations of a lorry or windy day. Sometimes the sensitivity decreases with age. As people grow older, their cerebral vascular system tends to become less reactive – and elderly people have far fewer migraines.

But what good reason could there possibly be in the first place for such a drastic series of events as a migraine may entail? According to Dr Sacks, who is consultant neurologist to several New York hospitals and has helped thousands of patients, migraines 'may be summoned to serve an endless variety of emotional ends'. He declares that most patients who experience severe and frequent attacks for which no obvious external cause can be traced are reacting to 'chronically difficult, intolerable and even frightful life situations'. It seems that such 'can't go on, can't opt out' situations lead to a build-up of emotional and physiological arousal that only finds relief when the migraine drives the patient into a retreat from the outside world and further stimulus, while a cathartic nerve storm takes place, and finally leaves the emotional landscape of the individual refreshed and renewed.

There is a part of the brain where mind and heart – thoughts and their physiological counterparts – are coexistent: the thought *is* the physiological response. This is not the case in the 'higher' parts of the brain, which give us the capacity of first examining thoughts and possible reactions, before deciding whether or not to implement them. These 'higher' parts, in the cerebral cortex, also seem able to block the movement of both thought and feeling welling up from the more 'primitive' areas. The migraine attack may be seen as a means of removing the cerebral block when the pressure from below becomes too great to bear.

Commonly the repressed thought and feeling is hostile; the migraine provides a means of expressing what can't be conveyed directly. The mother who has bottled up anger and frustration over her husband or children, or the employee who cannot tell his odious boss what he thinks of him for fear of the sack, might both be served by their migraine in this way.

More seriously, the migraine may be a means of discharging thoughts and feelings of self-hatred or low self-esteem, which have reached such levels as to be intolerable to the conscious awareness. When they threaten to break through, the punishing and overwhelming impact of the migraine helps to obscure the agony; just as it is easier to enter a cold sea running and shouting and with arms flailing than to let the water rise over the skin inch by inch.

If migraines are necessary in the physiological or emotional economy of an individual, they will continue to occur whatever particular 'trigger' mechanisms are eliminated. But one more mechanism should be mentioned, which has rarely been linked with migraine in the past but which may be a crucial means whereby an individual translates a potential migraine stimulus into a full-blown attack. This is the phenomenon of hyperventilation, or overbreathing, in which shallow and irregular but rapid breathing leads to too much carbon dioxide being 'blown out' of the system.

Dr Claude Lum, former consultant chest physician at Papworth Hospital, near Cambridge – famous for its heart transplants – is a world expert on this topic. He discovered while in charge of heart and lung by-pass machinery, which makes major heart surgery possible, that the flow of blood to the brain is partly controlled by the amount of carbon dioxide the blood contains. When the pressure of the dissolved gas is too low, brain blood-vessels contract and circulatory flow is reduced; overbreathing for just four minutes can produce a forty per cent fall in cerebral circulation. Furthermore, carbon dioxide is present in blood as carbonic acid. When this is lost, the blood becomes excessively alkaline, producing a chemical onslaught on a wide range of body systems, with symptoms such as pins and needles, muscle spasms, and an inability to digest and absorb food.

Paradoxically there is also breathlessness, dizziness and, before long, great tiredness. The overbreathing does not increase the amount of oxygen available to the tissues, as might be assumed, but in fact reduces it, since the ability of blood haemoglobin to release its oxygen for normal restorative purposes is impaired. However, while the cerebral, 'thinking' areas become starved of oxygen and therefore less responsive – they are anaesthetized, in effect – nerve cells in the autonomic system controlling movement and sensory alertness are put into a state of high excitability and readiness for action. Carbon dioxide is the main regulator in these cells of their internal acid–alkaline balance (pH), which determines their readiness to fire. At first the overbreathing causes their pH to rise, making them more excitable; but then it falls again, with lactic acid appearing as a by-product of their increased activity.

Hyperventilation is a natural mechanism forming part of the body's alarm systems, speeding up reaction times and reducing cerebral inhibitions in the face of demands for immediate action. But sometimes when the alarm rings fiercely, the individual is unable to respond to it – whether because of being trapped by external circumstances or internal psychological constraints. At such times, overbreathing could be an important link in the chain of events that culminates in a migraine attack in susceptible individuals.

One of the simplest methods of raising the carbon dioxide content of the blood is to breathe into a bag, and then rebreathe the expired air. Interestingly, this technique has recently been found to help a number of patients at one of London's migraine clinics.

Migraine is not only the commonest disorder with which family doctors are confronted, but one of the most perplexing for both doctors and patients. This is not too surprising, bearing in mind the delicate, intricate and rather beautiful mechanisms elaborated above – themselves probably only a fraction of the whole story – and their intimate relationship to the victim's circumstances and emotional responses. Sometimes the emotional strains are clear and readily admitted by the patient. Sometimes they are hidden and doctor and patient conspire to keep them so, perhaps putting disproportionate effort into the search for a purely physical explanation of the illness – and for a physical remedy. Whereas much research goes into examining the role of scientifically controllable triggers like certain foods and drinks, a majority of sufferers acknowledge and insist that excessive tension and worry are the main cause of their attacks. These are factors which the average doctor considers, rightly, to be beyond his powers of control, though they need not be beyond the control of the patient.

So drug sales for migraine are vast, and advertisements for migraine pills among the commonest in the medical press. Victims generally assert, however, that no pharmaceutical solution to their ordeal has been found, and that simple self-help remedies like resting in a darkened room are more effective than today's arsenal of pills. This was one of the main findings in a British study in which scores of researchers spent several months questioning a random sample of 3500 people across the country, and following up the results.

One migraine drug in common use, ergotamine tartrate, can even *cause* headaches. And patients who have been taking ergotamine in excess over long periods are made so ill by it that they have to be admitted to hospital to get them over the effects. This absurd situation came to light as a result of the establishment of special migraine clinics. Staff found to their amazement that in up to ten per cent of those attending, the symptoms of nausea and headache were the result of ergotamine poisoning rather than of the migraine itself.

Neither patients nor doctors had realized, because ergotamine pills do relieve an acute attack of migraine – for a while. The drug is a vaso-constrictor: the blood-vessels in the head, painfully throbbing and dilated in the wake of the 'nerve storm' described above, are driven into new constrictive efforts. The trouble is, as the effects wear off, the headache is liable to return even more agonizingly than ever. It seems like another migraine attack, so the victim takes more of the drug . . . and a vicious circle is established. This not only has happened, but at the time of writing is continuing to happen to many patients, although fewer since the maximum recommended doses of ergotamine tartrate were reduced by the manufacturers in response to protests from migraine specialists.

It is claimed that ergotamine should stay on the market since it still helps some patients over a crisis, but in view of the way it works – replaying the vascular events that precede a migraine attack – I would be most loathe to take it myself. Apart from the question of addiction, what effect does it have on brain tissues, I wonder, as it reconstricts cerebral blood-vessels that may already be trying to recover from the trauma of the migraine attack itself?

Drugs in the 'beta-blocker' class such as propranolol are being taken by some patients suffering regular migraines as a means of warding off attacks. They block chemical receptor sites – beta-adrenoceptors – in the heart and a multitude of other sites, preventing them from responding to the arousal hormones. Again, it seems obvious in the light of the delicate machinery involved in the migraine syndrome that this interference could have most disruptive consequences, and I would be unwilling to experiment on myself in this way. True, I have rarely if ever suffered a fully fledged migraine attack myself. If I was a frequent victim, and I found that any of these drugs really worked for me, I might think differently. But according to patients – who in any case are not usually aware of the long-term hazards – real relief is rare.

Beta-blockers are a chemical straightjacket restricting the expression of emotion. Apart from being able to precipitate heart failure and exacerbate circulatory disorders, they can have profoundly depressing effects on mood. To the extent that they succeed in aborting the 'nerve storm' of migraine, they may also ensure that the storm clouds never clear.

Very rarely, migraine attacks are so disabling that special medical help is needed. But for most patients, the greatest need is for kindness, not alarm and fuss, along with a sympathetic ear, an outline of the mechanisms of the illness, reassurance, advice on rest and relaxation, and perhaps an occasional gentle pharmaceutical hand, such as a tranquillizer or anti-emetic, to help a crisis pass.

Self Help

What can victims do to help themselves? First and foremost, acquire an understanding of the condition and the circumstances that can bring it on. To recap, migraines may serve one of two broad categories of purpose. They may be a response to relatively straightforward chemical and physical stimuli; or they may be a safety valve protecting against excessive internally generated arousal, providing a relatively harmless channel for the release of physiological and emotional steam for which no other outlet is available. Most often they are both, with the physical trigger providing a cue for the internal release.

Examples of common triggers not yet mentioned, and the chief mechanisms involved include:

Fasting Appetite is a form of physiological arousal which if frustrated for long enough can push the system into a migrainous protest. As blood sugars fall, energy supplies have to come increasingly from stored fat. The presence of these fats and their by-products in the bloodstream increases the clumping of platelets, making the blood 'stickier' and releasing chemicals that can put both body and brain tissues on general alert. So if you must fast, you should do so at a time when you can keep all other sensory and emotional stimuli to a minimum.

Intense pain from skin or muscle, and the trauma of violent exercise, can also provoke the general nerve sensitivity and platelet clumping that predisposes some people to a migraine attack.

Cold weather causes the blood vessels on the body's surface to constrict in order to conserve heat. The vessels in the head are particularly likely to be exposed to the cold, and so may have to do most of the work of constriction, after which they can flop back exhausted. The body also turns on its fat-fired central heating on very cold days. So as well as protecting against the cold, a balaclava helmet, for example, can reduce the chances of subsequent headache. And when you come back into the warm, soaking your feet in hot water will improve circulation in the extremities and relieve the pressure in the cranial arteries.

Hot weather The expansion of surface blood-vessels for cooling can overshoot, especially if you have been physically active in the heat. The resulting loss of tone in the tiny muscles responsible for constriction and dilatation may lead to overdistension and pain.

Coffee and tea tighten blood-vessels. If taken in excess, pounding headaches may set in as a reaction as the vessels in the head dilate exhaustedly.

Oversleeping can cause body arousal to fall so low that the cranial blood-vessels easily overdilate, causing a headache – though not necessarily a migraine. Physical exercise is one of the best remedies. It will stimulate production of noradrenalin and feelings of alertness and well-being will return. A cold shower will do the same.

Exhaustion after prolonged effort also commonly triggers headaches, and fully fledged migraine attacks. 'Weekend' migraines are well known: the individual does not allow the attack to come while effort is still essential, but 'saves' it until the rest and quietness that the migraine demands can safely – and necessarily – be accepted.

The fact that victims can seemingly choose when to have their migraines reminds us again of our own role in generating illness. But do those sufferers who are reacting to the internal strain arising from their 'chronically difficult, intolerable, and even frightful life situations' really have any choice in the matter?

Oliver Sacks declares that in the most important category of all – those patients in whom rage or other violent emotions may precipitate a migraine – the choice is not open. He quotes the eighteenth-century English surgeon John Hunter, who observed with regard to his own emotionally induced attacks of angina: 'A man may resolve never to move from his chair, but he cannot resolve never to be angry'. However, Hunter also once observed that 'my life is at the mercy of any fool who shall put me in a passion' – and later proved the point by dying in the course of a meeting of the board of governors of his hospital. The story makes me wonder who the real fool was. Anger is not natural and inevitable. It is a reaction that we learn to employ because it often seems to get quick results, when other strategies for obtaining one's own way have failed; but if it is proving to be self-destructive, it can be un-learned.

It *is* open to migraine victims to identify, if they wish, the emotional reactions to circumstances that cause them to become so steamed up: that is, the part that they are playing in generating their illness themselves. And once this is done, a number of options are available, of which the following are among the most important:

1 To try to avoid or change the circumstances.

2 To seek ways other than a migraine of displacing or removing the pressure, such as through sport or other activities in which achievements can be logged, self-regard restored, and the need for punishing headaches removed.

3 To check for and avoid overbreathing.

4 To take a conscious decision to practise not wasting energy in useless emotional reactions, and gradually to 'analyse out' the feelings by stepping back from the situation mentally and watching yourself and your relationships from a more detached vantage point. For this, a valuable aid is the ability to find at least a few minutes every day for stillness, silence and introspection.

Mostly easier said than done, of course. But in the end the decision, and the responsibility, do rest with the migraine sufferer. H. G. Wolff, author of *Headache and Other Head-Pain* (Oxford University Press, New York, 1963), wrote somewhat tartly, perhaps because of being a victim himself:

One must appreciate that elimination of the headache may demand more in personal adjustment than the patient is willing to give. It is the role of the physician to bring clearly into focus the cost to the patient of his manner of life. The subject must then decide whether he prefers to keep his headache or attempt to get rid of it.

The choice is real – once understanding has been achieved.

12 Multiple Sclerosis

Late one day in October 1980, I was asked by my news desk to write a few sentences about multiple sclerosis. The item was to go with a story in the following morning's paper about Vivien Neves, formerly a top model, who had been diagnosed as having the disease. This wasn't a subject I had studied, but there were some releases and medical cuttings about it in my files, and I drew on these for my facts (as I believed them to be) about the condition.

The article, headlined 'A crippling disease that has no cure', read as follows:

Multiple sclerosis is a baffling and unpredictable disease of the brain and spinal cord which is particularly distressing in that it tends to strike in the prime of life. There are about 40,000 victims in Britain.

Its cause is unknown, although it is thought to be due either to an infection, or the body's defences attacking the nervous system, or to a combination of both. Emotional stress also plays a part in its development.

A protective sheath surrounding the nervous system cells becomes progressively worn away, stopping various parts of the body from working properly.

The disease strikes without warning. A person may wake up in bed one morning to find some weakness or loss of feeling in a hand or foot, or notice blurring of vision or slurring of speech.

Often these early symptoms disappear, leaving no trace of illness – only to come back later, perhaps in a worse form. Once the disease is established, it is likely to become extremely crippling.

There is no cure, but changes in the diet seem to slow or halt the progression of the disease in some patients.

Both environmental and genetic factors are thought to contribute to multiple sclerosis. The environmental factors, as yet unidentified, are probably most important, because the disease is far more frequent in western Europe, southern Canada, the northern United States, southern Australia, and New Zealand, than in Asia, central America, and most of Africa.

The problem may well arise during the first 15 years of life. People who move from high-risk to low-risk areas carry much of the risk of their native land with them – but not if they move while they are still children.

I felt quite pleased with this summary, and congratulated myself on having kept my files up to date. But a few days later a letter arrived that gave me cause to be much less sanguine. Addressed to the editor, it took me to task for 'perpetuating the classical medical mythology' surrounding multiple sclerosis. The letter was from British playwright Roger MacDougall, a professor in the University of California's theatre department. As a wheel-chair-bound multiple sclerosis victim himself at the age of forty-five, he had been given only a few years to live; but at the time of writing he was seventy, in good health, and with no signs of disability.

His letter sets out very clearly some of the issues to be explored in this chapter. It also embodies a vital, health-promoting, self-reliant way of thinking, the value of which was not recognized, I am afraid, in my original regurgitation of 'medical mythology'. After referring to the Vivien Neves story, Professor MacDougall continued:

Some of your older readers may remember similar stories being written about me some twenty-five years ago. I had become reasonably celebrated then as the author of several 'hit' plays like *To Dorothy, a Son* and *Escapade* and of numerous movies like *The Man in the White Suit* and *The Mouse that Roared*. Then I too succumbed to multiple sclerosis. By the age of 45, however, I had degenerated much more seriously than has Ms Neves and had become a human cabbage in a wheelchair, given only a few years at most to live.

How come then at the age of seventy I am living a healthy, happy, symptom-free existence in sunny California? Simply because I refused to believe in the medical myth. To my legally trained brain, schooled not only in legal reasoning but in formal logic, it contained too many fallacious pieces of reasoning, made too many unwarranted assump-tions. I reasoned out the condition afresh, starting from scratch, realized that I was not, as doctors tend to postulate, a sort of living cadaver, but was more usefully to be regarded as a biochemical process.

Obviously something was going wrong with that process. It was failing to manufacture an adequate supply of healthy replacement tissue to make up for the normal wear and tear of living – rather as the body inevitably comes to do in extreme old age. I set about discovering and correcting the various food allergies and chemical deficiencies which were preventing my metabolism from functioning properly. Over the next ten years or so my symptoms gradually melted away, like snow in summer, until now I am normal again – much more 'normal' than many seventy-year-olds I know.

I am, of course, not 'cured' – simply restored to normalcy. Were I to revert to my old bad eating habits, I would once again suffer from the so-called disease of multiple sclerosis. In other words I am genetically prone to that particular way of becoming old (either prematurely or at full term).

As you will readily believe, many hundreds of people are following my example and reversing their descent to paralysis. Recently, the most striking proof of this has come here in Santa Monica where two sufferers from amyotrophic lateral sclerosis (Lou Gehrig's disease) are confounding the medical pundits by improving in a quite unprecedented and medically unbelievable way.

Your correspondent's choice of headline – 'A crippling disease that has no cure' – exemplifies some of the fallacious reasoning to which I referred. You can no more cure a sclerotic of his illness than you can cure a Chinaman of being Chinese. In both cases the condition is endemic to the very nature of the individual concerned. That is why the only 'cure' which will become possible is many years away. It awaits mankind's eventual ability to manipulate his own genes. It awaits the arrival of genetic engineering as a method of combating these degenerative conditions.

In the meantime why shoot for a cure? Why not gratefully accept 100 per cent control, as I have done. Neurologists are wasting their time researching the condition. It should be left to the biochemists. Neurologists would do their patients much more service if they would forget the nervous tissue which is where the condition ends and concentrate on the metabolism – on nutrition and chemical make-up. That way they might learn to help people instead of simply diagnosing them and then shrugging helplessly as they watch them degenerate.

In stubbornly regarding his illness as a process rather than a fixed sentence of wheelchair imprisonment and early death, Roger

MacDougall exposed a fundamental weakness in the medical model. Multiple sclerosis has remained 'baffling and unpredictable' to doctors for the very reason that medical science has persisted in analysing it not as a process but as a state. It is true that there has had to be acknowledgment of the fact that it comes and goes – that there are 'exacerbations' and 'remissions'. But these are seen as a kind of conjuring act of the 'now you see it, now you don't' variety: the 'it' is taken to be present throughout, while the comings and goings have tended to be regarded as illusory – and therefore just as baffling and unpredictable as the onset of the disease.

The situation is very like that governing the treatment of damaged blood-vessels. 'Sclerosis', or scarring, of the coronary vessels, when discovered in a patient who has complained of chest pain and breathlessness, is liable to be taken as a sign of irreversible disease, and this 'snapshot' thinking has led to vast numbers of people receiving major surgery and long-term drug treatment unnecessarily (see Part Two, particularly Chapter 5).

As in 'coronary atherosclerosis', 'multiple sclerosis' is really a description, not a disease. It simply means that the victim has scarring in the protective coating surrounding nerve fibres in the brain and spinal cord. This degeneration does have an effect: it reduces the speed at which the nerve fibres can transmit information. But the way people respond to this impairment varies greatly.

Many people have widespread damage of this kind without knowing it. They may have suffered temporary weakness or clumsiness in hands or feet, blurring of vision, or even paralysis because of it, but have recovered from their attack and returned to normal function without consulting a doctor, or at any rate without a diagnosis of multiple sclerosis being formed. This became clear from work at Basle University Hospital, Switzerland. All patients dying at the hospital – whether because of diagnosed illness, an accident, or 'old age' – undergo examination by a pathologist unless they have formally refused permission for an autopsy. In some, quite unexpectedly, the typical changes of multiple sclerosis are found; and in almost all such cases, the patient has never been seen by a neurologist nor even by a general practitioner.

Multiple sclerosis victims sometimes criticize family doctors who, despite suspecting the condition, are reluctant to refer a patient for neurological tests to have it confirmed. But one wonders what value such a diagnosis holds. There may be practical reasons, such as ease of claiming benefits, for having a formal-sounding label pinned on a condition that has become severely disabling. Patients may also have a profound need to be formally designated as seriously diseased, in order to use this new 'status' to help them break free from distressing and otherwise inescapable circumstances. But later, when that need is no longer there, the idea that they are in irreversible decline may stand in the way of recovery. Faith can injure as well as heal. When people mistakenly put faith in the judgment of an expert who declares, in the seemingly incontrovertible language of science, that they are doomed to an early demise, the prophecy can easily become self-fulfilling.

Lack of understanding produces frustration on both sides, with doctors becoming upset and defensive over their inability to meet patients' expectations of a cure, and patients unwilling to accept that nothing can be done. Judy Graham, author of a very informative self-help guide to the management of multiple sclerosis (Thorsons, 1981), tells of experiencing neurologists as 'remote, arrogant, and totally lacking in helpful advice of any sort' when diagnosed as a sufferer herself, and like Professor MacDougall she exemplifies what can be achieved when the individual rejects the professional pessimism that comes from viewing the condition mechanistically. At twenty-seven, when the diagnosis was reached, she felt as though she was 'wearing Wellington boots up to the thighs while walking through a quagmire in the Arctic Circle'. Seven years later, while still showing symptoms of the condition, there was improvement rather than deterioration: 'I can still walk the dog briskly across Hampstead Heath, but I would be pushing my luck to sprint across a road.'

Judy Graham wrote that to make a diagnosis the National Hospital in London used what seemed to her to be the entire armoury of its technological equipment.

Despite all that, I felt as though I might as well have been living in the

Dark Ages, for all the help modern medicine could offer me. The time I spent in a ward, of what is considered to be the top-notch neurological hospital in Britain, was nothing short of dire. I have never felt so ill in all my life as the week following the lumbar puncture [a diagnostic procedure in which a sample of fluid is taken from the spinal column]. In fact, the whole episode in hospital was so thoroughly unpleasant that I resolved never to be a hospital patient again.

The truth is that we have indeed been living through the Dark Ages as far as an understanding of disease processes is concerned. Much information has been acquired about what happens at the cellular and sub-cellular level in multiple sclerosis, as a result of the millions of pounds spent on research. But the more the specialist's vision has focused on the details, the less he has been able to see the patient as a suffering, ill human being. Suffering, and its physiological consequences, are the context in which the detailed information that has been gathered needs to be set before it can begin to make sense and be of real practical use.

The Theories

It has been established that there are various immunological changes in multiple sclerosis victims; and one of the front-runner theories as to how the damage to the myelin sheath that surrounds and insulates the nerves occurs is that it is the result of an autoimmune – immunologically self-destructive – condition, in which a part of the patient's own body is reacted upon and attacked as if it were foreign to the body. Several possible explanations for this reaction are on offer.

One is that cells become 'foreign' to the body as a result of a chronic virus infection lurking inside them (measles and distemper viruses have both come under suspicion). Another is that the immune reaction is linked to a genetic abnormality that makes myelin components susceptible to attack. A third is that dietary deficiencies in childhood (starting, perhaps, with bottle instead of breast-feeding) contribute to the laying down of defective myelin, which later becomes vulnerable to auto-immune attack.

It may well be that not just one but all three of these mechanisms are involved in generating vulnerability to multiple sclerosis in different patients. But once the vulnerability is there, what to do about it? Should the immune system be suppressed, so as to reduce the intensity of the attack? This treatment has been tried; it can have unpleasant and dangerous side-effects. It may even be the reverse of what the body needs: there is evidence that a group of immune system cells known as suppressor T-lymphocytes, which may hold the degenerative process in check, decline in number and activity just before an attack, but are present again at increased strength as recovery sets in. As a 1980 *Lancet* review of immunological treatment in multiple sclerosis commented, 'there is no certainty whether the immune response should be suppressed or stimulated'. It is not even known whether the immune reaction is a cause or an effect of the myelin disintegration.

It was because such work seemed to be adding to the confusion rather than reducing it that in 1974 a multiple sclerosis 'ginger group' was formed in Britain to try to give new leads in research. It was comprised of sufferers or friends of sufferers. Judy Graham, one of the founder members writes: 'We were a group of very angry activists who were outraged and enraged that nothing could be done for us. So we decided to do something for ourselves.' The group, called ARMS – Action for Research into Multiple Sclerosis – is now big business. It has an income of over half a million pounds a year, raised by members in branches right across the country. It is an extraordinary success story, because it was set up as a rival to a pre-existing fund-raising and caring body, the Multiple Sclerosis Society. This has been responsible for much good and honest work, but in the view of the 'activists' it has become too dominated in its research policy by an overly narrow scientific approach. In the words of the MSS itself, money is spent 'on the careful and considered advice of its Medical Research Advisory Committee, which is made up of the most distinguished and experienced scientists and clinicians working against multiple sclerosis'. ARMS felt that this medical dominance of research spending was perpetuating the journey down blind alleys, and set out to explore some fresh avenues; in particular avenues that seemed more directly oriented towards helping patients immediately, rather than searching for a 'final solution' to crack the mysteries of multiple sclerosis and banish it for all time. Its success in terms of membership – well over 6000 at the time of writing, with forty-two regional groups – and income testifies both to the energy and clear-sightedness of its founders and to the level of dissatisfaction with previous approaches.

Like Roger MacDougall, ARMS has put great emphasis on exploring dietary approaches to the alleviation of multiple sclerosis symptoms. It has backed research into the theory that the primary disorder is in the body's ability to manufacture and utilize enough of the essential fatty acids (EFAs) vital to the growth and repair of myelin and other brain tissues. Dietary modifications aimed at making good this deficiency have certainly helped some patients.

However, studies of the effects of diet alone on the progression of the disease seem to have brought disappointingly undramatic results overall. So could ARMS be heading down another blind alley? There may be a clue to the answer in the parallel case of coronary atherosclerosis. A diet rich in animal and other saturated fats does appear to contribute to the development of the porridgy plaques that are liable to clog the coronary arteries of westerners. But diet has been shown to rank way behind the emotions in generating the blood conditions conducive to coronary artery damage and heart failure.

We have seen that the cascade of changes in blood chemistry that accompany chronic emotional arousal have far-reaching effects on fat metabolism. The catecholamines adrenalin and noradrenalin mobilize fat reserves, literally thickening the blood; and if these are not burned off in activity they become a cue for blood platelets to clump together, further increasing blood viscosity. There are raised levels of cholesterol, and of the clotting agent thrombin, the fibrous protein collagen, the energy-releasing enzyme adenosine triphosphate, and the prostaglandin thromboxane, which causes platelets to aggregate and blood-vessels to constrict. Thromboxane is opposed by another prostaglandin, prostacyclin, which forms in the linings of healthy blood vessels and prevents deposition of platelets. It also dilates the blood-vessels as soon as the arousal storm has passed its peak.

In heart patients, the catabolic – energy-releasing – emergency response is often seen to have overwhelmed homeostatic safety-valve defences (such as the prostacyclin/thromboxane system), so that blood-pressure rises so high and the blood thickens so much that coronary vessels become damaged; and the labouring heart cannot get the oxygen and other nutrients it needs to continue to do its work.

It seems to me that there is every reason for considering a similar mechanism to be at work in multiple sclerosis. The 'blood-brain barrier' that guards brain tissue against noxious substances in the blood does not give absolute protection, and is likely to be weakened when the system is working under high pressure. When blood viscosity increases, pressure has to rise to maintain the flow. Above a critical point, plasma proteins can pass out of the fine network of blood-vessels serving tissues and enter the tissue fluid itself. White blood cells of the immune defence system also migrate from the circulation into the tissues to catch and remove the fugitives. When this happens in the brain, the scavenger cells may become overenthusiastic and digest a vital component of the myelin sheath as well. It is possible that this attack only occurs in people who have an abnormal component in their myelin, laid down in childhood – whether for reasons linked to genetics, diet, infection, or trauma. The crucial point is that such attacks are only likely to occur when blood-pressure rises too high and/or the blood becomes flooded with the products of prolonged emotional arousal.

So here we have a scheme of things that would take multiple sclerosis out of the realms of the 'baffling and unpredictable' and into the territory of the predictable and controllable – but by the patient rather than the doctor, because it is the patient who knows whether he or she is feeling contented or abnormally sad, benevolent or fiercely hostile, peaceful or filled with anxiety and fear. To the extent that the doctor is able and willing to judge these matters too, the disease will lose its mystery for him also.

Most of the pieces of the jigsaw already assembled fit into such a scheme. The diets that have helped patients are low in the saturated fats that animal products contain (which have a high energy content for high-arousal living) and high in essential fatty acids or their precursors, found mainly in vegetables and fish.

These favour prostacyclin formation, as well as being the building blocks of the central nervous system. Such diets are clearly a step towards healthier function in the struggling individual, though the benefit will be lost if hormone and circulatory systems remain overactive.

We can also see why many patients find exercise helps to protect them against further attacks, too. It burns off the products of arousal and increases the oxygen-carrying capacity of the blood, reducing as a result both blood-pressure and viscosity. It further eases blood-pressure and improves blood-flow rate by opening up and relaxing the vessels serving muscles.

The overarousal hypothesis also provides possible answers to the long-standing puzzle of what triggers the immune response seen in demyelinated areas of the brain. This could either be a consequence of unwanted protein escaping from blood-vessels into the vicinity of the myelin sheath, as we have seen; or of the sheath decaying because of becoming inadequately supplied by the struggling circulatory system with the oxygen and essential fatty acids that it needs for its sustenance. The breathing of pure oxygen in a pressurized chamber has been shown to reduce infirmity in some multiple sclerosis patients, though the effects are generally short-lived.

Emotions: the Missing Link

The crucial question is, does evidence exist to suggest that emotional arousal plays such a crucial role in initiating multiple sclerosis attacks? The answer is definitely yes, though one would not think so from the amount of attention this factor generally receives. Individual doctors – and patients – have noticed that multiple sclerosis is often related to prolonged grief or vexation, but there have been few studies to confirm this impression.

One such was reported as long ago as 1958 by G. S. Philippopoulos, Assistant Professor of Neuropsychiatry at the University of Athens, and a team at McGill University, in Canada, to which he was temporarily attached. They found that out of forty patients, thirty-five had suffered prolonged traumatic disturbance before their symptoms emerged, and when they relapsed into new attacks this was often associated with fresh sources of emotional disturbance. They also found that multiple sclerosis often followed an unhappy relationship with a parent, usually the mother, leaving a residue of anxiety.

Brian Inglis, referring to this trial in *The Diseases of Civilisation* (Hodder and Stoughton, London, 1981), writes: 'If these researchers at McGill had discovered a *chemical* change related to the onset of MS, or to relapses, they would have sparked off frenetic research all over the world. But laboratory scientists cannot be expected to investigate anxiety, and neurologists have felt ill at ease with this psychosocial element. The research was backed by the Canadian Multiple Sclerosis Society, but it has not been followed up elsewhere.' The possibility that psychotherapy might have some specific role to play in helping to manage the condition, though raised in a *Lancet* editorial, was one 'in which those MS fund-raising organizations dominated by neurologists and laboratory-orientated researchers have shown little interest. The only psychological aspect of the disease which has attracted much of their attention is how to help people cope with the emotional disturbance, which can be severe, consequent upon the diagnosis of MS.'

I believe it is a measure of the error in orthodox research strategy that while such very promising leads remain unexplored, the Multiple Sclerosis Society should recently have made a grant of £1,066,000 for a nuclear magnetic resonance scanner, supposedly to aid accurate early diagnosis by showing up small areas of damage in the nervous system. Such machinery is more likely to add to the sum of suffering than reduce it as long as those in whom multiple sclerosis lesions are discovered are offered little more than advice on planning for a restricted future. Machine or laboratory diagnosis can be so impersonal, so seemingly final, and so misleading. Unless properly and humanely interpreted, it creates fear. It draws attention away from the mind, which holds the key to the healthier emotions that reduce arousal and promote healing, and focuses it instead on degenerated matter. Mind and body, already lacking harmony in the 'dis-eased' individual, have their mutual lack of communication and cooperation reinforced.

This brings us back to the point made by Professor Mac-Dougall, with which this chapter began: that while the weakness, however it arises, which makes someone vulnerable to multiple sclerosis attacks may have to be regarded as a relatively fixed *state*, the disease that exploits this weakness – and determines whether symptoms become noticeable, grow worse or gradually recede in their impact on the victim's life – is not fixed at all, but a moving process. People who have these sclerotic lesions may also have to acknowledge the likelihood of a degree of long-lasting handicap, depending on how serious the damage has become; but there is much evidence that the process which produced the damage in the first place can be greatly slowed or else halted for good. And sometimes nerve function is fully restored.

Possible Ways to Recovery

People like Roger MacDougall and Judy Graham have shown the way not, I believe, principally because of their dietary change, but because they have made up their minds to banish illness from their lives. Healthier eating patterns accompany such a determination almost automatically, along with a generally healthier living pattern involving regular exercise, plenty of sleep, and a positive and cheerful outlook. Most protective of all in the case of these two particular individuals, I suspect, is the sense of purpose, satisfaction and relative peace that have come from helping others also to recover their health.

Judy writes of the immediate improvement in physical symptoms that accompanies mental peace and a sense of well-being. She recommends pursuits such as yoga, which is directed towards improving knowledge and acceptance of the self as well as smooth physical functioning. 'Some remarkable people who have been struck with multiple sclerosis have taken it as a blessing in disguise. They find it gives them the opportunity to find the true essence of life; to strip life of all its superficialities and banalities, and experience the true joy of living.'

Why is there such fear of multiple sclerosis? Brian Inglis suggests it is mainly because of the system by which patients with disturbing symptoms of nerve dysfunction are sent to a hospital for specialist diagnosis and treatment. The consultant neurologist tends to see patients when their symptoms are at their worst;

patients whose symptoms disappear may never set foot in hospital again. In other diseases such cases can be claimed as cures, but since no effective drugs or operations are available in multiple sclerosis, the belief that it is incurable is so strong that when symptoms disappear it is assumed that the diagnosis must have been wrong in the first place.

Sufferers who are not ready to bring about self-change and to embrace health and the 'true joy of living', but instead prefer to court sympathy from others or wallow in bitterness, may also conspire with their doctors to sustain the 'incurable' fiction. Yet the facts are that people do get better; fewer than ten per cent of multiple sclerosis patients ever require a wheelchair; and the condition does not appreciably shorten life in most patients, even despite what may well be a high level of misunderstanding and mismanagement.

I am sorry that I gave such a misleadingly negative instant sketch of the condition in my newspaper article in 1980, and hope that the ideas and information set out here may help to de-'hex' the multiple sclerosis label and encourage some present victims to cast it off altogether.

Part Four

Cancer

Introduction

Cancer is a disease like many others: sometimes harmless, sometimes inconvenient, sometimes painful, sometimes fatal. Like an infection, it is capable of coming and going: one moment seemingly racing through the body, so that a patient's days seem numbered; the next, completely disappeared, only to return again months or years later, or never to be seen again. Nothing is certain in cancer. And yet, people dread it more than any other illness, and doctors tend to regard it as their greatest enemy, to be fought with every weapon at their disposal. Why is this? It brings death to many thousands; but not so many as heart disease. It sometimes strikes in middle age or even childhood; but the great majority of deaths are in the old.

But cancer is a loaded word, a metaphor for purgatory. The disease has a natural history of its own, but we use it, I believe, for a very specific purpose: as a means of forcing ourselves to confront death, which also means confronting ourselves. The heart attack is popularly deemed to be quick and clean, a happy way to go; but cancer allows weeks, months or years of living with and coming to terms with the notion of one's mortality, and perhaps with one's failed hopes for the self and others.

Cancer is not evil or sinful in itself. It is just a physical disorder. But the way we react to it is a sin. Treating it as if it were a monster, monstrous things are said – or not said – and done to patients. Averting our eyes from suffering – trying to ignore the living mind, the human soul, and acknowledge only the body – we develop an inordinate fear of death.

Doctors are more distressed and confused over what to do for the best in most forms of cancer than probably at any other time in their profession's history. As the darkness has deepened, the human ability to respond to suffering wisely and with kindness has been obscured by a cloak of professional objectivity and scientific respectability. And cancer patients, who are sometimes – but by no means always – abject and defeated, have so often willingly embraced a cruel dependency on doctors and hospitals. Not seeing any alternative, such patients have taken refuge in this dependency. Fooled by the rest of us – using doctors as our chief spokesmen – into regarding cancer as a death sentence from which only science may discover a reprieve, they have sacrificed themselves on the altar of science to some extraordinary, sometimes agonizing, rituals performed in our temples of technology, in return for the hope of an externally imposed cure.

In the chapters which follow, that hope is shown to have been a vain one for the majority of cancers. Not that people don't survive – many do. But the case is presented that the main forms of treatment are being so misused as to cause vast, unnecessary, and unjustifiable suffering. Most importantly, a dependency on technological approaches to cancer has diverted attention from the patient's inner life and sense of purpose in living, in which, it will be argued, the chief arbiter of life or death resides.

13 Surgery

A few months after becoming a medical correspondent, I came across a story that had a deep impact on my thinking, and caused both me and probably a lot of readers much concern. Surgeons at the breast unit of London's famous cancer hospital, the Royal Marsden, had found that a group of women who refused to have a breast removed because of cancer, but instead insisted that surgeons cut out only the lump, had tended to fare much better than women in other studies who had had a full-scale mastectomy operation. There were thirty-one women in the group, identified during a review of 1500 cases dealt with at the hospital between 1968 and 1974. For various reasons – almost invariably involving the patient's own strong preference – these thirty-one had neither chemical nor X-ray treatment, as well as only the very limited surgery.

Their fate, reported in 1978 in the *Journal of the Royal Society of Medicine*, was strikingly different from the stereotype of the cancer 'victim' as a helpless creature swept along by a tide of disease and untimely death. At the time, it was almost unheard of to challenge the wisdom of the mastectomy procedure, let alone to reject other weapons in the fight against the dread killer. According to the stereotype, these women should have been rapidly consumed by their disease. Yet careful follow-up revealed that only *one* patient had died of breast cancer – six years and four months after her operation. Three had died of other causes (heart attack, bronchopneumonia, and cancer of the parotid), aged 104, seventy-eight and fifty-nine. Out of sixteen who had received their operation five or more years before the time of the review, fifteen were still alive.

This was and is a considerably better survival rate than usual.

Contemporary studies from two other leading London hospitals, Guy's and King's College, had shown that twenty per cent of a group who had partial mastectomy with radiotherapy, and twenty-two per cent of patients who had a full mastectomy – some with and some without radiotherapy – were dead after five years. Generally it is reckoned that about a third of breast cancer patients will die within this period. Of the fifteen five-year survivors at the Marsden, five had developed a new lump at some stage, and most of these had then agreed to have a mastectomy. But the recurrences were less frequent and came much later than most surgeons would have predicted.

When I rang the director of the breast unit at the Marsden to explore the significance of these findings, he urged that they should not be published in a mass-circulation newspaper. He explained that he was trying to win the cooperation of colleagues around the country in staging formal trials of different treatment 'regimes', and that any current controversy could jeopardize such plans, as well as alarming and confusing patients. I considered these objections with senior colleagues on my newspaper, but it was decided that they were outweighed by the possible value of the findings to future patients. With due caution expressed over the small numbers involved, the story was published under the headline: 'Should we think again over cancer?', with the sub-heading: 'Major breast surgery may not always be for the best, say group of surgeons.' The cautious tone did not forestall a complaint from the house governor at the Marsden – not contesting the accuracy of the story, but the fact that it was published at all.

More distressing were protests from relatives of women who had received full-scale surgery for a breast lump, and who were upset at being confronted with the possibility that this mutilation, and the accompanying treatment, might not only have been unnecessary, but could actually have lessened their chances of survival (though as will be argued below, any such effect is probably less than the study would suggest).

These protests were offset to some extent by letters from a number of women who had unquestionably suffered appallingly as a result of mastectomy, and who wanted it to be more widely known that such suffering could accompany the operation. Here are extracts from two of them. They make distressing reading, but serve the purpose, I hope, of illustrating graphically what a dark age of cancer medicine we have been experiencing, in which the treatments have all too often caused far more suffering than the disease.

One woman wrote that she had entered hospital six months previously as 'a strong, healthy, active seventy-six-year-old, running whist-drives for my fellow senior citizens, giving lectures, playing the piano for my club mates, writing poetry, essays, music, etc.' Now, however, she was 'a physical wreck, housebound, unable to walk, and in constant pain, thanks to my operation and the poisonous drugs I was forced to take'. She continued:

Knowing that other women had suffered damage to their arm because of the operation, I was promised by the surgeon 'on my honour' that the operation would not affect my right arm and stop me writing. Today I have an arm like a ton weight and in constant pain. (The writing of this letter will give me a whole day's agony.) . . .

For twelve years I had a lump on my breast about the size of an almond. It never got any bigger and I had no pain from it. Unfortunately, my doctor discovered it when he was examining me for something else. He assured me it was only a mastitis and there was nothing to worry about, but he would like me to see a surgeon to make certain. So muggins went to see the surgeon, who came secretly round the back of me and rammed a needle into my breast. From then on the lump grew and grew and started giving me pain. Only then did I agree to the operation . . . .

The part of my body that isn't dead is one big pain, day and night. I had looked forward to living to 100, but I shall be lucky if I reach 77.

Another woman wrote:

I didn't have a lump and I had very little pain, which my doctor put down to mastitis, but I did notice the nipple was a little tilted, so I reported it to my doctor who then sent me to see the surgeon. I was admitted to hospital, taken to the theatre, and my breast was removed. They had difficulty bringing me round as I could see everyone but I could not get my breath. I kept passing out. They finally settled me down about eleven hours later.

There was a very ugly scene for me to see about three days later. They had probed right down as there was only a tiny trace of cancer in the duct, and the specialist I had to see after the operation was disgusted at the sight. He asked me if they had used an axe as I was terribly bruised inside . . .

I have been in agony for 20 months with a terrible pain in the right arm. I was told I would have to learn to live with it.

A week ago they suggested I go in for four days for another course of injections which had very bad side-effects. They told me I would lose my hair. I went to pieces, I couldn't take any more and I was very ill and depressed, so I refused to go in. I am now cut off from the hospital and treatment. I decided to go to a physical culture and health centre where I am having physiotherapy. I am still in great pain at times, although I admit this person is after a week making some progress with me.

I was told I was completely cured of cancer, but in God's name why am I still suffering?

Such stories are not exceptional. Writer and broadcaster Brenda Kidman tells in *A Gentle Way with Cancer* (Century, 1983) of how in 1977, frightened by a well-meaning friend into having a pea-sized lump in her breast examined surgically – it had been there for at least a year without growing – she awoke feeling 'as though someone had clamped a branch of holly under my left armpit and the rest of my body had been reduced to a helpless pulp'. Moving her right hand to her left shoulder, she found a flat gauze dressing and tubes. The breast had gone.

Brenda was a victim of a procedure in which surgeons often insist on the patient signing a consent form allowing them to remove whatever they consider necessary immediately after examination of a sample of the growth. If an instant laboratory test on the sample – a biopsy – shows malignancy, then they may proceed with full amputation. (In fact, the patient is within her rights to insist on biopsy only, though the surgeon is within his rights to refuse to operate at all.) Part of the rationale for doubling up in this way is that in a case of malignancy, the biopsy procedure itself could cause the cancer to spread, and that therefore speed is essential. But there is another view: that the body will be in a better position to destroy stray cancer cells if it is not at the same time having to recover from the trauma of mastectomy. Besides, there is a bigger risk of cancer being falsely diagnosed when the procedure is rushed in this way. And the emotional strain and shock for the patient on waking to find the breast gone, without warning, must be enormous. On the other hand, some patients might prefer to avoid the ordeal of two operations.

Should uncertainties over treatment methods be aired publicly? There can certainly be advantages to such matters remaining secret. Most cancer patients, already in a low state psychologically and physically, are more likely to be cheered by confident and determined medical action against their disease than by being confronted with a wide range of doubts and uncertainties. But when that medical action is such as to suggest a loss of both rationality and humanity, the confusion that arises from challenge and debate may well be the lesser evil.

The original justification for radical mastectomy – in which lymph nodes in the armpit and muscles beneath the breast are removed, as well as the breast itself – was the belief by nineteenth-century surgeons that cancer was disseminated via the lymphatics, part of the body's immune defence and drainage system. In fact, cancer cells spread principally via the blood-stream – but are usually tracked down immunologically and eliminated. So as well as causing unnecessary pain and mutilation, in the probably futile hope of excising all remnants of cancer locally, radical breast surgery which includes removal of the lymph nodes may weaken the patient's chances of avoiding a recurrence of the disease.

'We now know that the organs of immunity must be preserved wherever possible,' the French oncologist Dr Lucien Israel tells us in *Conquering Cancer* (Allen Lane, 1979). 'These include the lymph nodes, spleen, thymus, tonsils, and appendix – all of which used to be frequently removed, before we understood their role.' Consultant surgeon Phyllis George said in the *British Medical Journal* in July 1980: 'Surgeons are confused about treatment, and however dogmatic they may sound about the correctness of their treatment, we don't know which method(s) are best because we don't have all the necessary facts for each patient.'

But faced with such confusion, why did radical mastectomy remain the most widely performed operation for breast cancer until very recently? It is not as if the controversy is new. The British surgeon Sir Geoffrey Keynes, writing in the 1920s about the origins and theory behind the radical operation – 'such barbarous mutilation of the human body' – declared that he was greatly relieved and excited to discover 'that the theory had been formulated by a distinguished surgeon who was rather old-fashioned in his ideas of the natural history of the disease, so that his concepts proved to be based entirely on fallacies and could be discarded'.

In 1937 Keynes published a paper showing that when 250 women were treated by simply having the lump removed and radium needles inserted in the breast to destroy remaining cancer cells, results were comparable to those obtained through major surgery. Yet it is painful to reflect that nearly fifty years later, with millions of breasts removed, the fact that there might be a case for lumpectomy – the simple removal of the lump – in 'early' breast cancer (that is, when the cancer has not become so advanced that no option remains but to remove the whole breast) has only just begun to be faced and tackled scientifically by the surgical establishment.

Dr Israel points out that the radical mastectomy was devised at a time when surgeons were consulted much later than they are now, and had to deal with large tumours that had always spread to the lymph nodes and were sometimes ulcerated. 'It is truly remarkable,' he writes, 'that in spite of increasingly early diagnosis and the almost universal application of post-operative radiotherapy, a majority of surgeons throughout the world persist in performing an operation that is so mutilating.'

A similarly chaotic and wasteful state of affairs exists in the management of other major cancers. 'It saddens me to think how little we understand the biology and proper management of many of our most catastrophic killers: lung cancer, breast cancer, and cancer of the colon are the outstanding examples,' Dr Jeffrey Tobias, a lecturer in radiotherapy and oncology at the Institute of Cancer Research at the Royal Marsden, wrote in *World Medicine* in 1980 (the lung, breast and large intestine are together responsible for half of all cancers). 'All these diseases have been with us for decades, as have the standard surgical procedures by which the primary cancer is excised. Yet how many surgeons can, with hand on heart, lay claim to know what is the operation of choice?' He pointed out that despite the organizational advantages of having a National Health Service, fewer than five per cent of all cancer patients in Britain are included in clinical trials.

The ease and relative safety with which operations can be performed nowadays have magnified the surgeon's capacity for doing harm by operating unnecessarily. The cancer surgeon's big mistake, his *hubris*, has been to think that his work can cure – and in many cases falsely to assure patients that an operation is almost synonymous with cure. The disappointment when a lump recurs must be bitter indeed. But if surgery were regarded from the outset as palliative – symptom-relieving – the disappointment would be nothing like so acute, and the surgeon, deprived of his belief that he can triumph over the disease alone, would be less likely to cut so deep and so readily. If the concept were one of easing the patient's lot, rather than saving life, the justification for radical surgery would diminish very greatly.

The hope of catching a cancer early enough for there to be no possibility of dissemination is usually forlorn. Rogue cells are liable to break off and travel elsewhere within a few days of a tumour's development. By the time a cancer is one centimetre in diameter, generally the earliest stage at which it can be detected in deep tissues, it already contains about one billion cells which may be infiltrating the blood-vessels in tens of thousands. To reach this stage, the original cancer cell will have doubled thirty times; and it is rare for untreated tumours to go beyond their fortieth doubling. So this 'early' cancer may already be three-quarters of the way through its 'natural' lifetime, and already have shed thousands of tumour cells into the bloodstream or surrounding tissues. That is not to say that the cancer will necessarily have spread. The wandering cells may all have been destroyed by the patient's internal defences before they could find fertile territory in which to take root. Nevertheless, in more than eighty per cent of cases, it is the distant spread of the disease that kills, and not the original tumour.

No proof exists that early detection saves lives. Though this is widely claimed, the record in terms of death rates gives no support to the argument. Because early detection catches tumours at an earlier stage in their history, the time between detection and death is naturally longer than when they are seen later. But treatment has nothing to do with this longer survival period. Furthermore, screening is more likely to identify slowly developing tumours than fast cancers. Again, this is often the real explanation behind claims that screening saves lives.

In fact, it has been demonstrated that patients operated on when their symptoms have lasted more than six months are *more* likely to recover fully than those whose symptoms are of recent origin. One reason is that the latter are more likely to be victims of fast-growing cancers. But it is also possible that patients with newly developed tumours have less resistance to the disease than those who have harboured it for long periods. In such circumstances, early surgery might expose the patient to greater risks of dissemination than the more leisurely approach of removing a lump after it has become an inconvenience. Early detection also has the great disadvantage – because of the fatalistic way cancer is regarded – of prolonging the period of fear associated with the disease.

There has been no improvement in mortality from cancer of the breast, but rather a worsening, throughout much of the world, to which present methods of treatment may have contributed. British figures are particularly disturbing: the number of deaths from breast cancer in England and Wales rose from 10,622 in 1969 to 12,513 in 1981.

Is Screening Useful?

The breast presents an easy target for examination and removal; and so also does the womb and, in particular, its neck or cervix. Hence when it was discovered more than thirty years ago that through taking a scraping or 'smear' of cervical tissue, and examining the cells under a microscope, early changes suggestive of cancer could be detected, a new field of medical endeavour was born.

By 1973, nearly half of all American women over seventeen years of age reported receiving the smear test during the previous year, and three-quarters had had one at least once in their lives. Britain was slower to start, but in the twelve years up to 1982, a total of twenty-six million cervical smears were performed. The cost of the screening service now exceeds £150 million a year.

The cost in human terms has been, firstly, a greatly increased consciousness – and fear – of cervical cancer among most women, and the discomfort and perhaps humiliation of the testing procedure in those who feel compelled to undergo it; and secondly, among those in whom cancerous or supposedly pre-cancerous cell changes are observed, an operation involving varying degrees of discomfort, pain, mental distress and loss of function, with hysterectomies having been performed especially commonly in the USA when cancer – either malignant or 'on site' – is diagnosed.

The only possible justification for these enormous financial, physical and emotional costs would be a big fall in deaths from cervical cancer. It was assumed by those who fuelled women's anxieties through health education programmes, and who acceded to the demands of the pressure groups seeking expansion of the screening programmes, that these savings would inevitably occur. Unfortunately, this assumption was never tested scientifically: no controlled trial was ever conducted at the time screening was introduced to examine the outcome in screened women alongside that in comparable groups of unscreened women. So the only clues we can obtain are from looking at trends in overall death rates, and from comparisons between intensively screened areas and those without formal screening programmes.

A look at national death rates shows, firstly, that cervical cancer is a relatively minor cause of death – contrary to the impression many have gained. It is listed as the cause of death for just over 2000 women a year in England and Wales, compared with 12,500 deaths from breast cancer and 91,500 female deaths from heart disease. Secondly, it becomes apparent that a steady decline in deaths from cervical cancer had been taking place before mass screening was introduced, and that this decline has actually levelled out since the screening programmes began. This could either mean that screening itself is somehow responsible for halting the decline in deaths, or that it has made no difference, or that its value has been obscured by an increase in the number of women at risk. Whichever of these is correct, its value is clearly not proven.

As for comparisons between high-screening and low-screening areas, varying results have been seen. Screening in New Zealand, for example, has been more intense than in England and Wales, but the disease has not become any less of a problem there than here. In Britain, women under thirty-five have been more intensively screened than older women (despite payment incentives to doctors to screen the older age groups), but death rates in the under thirty-fives doubled during the 1970s. (The figures are still low, however – only 118 out of a total of 2015 cervical cancer deaths at all ages in England and Wales in 1981.)

According to a review in *World Health Forum* by Anne-Marie Foltz, of New York University, and Jennifer L. Kelsey, of Yale University's department of epidemiology and public health, it does seem that in areas where the smear test has been used extensively for a long enough period, there is a 'small but real' decrease in death rates attributable to it. But even that cautious conclusion is questionable. Professor Walter Holland, Professor of Community Medicine at London's St Thomas's Hospital, believes that aggressive treatment, common in Canada and the USA, has distorted the mortality statistics. When the entire womb, which of course includes the cervix, has been removed, a subsequent death from cancer – even though it may have originated in the cervix – is liable to be attributed to some other site.

If screening for cervical cancer were of benefit, people diagnosed as having it ought to be living longer now than before the tests were introduced. But this has not happened, at least in regard to the disease in its invasive form. Of patients diagnosed during 1964–66 in England and Wales, sixty-two per cent were still alive five years later – while for those diagnosed during 1971–73, after screening came in, the five-year survival rate had fallen to fifty-four per cent.

Furthermore, the reliability of the smear test is not well established. Subsequent checking shows that false negatives are common, with between a fifth and two-fifths of cases with abnormal cells being missed. Sometimes this can happen because of the way the smear is taken, sometimes because of laboratory failings. A Yorkshire GP, concerned that some slides were not being examined properly, sent off scrapings from inside his nose to test the system. The laboratory simply reported: 'Normal smear, no malignant cells.' With northern bluntness, the doctor told *General Practitioner* newspaper: 'Cytologists ought to be able to tell the difference between a cervical smear and a bit of snot.' They ought indeed, because women who have had a negative result may ignore obvious signs of ill health, such as bleeding or heavy discharge between periods, thinking that this cannot be a matter for concern.

And when positive results are obtained, some women are receiving surgical treatment or radiotherapy unnecessarily. Only a small proportion of cases of abnormal smears go on to become cancerous, and the abnormalities themselves often disappear. One study of women under twenty showed that sixty per cent of smears returned to normal without treatment. In another, it was found that of sixty British women with positive test results – defined as invasive cancer or cancer 'on site' – who refused to have an operation, one-third had negative test results when they were traced and examined an average of five years later. The cancer had simply disappeared. (The women in whom this happened had all been under forty at the time of the original test.)

In the complete absence of proof that regular smear tests – and treatment for abnormalities found – will prolong a woman's life, the continuing high level of propaganda for this measure seems to be doing more harm than good. It creates an unnecessary worry for millions. In common with other forms of cancer screening, it turns the minds of healthy people towards disease and death. And to the extent that it reveals physical abnormalities which rarely develop into overt disease, it lands people with a frightening, sometimes disabling, and generally unfruitful experience of doctors, hospitals and operations.

14   Radiotherapy

Radiotherapy is the second main line of conventional warfare against cancer, after surgery. Over fifty per cent of all cancer patients are irradiated at some time during their illness. This is an astonishingly high figure, because there is no evidence of any improvement in overall survival rates arising from its use. In fact, it has been shown to have no effect on survival among victims of the major cancers such as breast, lung, and colon.

How can this possibly be the case? Surely this expensive treatment, which can cause weakness, sickness, pain and worse, would not have achieved such popularity without good cause? The answer is that for decades doctors have persuaded themselves that the more weapons they throw at the body in an attempt to seek out and destroy cancer cells, the greater the chances of success must be. The flaws in this philosophy, which is based on misunderstandings both about the nature of cancer and the nature of human beings, have long been trying to force themselves to the profession's attention. But when not only your livelihood but your life's meaning and purpose is threatened, it takes courage beyond normal human resources to face the truth. This is why, for the present, the sanest course for cancer patients is to obtain the maximum information possible about their condition and then decide for themselves what treatment to accept.

They will not always find this an easy or straightforward matter. Doctors whose treatments provide genuine help obtain satisfaction from their work that sustains their self-esteem and, with that, their humanity and openness. But those whose work is essentially useless, and who are sufficiently advanced in their careers unconsciously to know it, develop an inhuman front designed to fend off awareness – either in themselves or others – of the futility of their work and the emptiness of their self-importance. Such doctors can also be spotted by their sensitivity to questioning.

Brenda Kidman writes tellingly of her first appointment for radiotherapy:

When my name was called, I went through the door in a wooden partition which divided the consultant's office from the rest of the cavernous room. An impatient nurse dragged my jumper over my head, slipped my vest straps off my shoulders and ordered me onto the examination couch. Only then did the consultant turn round from his desk under the high, green, whitewashed window and without uttering a word, marked four ink crosses on my front and back with a felt pen. Then, dressed in a striped hospital robe, I was sent back to the waiting area.

Another breast cancer patient, Mrs Joan Craddock, told in the magazine *Cancer Naturally* what happened when she tried to have an 'objective discussion' with the consultant radiologist:

This was a complete disaster. All my queries about how radiation helps, its risks, side-effects, etc., were interpreted as criticism. The interview ended with the gentleman in question storming out of the room after having been very rude and leaving me with the comment that if I didn't want his service, there were plenty of other patients who did. This made me feel defeated, isolated and emotionally unstable because I had gone in good faith in case radiation was perhaps something I should try.

Mrs Craddock had been told by her surgeon that she should have a course of 'strong' radiation because she was considered to be at very serious risk, having refused a radical mastectomy. She had already had a partial mastectomy, but twelve months later another lump had appeared, and the brave woman insisted that this should simply be removed and not become a reason for major surgery. She stuck to her position despite intense pressure from a team of doctors at her bedside; and after the radiologist showed how deeply *he* appreciated the risk that this supposedly very sick woman ran – by walking out on her – she abandoned the National Health Service and adopted natural healing methods. These involved a wholesome diet, meditation, and developing an awareness of the need to avoid excessive stress. She was introduced to these methods of health maintenance by a doctor in Denmark. She wrote:

I feel quite justified in complaining about the marked difference in response to my problem shown by the two types of medical practitioners whom I consulted. The doctor in Denmark treated me as an 'intelligent and integrated woman' (his words) who needed significant answers to vital questions.

It is a pity that despite paying into a National Health Service for over thirty years, I had to find the money myself and travel so far from home to save my life.

I further regret that there was such a tremendous loss of faith and goodwill between myself and the British consultants simply because I questioned their recommendations.

. . . I still continue to stick to the basic principles of my diet and the wholistic approach to my health. My greatest triumph is that I have avoided mutilation and am living a better quality of life as well.

That account was written in August 1981. Today (autumn 1983), five and a half years after her original operation, Mrs Craddock is still completely free of disease.

Radiotherapy destroys cancer cells by interfering with their molecular structure. As with surgery, it can be of great symptomatic value to the patient. It can postpone death, when a tumour is life-threatening. It can buy time. It can also be used where surgery is no longer possible. But it has a number of disadvantages which are rarely taken into sufficient account, least of all by patients deprived of the information needed for rational choice.

The particles delivered in radiotherapy transfer their energy to electrons, resulting in the production of free, reactive chemicals ('radicals') in the matter that they reach. This chemical reorganization causes changes in the fundamental biological properties of the cells, altering the DNA and RNA. Sometimes the cells die as a result, or stop dividing. The higher the dose, the more likely it is that the cells will die and the tumour shrink or disappear. But the dose is limited by damage caused to healthy tissue.

When an area is bombarded with rays, Dr Israel tells us, roughly a third of the cells remain unaffected. The next bombardment will remove only two-thirds of that remaining third. And so on.

Consequently, the radiotherapist wears himself out trying to hit the last cells and can't do so unless he totally destroys the neighbouring tissues. If one cell out of ten thousand escapes, and if the tumour had 10^{11} cells (that is, weighed 100 grams) in the beginning, there remain 10^7 cells, which continue to proliferate and will become 10^{11} cells again in 13 doublings. The probability of radically sterilizing a tumour by radiotherapy rises in direct proportion with the risks one takes with regard to the healthy tissues, but it is never equal to 1.

What are these risks? Radiation can cause burns of the skin and mucous membranes, but these generally repair themselves. It can also irreparably damage blood-vessels, leading to permanent loss of function in sensitive organs. Even moderate amounts of radiation to the sex glands can cause sterilization, or lead to genetic mutations affecting subsequent generations. Some of the effects only appear well after the course of radiation treatment has finished. In the gastrointestinal system, the late effects of radio-therapy are 'many and diverse', a *Lancet* editorial (15 May 1982) tells us. 'They include strictures, especially of oesophagus and rectum, chronic ulceration, enteritis, fistulas, adhesions, hepatic changes (including vasculitis with portal venous obstruction), and pancreatitis.' (In other words, your innards are liable to go haywire.) On the bladder, late effects include chronic cystitis, bleeding, and obstruction. Nerve tissue and hormone system damage, fatal lung diseases, and inflammation of the heart and other organs are also documented.

When radiotherapy is applied in the hope of 'mopping up' remaining cancer cells after a large tumour has been removed surgically, the chances of the tumour recurring locally do seem to be lessened. But this is not the case when a small lump has been removed, as with Mrs Craddock. Furthermore, a number of studies have shown that metastases – the distant spread of the cancer – appear to happen more often when radiation is used in this way. There are two good reasons for expecting such an effect. One is that radiation throws the patient's own immune defence and cell repair mechanisms into disarray. The immune deficiency can be both severe and prolonged. Another is that among the cell mutations that it causes, some may actually result in the production of new cancers.

In view of the multitude of risks, both proven and likely, and the lack of proven benefit in most cases, it seems irrational, not to say criminal, that half of all cancer patients receive radiation treatment.

There is something horrifically symbolic about radiotherapy machinery. Photographs of human beings lying alone in a sea of metal and glass, being subjected to radiation doses way in excess of those considered safe for 'normal' people in an attempt to sterilize tumours, emphasize the alienation of the cancer patient, and the fear which the 'enemy within' inspires. It is as though the internal disorder which gives rise to cancer has found reflection in this wild, unrestrained, external growth of medical technology. Radiation therapy in its early days consisted of the administration of relatively low-voltage X-rays or the implantation of radium directly into the tumour. Through a series of steps like the doublings in a cancer cell, its latest manifestation is the cyclotron – a machine which accelerates certain types of sub-atomic particles to extremely high velocities. One such machine, being installed at the Mersey Regional Centre for Radiotherapy and Oncology, at a cost of more than £4 million, is expected to come into operation in autumn 1984. It will provide 'the most penetrating and most precisely deployable beam of neutron radiation available in any hospital anywhere in the world'. But will it help patients? There might be some who could benefit; but on the basis of the above analysis, their numbers will not be great.

The trouble is, just as cancer cells cannot recognize when to call a halt to their activity, so the very existence of such a monstrous device – costing over £200,000 a year to staff and run – will encourage self-justificatory, undiscriminating activity. 'It will be possible to study the efficacy of neutron therapy in the treatment of deep tumours such as those of the gastro-intestinal tract (stomach, bowel, rectum, pancreas),' say the project organizers. Years later, I would predict, the efficacy will be found to differ only marginally from present techniques, and the side-effects 'many and diverse'. It is claimed to be an advance on existing radiation treatments, but when these are often worse than useless, a hypothetical improvement still provides little incentive for allowing oneself to be the guinea pig in such an experiment.

15   Chemotherapy

As if the tale of surgical and radiotherapeutic folly was not bad enough to teach us our lesson, chemotherapy came on the scene. This involves the use of toxic chemicals to try to kill malignant cells wherever they exist. Chemotherapy has the theoretical advantage over surgery and radiation in that, because it affects the whole system, it may reach cancer cells which have spread to distant parts of the body as well as in the original tumour. By the same token, however, it has a high capacity for causing widespread physiological havoc.

The chemicals discriminate in their toxic activity towards those cells that proliferate fastest. This is likely to include cancer cells, but the drugs also kill cells in the bone marrow, which manufactures blood components essential to immune defence and general body maintenance; in the digestive tract, responsible for assimilating everything the body needs for its nourishment; in the scalp; in the skin; and in certain endocrine glands responsible for maintaining body homeostasis. So it is not surprising that the cytotoxic – cell killing – treatments have added immeasurably to the suffering of many cancer patients, poisoning their systems, often producing nausea and vomiting, chronic nutritional deficiency, loss of hair, skin disorders, vulnerability to infection, gastro-intestinal upset, painful ulcers, nerve damage, and in the case of one or two of the drugs, lung and heart disorders. Sometimes the effects are fatal. Above all, patients are liable to feel thoroughly miserable and unwell.

'Drug toxicity is necessarily very common during cancer chemotherapy,' says the *Drug and Therapeutics Bulletin* (June 1983). 'Doctors need to be familiar with its forms to make a diagnosis so as to decide whether to treat symptomatically or to refer urgently to hospital. Occasionally this can be life-saving. It is important to keep the relatives and the patient informed.'

Patients should also, in my view, be told very clearly that in most instances the drugs are of unproven benefit. They are experimental. The proven side-effects, and the evident risks that the treatment will injure, delay recovery, or even kill, are undergone by patients for what is usually only hypothetical advantage. Would they agree to treatment in such numbers as at present if these facts were made plain? It is true that some cancer patients do want to throw everything that medical science can offer at their bodies, believing themselves to be under a sentence of death. But why do they believe this? How often is it because their doctors tell them so, as in the case of Mrs Craddock?

Patients are often subjected to futile chemotherapy, with 'many, many patients being given cytotoxics that cannot possibly help them', Professor Timothy McElwain, consultant physician and Professor of Medical Oncology at the Royal Marsden (and a member of the World Health Organization's Expert Advisory Committee on Cancer Chemotherapy) said recently in London at a meeting of the Society for Drug Research. So called 'response' to these drugs was of interest to experimental chemotherapists, but was often of no benefit to patients. Drug therapy, he said, had not made any major impact on survival in patients with common solid tumours. It was still important to try new drugs and new combinations, but if patients were to be given drug therapy, they should be put into controlled trials of treatment, rather than undergo the current indiscriminate use of unproven treatments.

In cancer of the colon or rectum, Professor McElwain asserted, the position is clear cut: the chemotherapy which some patients receive as an adjunct to surgery is of no benefit. It does not delay the return of the cancer, or lengthen the life of the patient. In breast cancer, the case is definitely not proven: the drugs used are toxic, cannot possibly be of use to all patients – since many stay well after surgery regardless of additional treatments – and may not benefit those in whom the risk of a relapse is present.

Chemotherapy had some early impact, notably in cancers affecting general mechanisms such as the bone marrow and lymph systems, where turnover of cells is high. The forty or so cytotoxic drugs available have all been shown capable of lending a helping hand to the body in the fight against various kinds of tumour. Like surgery and radiation, they do have some capacity for doing good. But they have been used unintelligently and indiscriminately. Instead of providing a judicious boost to self-healing mechanisms, they have been thrown into the attack in so violent a way as to wreck the indigenous defences.

Most anti-cancer drugs block the growth of white blood cells, reducing the body's resistance not only to infection but perhaps also to the spread of cancer cells, making them potential pro-moters of cancer. Most are also mutagenic – they alter the genetic material of cells, making them a potential cause of cancer.

When tumours are first detected, many are found to have a considerable degree of order still reigning within their population of cells. The cells retain some or most of the specialities of the tissues in which they have arisen, so that they cannot easily metastasize – take root elsewhere. They are of low malignancy. And being only slightly abnormal, they remain responsive to most of the checks of growth inherent in the normal cell.

However, a phenomenon known as 'tumour progression' is often seen in which the offspring of the original tumour cells are more delinquent than their parents. They are less differentiated – they lose their sense of specialized function – and consequently are a lot more capable of insidiously but aggressively colonizing unrelated parts of the body. On the basis of experimental evidence, it seems entirely possible that the use of mutagenic cancer therapies, both drugs and radiation, may well hasten the development of the more malignant cells.

'The indication from a number of studies that treatment does not alter the lifespan of cancer patients is compatible with this view,' according to a *Lancet* article by Dr R. S. Kerbel, of the Cancer Research Laboratories Queen's University, Ontario, Canada, and Dr A. J. Davies, of the Chester-Beatty Laboratories, Institute of Cancer Research, England. If reducing the size of a life-threatening cancer does not prolong life, they argue, 'it could be that the growth rate and malignancy status of the tumour have been changed by the treatment.'

A similar theory has been proposed by American researchers George Poste, of the University of Pennsylvania, and Isaiah

Fidler, of the Frederick Cancer Research Center, in Maryland. Malignant tumours often contain groups of cells with widely differing capacities to metastasize – some benign, some deadly. And the benign ones exert a modifying influence on the anti-social tendencies of the others, creating a kind of ecological order. But when this equilibrium is upset by a sudden attack on the tumour, survivors multiply wildly, and new types of cell groups develop. Finally the tumour attains a new equilibrium. The possibility that such attacks – whether with chemicals, surgery or radiation – can sometimes hasten the development of malignancy is now being examined very seriously.

In *Conquering Cancer*, Dr Israel acknowledges that when used without discernment, the cytotoxic drugs 'are veritable poisons, acute or chronic, that add immensely to the discomfort and suffering of patients in exchange for a dubious improvement . . . First generation chemotherapy is still too often practised by physicians and surgeons who are not up to date,' he adds. 'The doses prescribed are inadequate, so that they are ineffective in addition to being toxic, and thus, through ignorance, is perpetuated the myth that chemotherapy is worthless as well as intolerable.'

He believes, however, that the latest techniques, involving massive, carefully timed doses of the drugs along with drug protection of the bone marrow to prevent loss of immune function are already making possible results 'that only yesterday would have seemed like science fiction'.

Certainly, in individual cases of advanced disease, his own unit seems to have achieved some notable successes in extending active life. But his therapeutic optimism and aggression – he writes, 'when it comes to the treatment of cancer, my motto is: When in doubt, do it' – are open to question.

Dr Israel made much play, in his book, on early results from two scientific investigations into the role of chemotherapy as an added safeguard after surgery for breast cancer. One of these studies, begun in 1973, involved a group of 269 women who had been operated on for cancer of the breast with involvement of the lymph nodes (stage two breast cancer) at units in Canada and America. Half received the drug L-PAM (melphalan) while half received an inert substance. In January 1975, the publication of the results (in the *New England Journal of Medicine*) 'burst like a bombshell': after twenty-four months, nine per cent of the women on the active drug had suffered a recurrence of cancer, compared with twenty-two per cent of those on the placebo pill. For pre-menopausal women, the difference was even more striking: three per cent against thirty per cent. 'This is an absolutely major breakthrough,' Dr Israel wrote. 'The study has proved, for the first time, that post-operative adjunctive chemotherapy is highly effective in the treatment of one of the "common" cancers.'

In a scathing attack on critics of the study, who argued that it was far too early to draw conclusions about the effectiveness of the regime, Dr Israel added: 'Let us remember that when patients are operated on for a breast cancer with involvement of the lymph nodes, and given no further treatment, metastases appear in nearly fifty per cent at five years, that is, in one case out of two. To persist in abstaining from treatment under these circumstances is incomprehensible, to say the least.' So far as patients themselves are concerned, he said, when shown the study results, 'they have no hesitation'.

Such absolute certainty, from a physician who has many harsh words for 'ideological prejudice' and 'charlatans' in medicine and who clearly prides himself on his own scientific rigour, was influential. The book, which originally appeared in France, was translated into English and published in both the United States and England. It was lauded by Susan Sontag, the author of *Illness as Metaphor*, as 'by far the most intelligent, informative and useful book ever written on cancer'.

But let us see what has happened since. In a superb review article on chemotherapy in breast cancer published in *Medical News* (29 September 1983), Dr James Le Fanu tells us that the 1975 paper was the last to be published about the study in any widely circulated journal. Follow-up reports could be found only in specialist oncology journals, or in symposia proceedings. So most doctors were in no position to question assertions that the trial had determined the worth of melphalan.

However, the most recent details of the fate of the women involved give little cause for confidence. They are contained in a report submitted to a meeting of the National Surgical Adjuvant

Breast Project, under whose auspices the study was performed. Marked 'confidential: not for publication or citation', the report shows continuing advantage for only one small section of the chemotherapy-treated group – pre-menopausal women whose lymph nodes were moderately affected by the cancer when the study began. In this group, after five years, twenty-one of thirty-one patients who received the placebo, and twenty-eight of thirty-two who received melphalan, were still alive. Meanwhile a controlled trial with the same drug, involving 370 British women also followed for five years, produced the following conclusion by a collaborating group of British surgeons and oncologists in April 1983: 'Our results indicate that there is no place for the use of melphalan as an adjunct to mastectomy in routine clinical practice.'

The picture is similar with other trials – of early promise failing to be confirmed by long-term results. Yet, as Dr Le Fanu points out, the majority of doctors still believe chemotherapy in breast cancer is effective. A questionnaire circulated at a 1982 conference on this topic asked: 'Have clinical trials established the efficacy of adjuvant chemotherapy in stage two breast cancer?' Eighty-six per cent believed that they had. Thus, hundreds of thousands of women continue to be medically poisoned without therapeutic effect.

This sorry story should make us question the ability of doctors to apply true scientific methodology in relation to such a complex issue as cancer. Dr Israel was not alone in greeting the 1975 study results overenthusiastically. 'The treatment reported in this issue of the *Journal* has produced results nothing short of spectacular,' a commentary in the *New England Journal of Medicine* proclaimed. It is not medical science that is at fault, but those responsible for interpreting its findings. They are human, like the rest of us. Oncologists have been 'willing' a breakthrough in the pharmaceutical fight against cancer. So on the most slender evidence, at the first hint of progress, too many of them indulge in chemotherapeutic evangelism. Clinical trials involving careful comparisons between treated and untreated groups can make available certain facts in a scientific way, but when the interpretation of those facts is left to people who have strong vested interests in a particular conclusion being drawn, objectivity gets lost.

Sometimes vested interests are financial, as when a researcher's livelihood depends at least partly on a drug company, for example. But more often the subjectivity stems from a false egotism, a fragile self-esteem, that lies hidden in the doctor's mind. Having pitched himself into the fight against cancer, having made that his *raison d'être*, the need for success becomes so great that he may sometimes grasp too readily at straws of encouragement. A *Lancet* editorial in April 1981, after reviewing the claims for chemotherapy following surgery for breast cancer, ended:

The unwelcome conclusion is that the precise role of adjuvant chemotherapy remains in doubt; adjuvant chemotherapy is still an experimental treatment, and should be confined largely to controlled trials designed to show what sort of patients benefit, for how long, and at what price. There has been much debate lately between the proponents and opponents of adjuvant chemotherapy. The existence of this controversy merely points to the shortcomings of existing data, which can be manipulated selectively to support either side of the argument.

These seem sensible words. But the uncertainty and manipulation continue today, with entrenched positions on both sides of the debate. Luckily (I believe) for British patients, our cancer specialists have shown considerably less inclination to wage all-out chemical warfare on tumours than American doctors who, in a situation reminiscent of the Vietnam struggle, seem to escalate the battle yearly. 'Polychemotherapy' – throwing five or six drugs at a time into the battleground of the patient's body – has now replaced the three-drug chemotherapy that sustained optimism after single-drug 'breakthroughs' began to be discredited. These trials require deeper justification than 'the advance of medical science'.

A study from the Royal Marsden in 1980, analysing side-effects from two cytotoxic drug regimes in breast cancer, found that apart from vomiting, hair loss and other well-known problems, the commonest side-effect – not reported in the usual medical literature – was being 'off colour'. And that is a euphemism, as one patient commented. 'It starts an hour or less after the injection. The unpleasant sensation crawls around the body. It is vile.' A Boston doctor, writing of his thirty-seven-week course

of chemotherapy for a neck tumour, observed that 'these powerful drugs interfered with body functions which most people take
for granted, making me feel as though I had surrendered bodily
control to a group of external agents. That helpless feeling, rather
than any individual side-effect, was what occasioned the need for
the greatest adjustment.'

16 Disarming Cancer

The reader could be forgiven for refusing to believe the evidence cited in the last three chapters. It may prove too much to take for those who counter fears of illness and death with a blind faith in medical science. But it seems to me that the case is unassailable: thousands upon thousands of cancer patients have undergone hellish procedures on an unproven, experimental basis. And the experiments have for the most part proved to be dismal, immensely expensive, time-consuming, life-disrupting failures.

That is not to say that all cancer treatments have failed. Surgery, radiation, and chemotherapy, when used to ameliorate evident symptoms of disease, have brought both physical and psychological relief. Where the surgeons, radiotherapists and chemotherapists have gone so wrong is to try to win the fight against cancer – to score a total victory, to shoot for a cure – without the patient's active cooperation and help. It has been this mistaken drive that has led many specialists to pursue more radical operations, more powerful radiation, more vicious polychemotherapy. And patients have so often been semi-willing victims, abdicating all responsibility for their body's welfare to hospital staff.

This abdication is liable to add to a patient's suffering rather than ease his or her burdens. It encourages those who are seeking to help to limit their vision to gross physical symptoms, or to statistics of narrow applicability and worth, so that progressively they lose sight of the human occupants of the bodies that come before them. In the end the body becomes just one more slab to be wordlessly blue-pencilled, as in Brenda Kidman's story, with the conscious being inside totally ignored. Such inhumanity is shared by the whole of a society that has allowed – encouraged – the medical profession endlessly to seek technical solutions to human problems. As one reviews the consequences of this error in the cancer field, one understands the accuracy of Ivan Illich's declaration in *Medical Nemesis* that 'the pain, dysfunction, disability, and anguish resulting from technical medical intervention now rival the morbidity due to traffic and industrial accidents and even war-related activities, and make the impact of medicine one of the most rapidly spreading epidemics of our time.'

The justification for devoting so much of this section to examining wrongful medical intervention in cancer is that the reader may thereby be led to ask, with interest and urgency, if there is any alternative to present strategies. If we cannot hand over responsibility for fighting illness to doctors, then who else are we to turn to? As indicated above the primary answer to that crucial question is our own selves; yet that does not seem like much of an answer, to a cancer patient who feels his or her self to be drained and fettered by illness and under a sentence of death.

Indeed, it is no answer while the patient feels that way. But *why* do we consider cancer a death sentence? Is the decline really as inevitable as generally assumed? There is much evidence suggesting that it is not, and to realize this, and exorcise the doom-laden connotations, is perhaps the biggest step towards recovery that a patient can make.

The first encouraging fact is that two of every three people who develop cancer live for at least five years after the diagnosis is made, despite present inadequacies in understanding and treating the disease. That figure conceals a very wide range of outcomes, of course. Some cancers tend to kill much more quickly than others, some patients die within weeks of diagnosis, while others, even with the same type of cancer, live a normal lifespan and die of something else completely. Post-mortem examinations show that many people who die in old age of causes unrelated to cancer have malignant tumours within the body that may have been quietly and harmlessly growing for years, and which – fortunately – never came to the attention of either the patient or the medical profession.

Secondly, cancers do not grow in an unpredictable, anarchic way. For much of its life a tumour has a constant doubling time. If it takes three months to double in volume, it will take another three months to double again. But this process does not go on for ever. Parts of the tumour may begin to find it hard to obtain nourishment, and will die. Furthermore, even given the most favourable circumstances for growth, the eventual size of the tumour is often limited by central feedback mechanisms. The genetic material that controls cell growth and function has been altered in cancer, but the cancer cells are not completely unfettered: they are usually obeying a new set of instructions, albeit of a mutant and physiologically inappropriate kind. It seems likely that many tumours deemed malignant when examined during their growth phase will stop being a threat (providing the patient lives long enough) once they have met the requirements of the altered instructions.

Thirdly, the causes of the crisis that proves fatal for a person with cancer are often obscure: that is, there are often no obvious biological or biochemical reasons as to why the patient dies at a particular time. Many never suffer from the obvious malnutrition, bleeding, or internal obstruction that form part of the stereotyped picture of the cancer patient, especially with the wide availability of surgery, radiotherapy or drugs to shrink tumours. Rather, death often comes to cancer patients gently, seemingly at their bidding, as when an old person decides there is no longer any reason to go on living and is said to have 'died of old age'. Death seldom coincides with rapid tumour growth. In fact, tumours often stop growing and begin to deteriorate when the fatal crisis approaches.

Fourthly, there is plenty of evidence that people do recover from cancer – fully. There are many stories of individuals who have been considered hopeless cases by their doctors, but in whom the disease has regressed and who have gone on to live a full lifespan without further trouble. In my view, patients should reject any assertion that they are suffering from an 'incurable' disease. It may be true that a tendency to cancer will always remain after recovery, but whether or not that tendency is given another chance to express itself later in the individual's life, if it has been quelled for the time being, then for the time being the patient is cured. Similarly, if the growth of a cancer is restrained to the point that it would only prove life-threatening if the patient lived to 150, then that too is a cure in the most meaningful sense.

What doctors mean when they sometimes declare cancer to be incurable is that they do not feel competent to cure it themselves. When a cure takes place, it is called 'spontaneous regression', indicating that this is regarded as some lucky stroke of fate, an abnormal occurrence, not deserving the word 'cure' because it has not happened as a result of medical intervention. But cases like these provide some important clues for developing a more rational strategy for coping with cancer.

If the human body is capable of killing and removing even disseminated cancers using only its own resources, as is undoubtedly the case, then those natural mechanisms deserve the strongest possible attention and support. What weakens them, causing them to allow a cancer to grow instead of killing it at its birth? What strengthens them, to such an extent that they can dispose of an advanced cancer? The exact mechanisms governing these events are not yet known, but there is enough information available to make some sensible guesses. And the joy of this approach is that it puts the patient, instead of the doctor, at the centre of the stage.

Immunotherapy

The first, most obvious candidate for examination is the immune system – the body's inbuilt defence mechanism for identifying and disposing of harmful entities. Animal experiments have shown that in animals, at least, it is involved in preventing the establishment of malignant disease. The experiments have also shown that when animals are put into stressful circumstances, their immune surveillance system is weakened so that they become more vulnerable to cancer. And transplant patients on drugs to suppress the immune defences, so that they will not reject their graft, run considerably increased risks of developing cancer.

These findings appear to have significance for the *prevention* of cancer, at the very least. They suggest that the immune system plays an important part in preventing mutant cells with carcinogenic qualities from becoming established as tumours. It also seems likely that immune defences help to prevent an established tumour from spreading to distant sites. The idea that cancer develops 'when your lymphocytes take a dive' because of emotional factors is appealing, inasmuch as it turns attention away from the tumour and towards the whole patient. And as we shall see, many indicators point to the mind and emotions as key factors in cancer vulnerability.

However, attempts to bolster the immune defences in order to combat established tumours have had generally disappointing results. When breast cancer patients receiving radiotherapy were treated with levamisole, a drug capable of stimulating production of the white blood cells involved in recognizing and destroying unwanted products, they were found to be more at risk of a recurrence of the diseases than patients who received radiotherapy alone. Attempts at vaccination – with virus particles and spleen cells, to produce a generalized stimulus to the immune system, and with white cells experimentally stimulated to combat specific tumours – have also failed.

Dr Carl Simonton, a radiation specialist in Texas, has for several years used 'mind control' techniques in the fight against cancer. Patients are taught to visualize a battle taking place inside the body, with white blood cells as sharks, for example, tracking down and destroying tumour cells. He also teaches the visualizing of peaceful imagery to foster relaxation and well-being and promote repair processes that way. He had some early indications of success, in terms of cancer patients using these methods generally living longer than usual after diagnosis. One study showed a two-year average survival – twice the USA national average for such patients. But when I met Dr Simonton in London recently, it seemed to me that he was taking pains to deflate any expectations that visualization therapy could defeat the disease. Rather, he was emphasizing what a high proportion of cancer patients seem to want to die. The main value in .iis therapeutic methods appears to be in allowing cancer patients to learn introspection and with that, a greater degree of self-knowledge and control – whether in living, or in dying.

Finally – and encouragingly, in a way – experience with radiotherapy and chemotherapy treatments suggests that the immune system does not play as crucial a role in cancer surveillance as some commentators have thought. For despite the severe damage to natural defences (and increased vulnerability to infection) caused by these treatments, studies with large numbers of patients indicate that survival is not much affected either way, though this might be because any benefits from the treatments are compensating for damage caused.

The Role of Diet

A second approach in promoting natural self-healing mechanisms concentrates on cleansing the body through a vigorously controlled diet. The thinking here is that western diets in particular can overburden body systems in such a way that poisons accumulate, either promoting carcinogenesis or interfering with anti-cancer mechanisms. Too much meat is considered particularly harmful, because enzymes needed to break down meat are also needed in the attack on cancer cells, and may become deficient. Other dietary demands on the system considered liable to render it vulnerable include food additives and preservatives; foods drained of essential vitamins, minerals, and fatty acids, by modern methods of production; and excessive alcohol, which damages the liver.

A pioneer in nutritional approaches to cancer was Dr Max Gerson, who achieved remarkable results in a medical career filled with controversy (he died in 1959). Working with 'terminal' patients, he took them off all drugs, including painkillers; tried to keep them away from every kind of possible chemical contaminant, including 'safe' ones such as are found in toothpaste or gargles; put them on a diet of vegetable and fruit juices, freshly made several times a day; and administered a coffee enema at least once every two hours. Difficult as it might be to believe, he wrote, 'frequent enemas completely eliminate the need for sedation'. As well as helping a number of patients who had been given up for dead to recover completely – several testified on Dr Gerson's behalf at congressional hearings into his methods as long ago as 1946 – the emergency detoxification appears to have brought relief of pain, nausea and vomiting; to have controlled infections, to which patients with advanced cancer are vulnerable; and to have enormously increased patients' morale. Gerson was described by Albert Schweitzer as 'one of the most eminent medical geniuses in the history of medicine', but he was vilified within the American medical profession, which mistrusted his uncompromising and probably rather egocentric individualism and feared the implications of his methods for orthodox approaches to cancer.

Recently, however, diet has begun to be taken seriously by some doctors as a factor in cancer vulnerability. A 1982 report from the US National Academy of Sciences, based on a review of no fewer than 10,000 other reports, advocated that we should eat more fruit, vegetables, and whole-grain cereals, and cut down our intake of fat, to lessen the risk of cancer. It concluded that 'the evidence is increasingly impressive that the cancers of most major common sites are influenced by dietary patterns'. Further recommendations were to eat very little salt-cured and smoked foods, such as bacon and hot dogs, and to drink alcohol only in moderation. The report identifies carotene, which converts in the body to Vitamin A, and Vitamin C, as perhaps having a specially protective role. Foods rich in these substances include oranges, grapefruit, dark-green leafy vegetables, carrots, tomatoes and vegetables such as cabbage, broccoli, cauliflower, and brussels sprouts. The committee recommended against taking high-dose supplements of individual nutrients.

These recommendations can be welcomed as sensible because they are in keeping with general good health, never mind cancer. A well-balanced diet, providing the body with all it needs while at the same time not burdening it with excesses, will help to protect against all kinds of disease.

But there is very little evidence of dietary inadequacies directly causing cancer. It seems more likely that poor eating habits – too much fat and refined sugar and starch, too little fresh fruit and vegetables – are just one of the aspects of a person's life that ut him or her at risk, through increasing the vulnerability of body tissues to the initiation of a tumour and to metastatic spread.

Equally, there is very little evidence for believing that dietary change alone can ever offer a cure for cancer. Rather, what may happen is that a general increase in well-being accompanying healthy eating promotes healing at a deeper level.

This distinction is important. If a naturopath or other practitioner of 'alternative' approaches to cancer becomes overenthused with the dietary approach, he or she will be falling into the same trap as the surgeons, radiotherapists or chemotherapists who go all out for a cure with their particular speciality – at the patient's expense.

Dr Donald Gould, writing in the *New Scientist*, has contrasted the approach that 'forces cancerous clients to drink gallons of fruit and vegetable juices, which must be prepared according to a detailed ritual if they are to be effective', with that of a woman doctor at the Royal Marsden Hospital who will tell a patient to go and buy himself a steak from time to time, and cook it on the ward, if she perceives that to be his pleasure. The doctor runs a ward devoted to the care of cancer patients for whom the therapists have decided they have nothing further to offer. But she has found that 'with sensible and compassionate help, many a cancer victim can go on living with the disease for a decade or more, finally dying (perhaps from cancer, perhaps not), long after the making of the "mortal" diagnosis'.

Although a vegetarian diet is advocated elsewhere in this book as a specific measure for fighting disease vulnerability, the advantages in cancer are less clear cut. Meat is stimulating, and nutritionally rewarding; cancer patients are often low both in vigour and vitamins. On the other hand, overindulgence in meat imposes metabolic burdens that could be an obstacle to recovery.

It is true that some vegetarian communities, such as Seventh-Day Adventists, enjoy much lower than average death rates from cancer. But the vegetarianism stems from and forms part of an outlook and general lifestyle that is also very different from usual, in which religious faith provides strong individual and social cohesion and purpose. These are qualities which, according to studies of the social and psychological profiles of people who develop cancer, are often missing in victims of the disease.

17   The Will to be Well

Because scientific methods of arriving at conclusions about the properties of the material world have proved so useful, we have developed a tendency to regard any aspects of reality that are *not* scientifically proven as unworthy of consideration. Thus, when Prince Charles visited a privately run cancer-help centre in Bristol and spoke open mindedly of the 'alternative' therapies employed, he was criticized very fiercely by an orthodox consultant radiotherapist at a local hospital. 'Their bogus science seems fine to the layman, but really it is based on nonsense and when tested is shown to have no benefit,' the woman consultant said. 'I do feel strongly about the Prince of Wales making a royal tour of something that is full of bogus notions.' But in view of the critique of conventional cancer treatments offered in this section, can the orthodoxy be considered to be any more scientific than such 'gentle' methods as faith-healing, meditation, and a 'cleansing' diet?

In one sense, it can: great efforts and resources have been and are being put into testing the effectiveness of the orthodox treatments in a scientific way. Indeed, the whole of the critique in this section rests on scientifically acquired evidence. But this is of little value to patients because the evidence points to the widespread ineffectiveness of these methods, as they are actually applied. They relieve symptoms, but at a cost in terms of suffering often disproportionate to the benefit gained. As one failed attempt to conquer cancer succeeds another, patients unwittingly become mere objects of study in an unending scientific experiment. So whereas this may be genuine science – as each generation of trials proves what *doesn't* work – it is thoroughly bogus medicine. It elevates the requirements of scientific investigation above those of patients.

Are we, then, to join a 'flight from science' and return to the irresponsible, money-making quackery of medical history? Actually, even a quack who takes money from a patient on false pretences of a cure, probably has less capacity for doing harm than the high priests of the hospital system with so much technology at their disposal. The quack at least has a personal, face-to-face relationship with patients, and depends on charm and persuasiveness to obtain their cash. He would not get far if he treated them in the dehumanized way that too many cancer patients have experienced. What is more, he would very soon find himself locked away if he caused as much harm to patients as orthodox doctors are able to do in the name of scientific progress.

It would surely help to restore balance in the treatment of cancer patients if it were recognized that present scientific methods are greatly limited in their power to improve understanding of a matter so infinitely complex as the human condition. However, we should still make whatever use we can of the clues science has provided. Then those involved may hope to come to a rational conclusion, however inadequate, and however much it may change in the future, about how best to proceed.

There is, in fact, a considerable body of scientific evidence which indicates that to the extent that the 'alternative' approaches to cancer focus attention on the patient's individuality and general well-being as opposed to specific symptoms, they are medically more sound than the orthodox strategies.

A number of studies have shown that cancer patients tend to have a weak sense of 'self', such that when their habitual way of life is unavoidably shaken by some major change of circumstance, the integrity of their being is lost. For example, when a professor of psychiatry at the University of Rochester tested patients with leukaemia and Hodgkin's disease, he concluded that in nine out of ten cases the disease develops when a person feels alone, helpless, and hopeless.

When the psychological profiles of a large group of American medical students were compared with their experience of disease over subsequent decades, a 'striking and unexpected' finding was that those who developed cancer were strongly similar to those who committed suicide: generally 'low gear' people, little given to expressions of emotion, whose relationships with their parents had been more remote than those of individuals who developed other kinds of diseases.

When a Glasgow researcher compared cigarette smokers who developed cancer with equivalent groups of smokers who did not, he found that they had different personalities: the cancer victims suffered particularly from denial and repression of their emotions, while the average smoker tended to be extrovert and to give freer reign to feelings.

When a New York psychologist, Lawrence LeShan, examined the emotional lives of more than 400 patients with various forms of cancer, he found that nearly three-quarters had suffered the loss of a central relationship in the period ranging from eight years to a few months before the onset of the disease – compared with only a tenth of a comparable group of people receiving psychotherapy for other reasons. The cancer patients showed a profound sense of despair, he said – feelings of futility and isolation, so deep as to be beyond emotion. They had often been in this condition for many years before becoming ill.

Those patients with cancer who do not feel this way are more likely to survive and surmount their disease. When sixty-nine women with breast cancer admitted consecutively to London's King's College Hospital had their responses to the diagnosis recorded, it was found that those who felt hopeless, or reacted with stoic acceptance, were much more likely to die over the ensuing five years than those who reacted angrily or who refused to accept that they had a serious illness. A similar study in the USA at the Johns Hopkins Medical School, found that women who expressed anger, not only about their disease but with their doctors, lived longer than those who were compliant and cooperative.

These findings are supported by, and shed light on, the remarkable outcome of the Royal Marsden study described at the beginning of Chapter 13. The patients who insisted on having only the lump in their breast removed, and who were subsequently seen to be enjoying a much better long-term survival rate than usual, were evidently a special group psychologically, with their powers of self-determination not merely intact but unusually strong.

There is enough of a common thread to these studies for it to be a sound hypothesis, and not 'bogus science', to suggest that the mind can play a big part in the development of cancer, and in determining whether or not the disease is to sweep an individual towards an early death. Vulnerability seems to be linked with feelings of loss and alienation, of helplessness and giving up. It is as though the disease offers a way out of the intolerable pain of 'non-being'.

A retreat into mental illness can be another way of resolving the irresolvable in a person's life, and it is significant that fatal cancer is rare in mental patients: one study showed that the disease kills only about a third as many mental hospital inmates as non-inmates. (Schizophrenic patients are especially unlikely to die of cancer.) It is not necessarily that these patients don't get cancer, but they are less likely to die of it when they do.

In a 1982 report headed 'Doing nothing can give you cancer', the *New Scientist* magazine drew attention to a Yugoslav study of the effects on health of conflict at the personal level. It showed that whereas some people have the habit of exerting their wishes on others – and tend to put themselves more at risk of heart disease if the effort of maintaining this dominance becomes too great – those who let themselves be pushed around had a higher incidence of cancer. The magazine concluded: 'The possibility that cancer, like heart disease, may depend in part on how we see the world, is too important to ignore.'

As in the case of mental illness, cancer and circulatory disease may be to some extent mutually exclusive – as a consultant pathologist, Dr Arthur Kittermaster, noted in a letter to the *British Medical Journal*. 'As a "morbid" pathologist,' he wrote, 'approximately 4000 necropsies have left me with a strong impression that the incidence of severe arterial disease is surprisingly low in patients who die of cancer – and that where death is due to atheroma anywhere in the arterial tree, it is exceptional to find concomitant neoplastic disease.'

But this does not mean that no matter how we respond to

circumstances and challenges, disease will get us one way or another. There is a need for balance between self-assertiveness and cooperation, activity and passivity, determination and flexibility, aggression and repression, the expression of authority and the willingness to adapt and learn. The cancer risk appears to increase when the scales of the personality are too heavily weighted towards the second of these pairs of opposing tendencies.

How could the mind influence the body in this way? The most obvious candidates for being linking agents are the corticosteroids, the powerful hormones produced by the outer part of the adrenal glands in response to heavy coping demands. The adrenals are linked to the brain both hormonally and through the nervous system, and in response to orders from the brain are capable of flooding the bloodstream with agents that in turn affect brain function: promoting a state of alertness and alarm which, when prolonged, can lead to a sense of defeat, depression, and emotional withdrawal. The physiological accompaniments of these feelings have been shown to include depression of lymphocyte function and other aspects of the immunological defences. So there is a reasonable theoretical basis already established for the belief implicit in the 'alternative' approaches to cancer that by paying attention to improving patients' psychological state, their outlook as far as the disease is concerned may also be improved.

But the effect of the mind goes far deeper than that. A chronically distressed person does not handle food as well as one who is relaxed and happy, so that the blood is more liable to become loaded with undigested fats and sugars. He tends not to exercise, but to be immobilized in misery. He may be more liable to smoke to excess, gradually destroying the capacity of the lungs not only to oxygenate the blood adequately, but to destroy both external and internal pollutants. These pollutants include circulating cancer cells that have broken away from a tumour and are looking for a home elsewhere. The healthy lung destroys a great number of these cells, sometimes all of them. Thus it is on many, many levels that distress and disordered living breed the soil in which cancers can take root and grow.

Are We in Control of Our Genes?

Evidence is growing that the *origins* of cancer also involve a multi-stage process, requiring a number of mutations in the genetic material of one or more cells. In a remarkable book published in 1976 (*The Biology of Cancer, a New Approach*, MTP Press, Lancaster), Professor Philip Burch, who holds a personal chair in the department of medical physics at Leeds University, set out a theory of cancer foreshadowing recent discoveries in the field of genetics and cancer.

He argued that the disease is initiated by mutations – probably DNA strand-switching events – in stem cells of a central system of growth control. These stem cells send out messenger materials – either other cells, or cell proteins – which locate and interact with target cells in different parts of the body in a homeostatic, negative feedback system of growth control. The interaction between the messengers and the target cells has to be very exact for the system to work properly, with information being passed to and fro between the controlling cells and the target tissues.

The target tissues themselves may be subject to mutations which promote carcinogenic growth, but do not cause it. Thus, the known mutagenic properties of tobacco smoke, or other environmental carcinogens such as asbestos fibres, might render an individual vulnerable to lung cancer, but the disease would only develop if the central mutation also occurred. Those diseases which show distinct stages of progression, Professor Burch argued, involve multiple mutations at the central, initiating level. As the central controls become less and less specific, the tumour cells become progressively undifferentiated, and increasingly virulent in their ability to spread.

Preoccupation with the cancer cell has obscured the key issue of inter-cellular relations. Professor Burch wrote: cancerous growth should be regarded as a breakdown, or aberration, in biological organization. The great majority of cancers in man, he believes, result not from the action of extrinsic carcinogens, but from spontaneous changes in cells of the central system of growth control (probably located mainly in the bone marrow), and, during the promotion phase of the disease, from similar changes in cells of the target tissue. It follows that, in the professor's view, the enormous emphasis on identifying external factors in the causation of cancer is a mistaken policy that will never have any significant effect on death rates. He also challenges the orthodox picture of cancer as a progressive growth and/or invasion of other tissues leading remorselessly to death, unless the initial tumour cells can all be removed in time. If it were true, death rates from a specific cancer would tend to be low initially, and to increase with time after diagnosis. But deaths rarely follow this pattern. On the contrary, with most cancers the average death rate from cancer itself remains roughly constant from the time of diagnosis onwards.

Professor Burch's fascinating, deeply researched and well argued work was largely ignored. But now – seven years after his book was published – great excitement is being expressed about discoveries relating to a genetic basis for cancer. One concerns a cancer-causing gene isolated from cells of bone, tendons, ligaments and brain tissue; this has been shown to cause uncontrolled production of a protein normally only present when injured tissues are being repaired. The other involves the unravelling of a two-stage process turning normal cells into cancerous ones: 'immortalization', in which genetic change frees certain cells from the body's built-in controls, and 'conversion', in which the cells become truly cancerous and invasive. These developments were so closely foreshadowed by Professor Burch's analysis that I feel confident to predict that more will be heard of his theory in years to come.

But if the professor is right, how could such a fundamental mechanism of cancer causation tie in with the observation that many cancer patients have had prolonged periods of depression, unhappiness and 'giving up' preceding the onset of their disease? At the risk of further alienating those readers who still find it hard to accept that the mind can have anything to do with becoming ill or staying well, I should like to mention a possible modification of the Burch theory for which I do not have any evidence, but which seems to me to be a reasonable hypothesis which may allow individual cancer patients to keep hope of a cure alive even when they are in an advanced state of the disease.

It is possible that the genetic events which initiate cancer as described in the Burch theory are not random, but that by some subtle means yet to be determined, the cancer victim himself or herself often causes the central genetic switch to be thrown. The disease then develops where there is a tumour-promoting weakness in particular target tissues. By this reckoning, it is no accident that many cancer patients have similar personalities to those of suicide victims: in many instances cancer is a slow form of self-destruction. Differences in exposure to environmental and dietary carcinogens will cause differences in the specific means of cancer 'suicide' according to geographical, occupational or behavioural differences, but once the 'self' decides to court death, it will find one means or another of doing so . . . unless at that same deep level there is a subsequent decision to reverse the disease process.

One immediate objection to this argument is that the growth of lung-cancer deaths this century, accompanying the growth in cigarette smoking, appears to indicate a clear cause-and-effect relationship between an external carcinogen and a specific form of disease. Surely, the mind could have nothing to do with that? But, as Professor Burch shows, numerous statistical anomalies challenge the idea of a direct causal link, and despite widespread belief to the contrary the causal hypothesis is by no means proven. Changes in diagnostic fashion may have accounted for a considerable part of the recorded increase in lung-cancer deaths this century. And to the extent that the increase is real, it may simply represent an alternative form of self-destruction by those with an unconscious wish to die. There is a striking inverse relationship between death rates in men aged forty-five to sixty-four years in England and Wales from pulmonary tuberculosis, and death rates from lung cancer, over the period 1916 to 1965. The rise in death rates from lung cancer is almost paralleled by an equivalent fall in death rates from pulmonary TB. There are almost certainly fashions in the ways we choose to die, as well as in the ways doctors describe the causes of death.

This is not to say that cigarettes, or other pollutants, play no part in the cancer story. The damage that they do provides that 'fertile soil' in which the individual can plant the seed of a particularly rapid and fatal form of cancer. However, deprived of that particular form of self-destruction, a person has plenty of other options available if he or she should be so minded.

For example, although doctors who reduced their smoking when the hazards become apparent suffered fewer deaths from cigarette-linked diseases, they became *more* prone to die of other causes. This was disclosed in a *British Medical Journal* report based on an analysis of occupational mortality tables for England and Wales, covering the years 1970–72. Mr Peter Lee, an independent research statistician (formerly employed by the tobacco industry), looked at deaths among male doctors aged under sixty-five because it was known that from 1951 to 1971, as a group, they reduced their cigarette smoking far more than other men in their social classes.

He found that they had only a marginal advantage in their death rates. A total of 665 of them died, compared with an expected 699 deaths if they had merely enjoyed the same improvements in death rates as other men. They showed eighty-three fewer deaths from heart disease, sixteen from stroke, eight from lung cancer. But these 'savings' were offset by sixty 'surplus' deaths – thirty from accidents and poisonings, twenty-six from suicide, and four from liver disease associated with heavy drinking. So the overall saving was only thirty-four; and even that was unlikely to be due to the reduction in smoking, because deaths from heart disease had been falling faster among doctors than among others in their social classes during the previous twenty years as well (1931–51) before they started to drop the habit.

Peter Lee's interpretation of these figures was that if someone stops smoking, he may feel a need to do something else – also hazardous to health – as an alternative means of coping with stress. This might be so, though the 'something else' would appear to have been drastically dangerous in the case of the increased numbers of doctors dying of accidents, poisonings, suicide, and so on. On the other hand, these figures do provide powerful support for the idea that when an individual has decided at some deep level that life is no longer worth living, behavioural habits and bodily developments may combine to offer a way out.

Fatal cancer is by no means always a disguised form of slow suicide. There are occasions – such as of massive occupational exposure to a powerful carcinogen – where the physical assault on the body causes such damage as to overwhelm the spiritual 'will to live', to hold the body together. Similarly, normal ageing processes gradually make the body uninhabitable and also, it seems, contribute to the genetic roots of cancer. In many cases, too, the will to live may falter – allowing the breakdown in biological organization that promotes the establishment of a cancer – only to return later. Such patients may be the very ones who respond best to whatever treatment they receive, and who go on to live a normal or near-normal lifespan. But the 'will to die' is a factor that deserves recognition – and respect.

Commenting on a two-part documentary called 'Mind over Cancer' shown on BBC television, *Guardian* reviewer Peter Fiddick wrote:

I was left wondering whether we were any further on than the notion of the 'will to live' which seems accepted as an important element in the recovery process in many other forms of illness and injury. And also, to what extent it is possible – or perhaps even necessary – to incite someone to find such spirit. Winnie, in the hospice, giving up the fight because the time had come to join her husband, did not seem the example of someone who now needed such help.

A similar point was made by a Glasgow radiotherapist, Dr Thurstan Brewin, reviewing a book on mind and cancer in the *British Medical Journal*:

To some earnest psychologists – discussing patients who face death – it seems that tragedy and heartbreak, serenity and sadness, defiance and despair, hope and humour, are only just being discovered. And given new names, of course, so that they fit more comfortably into the ugly jargon of pseudo-science. It is as if all the literature of medicine and mankind – and all the great stories of humour and courage in the face of danger – had never been.

In Conclusion

After this long journey of exploration, have we too only managed to arrive at a point where we see that those patients who survive and surmount cancer do so because they retain their will to live, while those who lose it irrevocably die? It seems an unsatisfactory conclusion from the point of view of medical science – rather like a passage attributed to the Greek physician Galen: 'All who drink of this remedy recover in a short time, except those whom it does not help, who all die. Therefore, it is obvious that it fails only in incurable cases.'

That passage was quoted in a letter to *The Times* by Professor Michael Baum, of the Cancer Research Campaign Clinical Trials Centre, as an example of non-scientific medicine which 'would therefore find its place amongst the many panaceas employed by the practitioners beyond the fringe'. The philosophy of alternative medicine dates back to Aristotle and is entirely inductive, he argued. It seeks only corroborative evidence, which continues to rationalize the original conceptual view of nature. Orthodox medicine, by contrast, is essentially deductive, with its concepts being constantly challenged by experiments seeking to refute or verify biological hypotheses.

In fact, vast areas of belief and practice in orthodox as well as alternative medicine rest on untested hypotheses. And as the reader has seen in the case of cancer, and will have found again and again in this book as we have examined a variety of diseases, when orthodox treatments that have seemed to work in clinical practice are tested in a thoroughly controlled scientific manner, they are seen to carry virtually no positive advantage one from the other; the differences rest mainly in the amount of damage that they do, and the extent to which they interfere with natural healing processes. With very few exceptions, the only advances that are made in cancer are the discrediting of treatments that may have been hastening the deaths of patients, or adding to their misery in the process of dying.

Nevertheless, if we accept Professor Baum's definition of orthodox medicine as being essentially deductive, our analysis does have some very large practical implications, for patients at least. Those doctors whose attention is focused on finding a 'scientific' cure for cancer are necessarily blinded to the most important influences determining the patient's welfare, because these influences – which culminate in 'the will to live or the will to die' – cannot be examined scientifically. Their impact is essentially subjective, individual, unrepeatable. The influences include the methods of both orthodox and alternative practitioners.

Some patients respond well to chemotherapy, enjoying the

fight against the disease, shared with the hospital team, or the challenge of coping with side-effects. Others have their sense of helplessness and agony increased.

Some patients respond well to mastectomy operations, the sacrifice of the breast giving them new hope; others are devastated by it and would do far better having only the lump removed.

Some patients respond well to radiotherapy, their faith in expensive technology giving them new faith in themselves; others feel themselves more lost than ever, as their body passes down the hospital production-line for processing by impersonal machinery.

Some patients benefit from strict dietary regimes and coffee enemas, perhaps feeling that along with the cleansing of the body goes a cleansing of the soul; others cannot bear such a regime, finding it deepens their sense of deprivation and joylessness.

Dr Malcolm Carruthers, director of clinical laboratory services at London's Maudsley and Royal Bethlem hospitals, a foremost researcher in the area of mind and body relationships, once sent me the following quotation by the American Edgar Cayce (1877–1945), who had a gift for 'divining' people's ills in a psychic manner:

For all healing comes from the One Source. And whether there is application of food, exercise, medicine or even the knife, it is to bring the consciousness of the forces within the body that aid in reproducing themselves [through] the awareness of creative or God Forces: All strength, all healing of every nature, is the changing of the vibrations from within – the attuning of the divine within the living tissues of a body to Creative Energies. This alone is healing; it is the tuning of the atomic structure of the living cellular force to its spiritual heritage.

When I first saw those words, they had a ring of truth, but did not appear to make sense in terms of scientific medicine, which at that time still seemed to me to offer great prospects for the future. Now, I feel Cayce's words to be not only true, but making evident good sense, and to be entirely in accordance with the known facts. And the story of cancer offers one of the best illustrations of this truth.

The great virtue of orthodox, scientific medicine is that it is capable of offering a powerful *illusion* of cure, which, if the patient is willing, can then be turned into a reality. 'By removing the symptoms, such treatments help to restore in the patient the 'idea' of being well; but that 'idea' must be adopted or tuned into by the inner self, and by the divine forces 'within the living tissues of a body', if true healing is to occur. The divine, as its name implies, is beyond the grasp of medical science, but that does not prevent doctors from employing scientifically developed tools that help to mobilize the hidden forces. Where they go wrong is in assuming that it is their science that cures, or is capable of curing.

'Alternative' health practitioners tend to be less blinded by science, and therefore better able to see the human needs for comfort, hope, and self-worth in those patients who seek out their services. To the extent that they are able to give the patient peace of mind, there will also be healing at some level, though not necessarily affecting the cancer itself. This is why cancer patients so often find that they *feel* better through the alternative treatments, even though objectively their cancer may remain unaffected.

Diet is also important, because it is so intimately connected with both bodily and mental well-being. Foods which are nearest to their living origins – fresh and whole – seem capable of providing not merely the right physical nutrients to the body, but sustenance for the soul. Again, orthodox doctors have tended to be blinded to this effect because it is unmeasurable, and therefore 'non-science'. Hence the appalling 'dead' food served in most British hospitals.

But all of these interventions – orthodox, alternative, dietary – are as nothing compared with the structure of the patient's own thoughts. Within the mind, I believe, lies the power of determining whether the tumour is to grow quickly or slowly, to disappear and then reappear, to vanish for ever or to sweep the patient towards death. Positive, harmonious thought – of happiness in life, love for others, satisfaction with the present and hope for the future – gives the power to heal; negative thought – of sorrow, anger, self-hatred and hopelessness – is antagonistic to life and health.

On the basis of this analysis, we enter ultimately into spiritual territory, beyond the power of science to reach. In cancer, perhaps more than in any other kind of illness, patients need spiritual sustenance: not in the sense of religious dogma, but of a change of approach and understanding that will strengthen the mind and produce happiness and vigour in life instead of sorrow and depression. The psychologist Lawrence Leshan tells of cancer patients who recovered after being enabled to 'sing their own song' – finding an outlet for positive strengths within them that had previously been denied expression – such as the former leader of a defunct teenage street gang whose Hodgkin's disease disappeared when he studied to become a fireman.

Some find new strength of purpose in working for a cause. There are many stories of cancer patients who have 'changed their vibrations within' through determined self-examination, and then stayed free of disease as they made it their life's purpose to tell others how to do the same. Others find strength through meditation and religious contemplation – filling the mind and heart with the love and peace of God. Again, well-authenticated cases of spontaneous regression in cancer are often associated with intensive prayer, meditation, or some equivalent deep-seated psychological experience. But whatever the future in terms of recovery, continuing disease, or death, fear is cast out and the quality of remaining life vastly improved when spiritual truth is experienced; that is, when the true spirit of the individual is perceived, acknowledged, and given expression.

The following passage, from *The Letters of Marcilio Ficino*, Vol. 1 (Shepheard-Walwyn, 1975), quoted in the magazine of the Association for New Approaches to Cancer, is a fine example of thought that heals. It was written in 1473 by the head of the Platonic Academy of Florence, Marcilio Ficino, who was a central figure within the Florentine Renaissance, as consolation to a friend on the death of a beloved.

If each of us, essentially, is that which is greatest within us, which always remains the same and by which we understand ourselves, then certainly the soul is the man himself and the body but his shadow. Whatever wretch is so deluded as to think that the shadow of man is man, like Narcissus, is dissolved in tears. You will only cease to weep, Gismondo, when you cease looking for your Albiera degli Albizzi in her dark shadow and begin to follow her by her own clear light. For the further she is from that misshapen shadow the more beautiful will you find her, past all you have ever known.

Withdraw into your soul, I beg you, where you will possess her soul which is so beautiful and dear to you; or rather, from your soul withdraw to God. There you will contemplate the beautiful Idea through which the Divine Creator fashioned your Albiera; and as she is far more lovely in her Creator's form than in her own, so you will embrace her there with far more joy.

Delusion makes us weep; or die, as the German writer Fritz Zorn said of the lymphoma that killed him at thirty-two, of 'an accumulation of swallowed tears'. Accurate information about the self is needed before right thinking can begin to be acquired, and with that right thinking, freedom from disease. The following ideas may serve as seeds for the kind of change in thinking needed to protect and heal in cancer:

1   A diagnosis of cancer is rarely a death sentence, unless we choose (or have already chosen) to believe it to be so. Any suggestion to the contrary from others, including doctors, can be rejected. Many people diagnosed as having cancer live a normal lifespan. Many people who die of other causes have cancer without even realizing it.

2   Screening for cancer is of questionable value. It may encourage cancer neurosis and is liable to prolong worry should cancer be diagnosed. There is no solid proof that it saves lives. But people have been fooled into thinking that it does because of the mistaken view that cancer always kills unless caught and treated early.

3   To view a diagnosis of the disease positively, as heralding an episode capable of sharpening the process of self-discovery or change, is more likely to lead to recovery than to accept it with bitterness or as a punishment for past sins, real or imagined. Blame and guilt are both antagonistic to the forces that heal.

4   Diet is important. Meat tends to feed aggression; fresh fruit and vegetables promote mental stability and feelings of well-being.

5   Viewing the body as a temple for the experience of happiness

and an instrument for giving happiness to others will help to make self-destructive habits such as heavy smoking and drinking fall away.

6 Orthodox medical approaches to cancer offer powerful methods of removing symptoms but can become the cause of unnecessary suffering when doctors try to use them to cure.

7 'Alternative' health practitioners, such as homeopaths, naturopaths, and faith healers, are no more able to bring about 'miracle cures' without the patient's willing it than mainstream doctors. But to the extent that they enable people to care more for themselves, for others, and for life, some tend to be better at prompting self-healing. It is through such a change of mind that the most lasting and valuable kind of healing takes place – even in the face of death.

Part Five

In Conclusion

18   Integrity

Half way through the writing of this book, I came across the following remark by the spiritual teacher J. Krishnamurti: 'All explanations are escapes, avoiding the reality of what is. This is the only thing that matters. The "what is" can be totally transformed with the energy that is wasted in explanations and in searching out causes.' Krishnamurti's point is that explanations arising from human thought are inevitably partial and fragmentary: they can never make whole, and therefore can never heal. To the extent that explanations about disease processes have been suggested here as an alternative to or amplification of orthodox descriptions, they must still be subject to this truth.

So has it been right or useful to continue to delve into such matters of detail as lymphocyte function, chromosome mechanisms, pituitary adreno-cortical pathways, and so on, in relation to the various processes examined?

For me, at least, the exploration has been valuable, if only to drive home to myself the truth of Krishnamurti's words. For at the end of the day, my own attempts to sketch a fuller account of these disease processes than modern medicine has acknowledged have brought me face to face with the 'what is', the point beyond explanations: the sense of purpose and joy in living that *are* the vitality that determines life and health.

There may also be value for others in what I hope is an irrefutable demonstration of the enormous shortcomings and waste of energy involved in present attempts to lessen the burden of disease through a search for purely physical causes and explanations and cures. If the reader has accepted this demonstration, then he or she may at least realize something of the perils involved, as well as the specific benefits to be obtained, in dealing with a medical system strongly biased towards analysis rather than synthesis, towards dissection rather than construction, towards examining the parts rather than helping the whole 'what is' to stay together. This realization is itself one important step towards wholeness and health. Perhaps, also, value will be found in some of the suggestions for general health maintenance contained in the various chapters, though these are offered tentatively and with the caveat that while they are likely to prove helpful for some, it is the spirit in which such measures are adopted that really counts.

Another word for wholeness is integrity, and this has great relevance to disease. To the extent that our thoughts and feelings are integrated internally, we will be free of the arousal-inducing and eventually debilitating effect of self-criticism and a biting conscience. And to the extent that the package of thought and feeling with which we live also allows us to integrate well with other human beings, we will be free of the heated emotional states that social friction engenders, and able to enjoy other people's good wishes instead. On the other hand, when personal integrity is shaky, events that threaten to expose this weakness will be seen as very intimidatory and will bring great suffering.

A smooth fit between the individual and the social environment is the best protection against disease. Anything that interferes with this fit, whether from inside the person or outside in the environment, will increase susceptibility to disease (though there is certainly a part for the abrasive personality, who may fit best in circumstances where that abrasiveness can knowingly be expressed).

We have seen how the loss of a close relative, or of a job, or of any other aspect of circumstances through which life has taken on structure and meaning, can bring about a catastrophic collapse in health. We have also seen that perceived threats to the structure of our lives, most commonly in the form of chronic difficulties at work or clashes in the home, can put us at risk of developing chronic illness. Some illnesses, such as heart disease, tend to arise from prolonged attempts to cope with such threats, when the accompanying physiological change eventually overtaxes the system and a change of strategy becomes essential. Other illnesses serve more obviously as mechanisms forcing immobilization and withdrawal, taking the victim away from the battlefield on a stretcher into invalidity or towards death when the fit between the individual and the environment – perhaps never very strong – seems to have collapsed completely. But even in these latter conditions, we have argued that doctor and patient have both been far too ready to regard them as incurable. Emergency repairs to the 'fit' that bring a renewed sense of purpose – allowing a soul to 'sing its song' – can enormously diminish the suffering experienced because of physical illness, and sometimes lead to a seemingly miraculous cure from within.

The development of a disease (and indeed the approach of death itself) is a cue for some form of adjustment, whether in a person's external circumstances or in internal responses to circumstances. Time, as well as effort on the individual's part, often helps such adjustment to come about, but when symptom suppression with drugs or other artifical measures (including those of alternative medicine) causes the cue to be missed, suffering is prolonged. Such measures should only be used with the aim of helping the adjustment to take place.

Limitations of time and space have restricted the number of disease conditions examined here, but the forces seen at work in those described are present in most other conditions as well. Even infections, for example, though particularly susceptible to attack with the weapons of science, are very clearly related to the ability of a particular environment to support the life it contains. Improvements in housing, nutrition, and other living circumstances caused deaths from tuberculosis to tumble long before the introduction of anti-TB drugs, and in fact the drugs only very slightly accelerated what had been a continuous decline for many decades. The severe gastro-intestinal diseases that still take the lives of millions of children in poor countries cannot be conquered with drugs that in wealthy countries seem outstandingly effective. In a flu epidemic it is the old, the exhausted, and the unhappy who are most at risk. Even the ubiquitous cold viruses tend to leave us alone while we enjoy harmonious circumstances and a cheerful outlook; but they quickly strike when our self-confidence (and immune defences) are impaired, most commonly through being confronted with some shortcoming in ourselves or in someone close to us with whom we identify.

Alcoholism, asthma, appendicitis, drug addiction, epilepsy, gallstones, gout, respiratory disease, skin trouble, stroke, tonsillitis, ulcers, warts, even accident proneness and tooth decay – just about every threat to health that exists (including illnesses of a directly 'mental' nature such as depression and schizophrenia) is susceptible to the same kind of analysis as in those presented above, where disease is seen to be the outcome of *unease* and discord in the relationship between a human being and the social or physical environment. In most of these conditions, too, there is much evidence that the present failure to recognize the roots of illness causes widespread application of inappropriate and harmful medical or surgical treatments – even though these interventions are sometimes useful, or indeed life-saving, in helping a patient over a short-term health crisis.

We live in an environment that is constantly changing, that presents numerous challenges and threats, and in which the speed of change is accelerating. Habits of thought and behaviour that may have served us adequately in the past become redundant, just as our occupational skills are liable to do. Hanging on rigidly to these old habits prevents adaptation and may invite friction and illness. An essential characteristic of the person who can fit smoothly and stay healthy and strong in such an environment is flexibility and adaptability. But this flexibility has to be accompanied by a recognition of fixed values also, or it degenerates into an aimless pragmatism.

What can provide personal integrity, the strength and understanding to retain that integrity in dealings with others, the flexibility and sense of occasion to come fresh to each circumstance, and the insight into eternal values to keep a constant sense of direction? The answer does not lie within the explanations and causal processes sought or offered by medical science – including the more elaborate ones explored in this book – but within ourselves. There is an 'I' within us, an essential self, that is able both to rise above the concerns of the moment and to show us how to handle those concerns with minimal strain. The greater our contact with this 'I', the greater is our experience of both internal and external peace, and the lighter the burdens on heart and soul.

Disease-prone people tend to be ill-endowed with the qualities of self-knowledge and 'seeing things in the round'. Theories and treatments of disease that overemphasize physical factors such as cigarettes, exercise, diet, or obesity, and even external factors such as poor working conditions, unemployment, or bereavement, may consolidate and confirm these blind areas and certainly do nothing to lessen them. They may perform a disservice to patients by drawing their attention still further away from the 'I' – the 'what is' – that must be cared for and encouraged and listened to with respect if health is to be restored and maintained.

So to strengthen body and mind, we need to strengthen our souls – to give ourselves new hope and happiness. For that, we need to find a mirror or mirrors with which to gaze at our existing strengths and shortcomings, and to begin to make good those deficiencies in thinking and feeling and behaving that diminish us and cut us off from other people.

Effective, 'real' communication with another can provide such a mirror. This 'dialogue', psychology professor James Lynch tells us in *The Broken Heart: the Medical Consequences of Loneliness* (Basic Books, New York, 1977), is the elixir of life. Those who lack it early in life can perish quickly, while those who lose it as children, adolescents, or adults feel acutely what they have lost, and struggle to get it back. Dialogue does not have to be through words. In fact, it is often non-verbal, through gestures and through the eyes. Obvious interruptions to a well-established relationship, such as the loss of someone very close and dear, can cause acute suffering; but more subtle and difficult to recognize is the chronic deterioration of dialogue that can happen when a person is trapped in totally impoverished relationships without being able to recognize what has happened or why. Since dialogue involves reciprocal sharing with other human beings, Professor Lynch writes, its deterioration must also be reciprocal, and in a failing marriage, for example, each person must share part of the responsibility. 'An individual can only receive to the extent that he gives, and, in that sense, dialogue is a mirror of his personality.'

Good communication with another person can provide at once both the nourishment – the contentment – for which our souls yearn, and a means of learning how to break free of narrow, selfish concerns. This is why human contact alone is a powerful force for healing. Whether that contact is with an orthodox doctor, an 'alternative' health practitioner, a counsellor, healer, or friend, to whatever extent the other person is sufficiently willing and skilled to address the whole person as opposed to superficial complaints, suffering will be reduced and restoration of health encouraged.

Wisdom, and human comfort, are not the prerogative of any one profession or group of practitioners. They can be found in all sorts of places. But in order to be helped, and for dialogue to be established, the patient has to give something of the self – to open the self up, as it were – allowing some truth about the real self to emerge. This is then reflected back and the individual's own vision is drawn towards the 'I' within. The process can be uncomfortable at first, not because of any ugliness within but because of the beauty that lies there, hidden for so long. There is pain in recognizing how much we have betrayed our real selves. So some patients maintain their emotionally anaesthetized state through continuing to exhaust themselves, or by taking medical drugs or alcohol, or even by welcoming the chance of major surgery in the often mistaken belief that this in itself will make them more fit for life.

An awareness and experience of the detached, observing self – the soul – and of the beautiful truths about life and God that become available to it as self-awareness deepens, have been taught in the past by great religious and spiritual leaders as a means of healing wounded spirits and helping the joy that is so protective of health to return. The upsurge of interest in the West in eastern systems of spiritual development through yoga and meditation, and a revival of interest in religious contemplation within Christianity, are valid expressions of the need for these forms of experience.

Positive human development is a process of becoming more and more complete in ourselves as individuals, in order that we may then fit easily and harmoniously into the whole of existence. 'The quest for perfectibility is not a presumption or a blasphemy, but the highest manifestation of a great design,' is how Norman Cousins puts it. The more we recognize this perfectibility, and taste completeness, the greater the peace and happiness in our hearts. In its most powerful form, completeness is felt through silent dialogue between ourselves and God, towards whom the natural world can lead us, as Krishnamurti describes:

In the silence of deep night and in the quiet still morning when the sun is touching the hills, there is a great mystery. It is there in all living things.

On a still night when the stars are clear and close, you would be aware of expanding space and the mysterious order of all things, of the immeasurable and of nothing, of the movement of the dark hills and the hoot of an owl.

In that utter silence of the mind this mystery expands without time and space. In the quiet stillness of the mind that which is everlasting beauty comes, uninvited, unsought, without the noise of recognition.

(*Krishnamurti's Journal*, Harper & Row, New York, 1982)

The ill person who recovers sufficient strength to learn how to silence the racing mind, to see more of other people, of nature, and of the self, and to experience from time to time 'the mysterious order of all things' will find that circumstances which previously seemed to offer undiluted misery are first transcended and then gradually, magically, transformed.